Entertainment
Theology

cultural exegesis

William A. Dyrness
and Robert K. Johnston, series editors

The Cultural Exegesis series is designed to
complement the Engaging Culture series
by providing methodological and foundational studies that address the way to engage culture theologically. Each volume
works within a specific cultural discipline,
illustrating and embodying the theory behind cultural engagement. By providing
the appropriate tools, these books equip
the reader to engage and interpret the surrounding culture responsibly.

Entertainment Theology

New-Edge Spirituality in a Digital Democracy

Barry Taylor

Baker Academic
a division of Baker Publishing Group
Grand Rapids, Michigan

Published by Baker Academic
a division of Baker Publishing Group
P.O. Box 6287, Grand Rapids, MI 49516-6287
www.bakeracademic.com

Printed in the United States of America

Library of Congress Cataloging-in-Publication Data
Taylor, Barry, 1956-
    Entertainment theology : new-edge spirituality in a digital democracy / Barry Taylor.
        p.   cm. — (Cultural exegesis)
    Includes bibliographical references and index.
    ISBN 978-0-8010-3237-0 (pbk.)
    1. Popular culture—Religious aspects—Christianity. 2. Christianity and culture.
    I. Title.
BR115.C8T38 2008
201′.7—dc22

2007042069

To everyone, everywhere, I have ever met, thank you.

"Whenever they enter a new era of history, people change their ideas of both humanity and divinity."

Karen Armstrong

Contents

Contents

Acknowledgments

I found a note in one of my journals referencing a Talmudic tradition that urged Jewish scholars to acknowledge the sources of their ideas in order to bring redemption to the world. I had no quotes or sources beside the note, but I wanted to honor this tradition and "name" a few of the many people who have helped me, either through their works or via personal interaction. It was Picasso, I believe, who said something like, "Good artists borrow; great artists steal." Many of the ideas in this book find their genesis in the thinking and writing of others, and I would like to give them the credit and gratitude they deserve. The endnotes and bibliography will alert the reader to influential works and sources, but I wanted to mention a few in a more direct and personal manner.

Graham Ward, Walter Truett Anderson, Karen Armstrong, and Douglas Rushkoff form the backbone of my overall thinking about religion, culture, and change throughout this book. Each helped me coalesce my thinking and provided me with categories to work in and through. They each inhabit different fields of study, but there was a convergence in their writings that I found to be of great assistance in pinning down some of the dynamics I was exploring. I should single out Ward's *True Religion* and Rushkoff's *Playing the Future* as key works in this area.

On the theological front, I must acknowledge a deep debt to John Drane, John Caputo, Mark I. Wallace, Roger Haight, and Leonardo Boff. It was not always the answers they offered as much as the questions they raised that were of the most benefit to me. John Drane has been a mentor for many years, and his generous and thoughtful interactions have helped me more than I can say. His insights into the dynamics of faith and cultural change have been central to much of my thinking in this book and go well beyond the references cited.

John Caputo's book, *The Weakness of God*, is a seminal work for me. His idea about "weak theology" not only gave me the freedom to approach Scripture and institution in new ways but also has become central to my own theological grid. Leonardo Boff's commitment to what he terms eco-theology—a holistic and integrated view of human life that seeks to collapse the compartmentalization of religion and spirituality from the rest of life—has become an inspiration for my own life and relation to creation. I have read his small work, *Global Civilization*, countless times in the past year or so and have found it very helpful when attempting to understand the implications of technological change in an increasingly global society. Mark I. Wallace and Roger Haight have also assisted in the formation of my own theological opinions, and their thinking influences much of what emerges throughout the present book.

I also need to say something about Slavoj Žižek, Gianni Vattimo, and Ken Wilber, whose "outside" voices helped me look at Christianity in new ways. *After Christianity*, Gianni Vattimo's provocative book that offers an alternative future for Christian faith, influenced the final portion of this book. Žižek has much to say about Christianity and religion in general, and the fact that he is not a believer only made his thinking on the subject more helpful to me. Ken Wilber, whose theory of integral spirituality has gained a lot of cultural traction in recent years, was very helpful in the middle section of this book where I tried to gather some of the shifting dynamics in the world of faith into categories, as was Walter Truett Anderson's book *The Next Enlightenment*, which made sense of the new developments in the relation between science and faith.

I must also say a word about Rob Johnston, who is one of the editors of the series in which this book appears but who is first and foremost a great friend and an always-thoughtful conversation partner. He has been supportive and helpful in my academic journey and has always challenged me to clarify my positions and perspectives. There is no particular work of his I drew on in this book, but our conversations were many and his help goes beyond cited materials.

I realize that this list is incomplete; many others could and should be added. But I offer this "naming" as a symbolic gesture about the genesis of ideas and thinking in my own life and work and as a mark of respect to all whose giftedness and creativity has marked me and makes me who I am.

Introduction

For the times they are a-changin'.
Bob Dylan, 1963

Things have changed.
Bob Dylan, 2000

There is a new mood in the air, a new interest in religion and the nature of belief and their role in what it means to be human. It is a realization, emerging in Western culture particularly, that the old values that have informed and shaped us for the past few hundred years are lacking in their ability to meet the deep yearning of the human heart. It is the recognition that the Enlightenment view (which held that scientific rationalism was the only viable means to the realization of full humanity) is, in fact, sorely limited in its scope and that our commitment to it has left us barren and adrift. It is also an acknowledgment that the balance of power has shifted in the culture. A growing number of people are increasingly unwilling simply to accept the pronouncements of institutions, whether they be religious, political, or otherwise, and are instead looking to themselves, to their peers, and particularly to alternative resource centers, such as Internet Web sites and contemporary media, in order to create new means for grappling with questions of ultimate reality. This is not to say that the day of traditional institutions is over, but it is to say that those institutions no longer have the last word or hold the authoritative sway they once did.

The emergence of a postsecular society (a result of the shift from a modern to a postmodern world) reflects a movement in the broader culture in which the voices of the marginalized and formerly overlooked are legitimized and power emerges from unexpected places rather than through the traditional avenues that shaped the previous era. As singer Patti Smith declared in the 1970s, the "people have the power." New technologies have shifted the balance of power in the realm of information. We are, as theologian Leonardo Boff asserts, witnessing the "beginning of the post-television era, as a revolution in which numerical, synthetic and virtual images takes place."[1] For quite some time I have referred to this process as "democratization," a term that attempts to capture the trend toward a less hierarchical and authoritarian exchange of ideas, ethics, information, and just about everything else in contemporary society.

Democratization seems to be at work in virtually every area of life today. In fact, in the wider culture there is a new term for this phenomenon: "crowdsourcing." This phenomenon is outlined in an article by Jeff Howe, titled "The Rise of Crowdsourcing," in the June 2006 issue of *Wired* magazine. The subtitle of the article is "The Rise of the Amateur," which sums up much of what is going on around us. As traditional structures lose their stranglehold, there appears to be an unleashing, a veritable tidal wave of people-powered content. Whether this is a good or a bad thing is not really the point as far as I am concerned; it is the reality we find ourselves in and the one with which we must dialogue. The Internet, and computer technology in general, has been central in this shift—innovations such as *YouTube* and *MySpace* have not only flooded the ether with mindless Web pages and homemade videos, they have also aided in the development of new perspectives on life and added yet another layer to the destabilizing of traditional authority and power structures. *Wikipedia*, the on-line encyclopedia, which is democratic in that anyone can contribute information, is another example of this dynamic. In a nod toward this emerging dynamic, which appears to be a defining characteristic of our time, *Time* magazine declared its 2006 "Person of the Year" to be "You." You, as in me, you, us, all of us. The cover of the magazine features a computer terminal with a metallic, mirror-like screen that reflects the image of the person who looks into it. Terming it the "digital democracy," *Time*'s editors overlooked a host of significant events and people in 2006 to acknowledge the growing phenomenon of people-powered culture shaping.

There is really no area of our lives that has not been influenced in some way or another by these new developments. Whether or not these changes are good or bad is not the focus here. Rather than rejoice or bemoan what is occurring, I simply choose to accept these new realities and see them as the setting for a conversation about how, and in what ways perhaps, we might understand what is going on and thereby further explore how Christian faith might look in such a context.

The focus of this book is the way the aforementioned ideas, as well as other dynamics, have affected the realm of faith and belief. To be sure, the traditional religions still appear to hold a monopoly on the mediation of all things religious, at least on some levels. Religions such as Christianity and Islam still attract billions of followers around the globe and continue to influence and shape much of the world's religious thought and perspectives. But there is something else going on. What I am attempting to capture in these pages is something of the new religious horizon. It has not completely come into view yet. It is the result of many things: cultural shifts, new opportunities afforded to many of us through technology, the compression of our world by those same technologies. It is not that the world is necessarily a different shape, but rather that we have access to more of it (new mediums for the exchange of ideas, and the list goes on and on). It is also the result of changing attitudes and opinions about the nature of belief itself.

For many people, the old religions no longer offer the comfort and consolation or guidance and insight they once did. The rise of many forms of religious fundamentalism has not helped. More and more people regard traditional religions as a source of conflict. Yet the desire for ultimate meaning continues. There are more and more resources available that offer "religion without the baggage." Baggage in most cases means the perception of unnecessary and definitely unwanted dogmatics—arcane and archaic views that seem inconsistent with much of the rest of life—and a feeling that the traditional religions are out of touch and incapable of responding quickly enough to the massive social and cultural upheaval that many sense themselves navigating. This mood is heard time and again in the expression, "I am spiritual but not religious," or words to that effect. What that means exactly will be taken up a little later, but for now, suffice it to say that it reflects a central dynamic of a shift this book focuses on: that the faith quest continues in a revitalized manner in the early years of the twenty-first century, but this faith quest has horizons and parameters that would surprise those who think they understand the dynamics and ingredients that contribute to a quest for meaning.

The spiritual landscape, rather than the religious tradition, has become the arena for theological exploration. And the theological excursion may no longer begin with God and work downward; rather, it will originate in the human experience of searching and seeking and move outward to embrace ever wider horizons of life and reality.[2]

A revolutionary dynamic is currently at work in the culture. Western culture is in the process of completely reevaluating and revising virtually every aspect of the human condition. As Douglas Rushkoff states, "The degree of change experienced by the last three generations rivals that of a species undergoing mutation. . . . What we need to adapt to, more than any particular change, is the fact that we are changing so rapidly."[3]

The two lyrics from Bob Dylan quoted at the beginning of this introduction exemplify what I am talking about here. Between the years 1963 and 2000, when those songs were released publicly, much has changed, not only in Western culture but also around the world. When Dylan's 1963 song was released it was seized on by a generation of frustrated and discontented young people who yearned for change and longed for a new way of being. Disillusionment over the Vietnam War, shifting sociopolitical and socioeconomic factors, and a host of other issues related to such diverse areas as technology, manufacturing, and changing production methods that affected labor were redrawing the cultural landscape. In 1963, the faint stirrings of an immense cultural shift were being felt. The idea that the times were changing was in the very air of the West.

By the time Dylan released his song "Things Have Changed" in 2000, those first faint stirrings had coalesced into a new paradigm in Western cultural history that many term the postmodern paradigm. I have no real desire to engage in a treatment of the modern/postmodern phenomenon; I have done that far too many times and find it an exercise in frustration at best. All things postmodern remain somewhat polarizing and would tend to steer us off track and down philosophical rabbit holes that are not pertinent to the conversation here. I am now more inclined to declare this shift "postsecular," but that is yet another word destined to divide us unnecessarily. So let me quote Mr. Dylan again: "things have changed." However it is termed, this is the reality.

It seems that we are entering a new age, a new time, governed by a new ethos and a new desire for meaning. But there is a tension. The titles of the two songs by Dylan seem to reflect a linear progression from changing times in 1963 to realized change in 2000. This is far from true; old ages die slowly, if at all, and new paradigms generally take a long time to establish themselves. However, I contend that things are moving at a rapid pace today, and the consolidation of a new cultural paradigm is emerging at a frantic pace and is quickly defining and delineating itself. It is within the realm of this new paradigm that the present book is set.

Entertainment Theology is an exploration of some of the new directions that faith and belief seem to be taking in our time. It is a look into key shaping factors and dynamics in contemporary religious exploration and practice. It also suggests ways in which Christian faith might more effectively engage in the current conversation about religion.

I wish to emphasize the word "current" for it is surely a new conversation, sometimes barely informed by traditional concepts of God, faith, or the nature of belief. The Chinese revolutionaries greeted each other with the question, "Are you living in the new world?"[4] In this book I locate the missional-theological reflection of the Christian faith in this new world. There are many things to explore in the twenty-first century; changes seem to be occurring in every realm of life. This book focuses on what is perhaps one of the more surprising dynamics of Western cultural life today—a return to God. But before we get too excited and gleefully rub our church-growth hands together, as we will see later, this return to God is not a return to premodern concepts and traditions but a movement *forward*. The return to God is in fact a shift into entirely new understandings of the religious dynamic.

I argue that "spirituality" is the new religion of our times. I sometimes call what is occurring "techno-spirituality" or "postsecular spirituality." Both terms are attempts to capture key elements of the new state of things, for surely what is going on in the realm of the spiritual is post or after the secular and decidedly influenced by technology of all kinds, from information technology to mass media in all their forms. I also use the term spirituality for specific reasons. Quite often in my conversations with people both inside and outside the church I hear comments such as, "I'm not religious," or "I'm not into religion," or "I'm not religious, I'm spiritual." This "I'm spiritual, not religious" comment represents a shift in approaches to religion and belief. It used to be that if we referred to someone as religious we would also say that they were "deeply spiritual," highlighting the perception that religion and spirituality were in harmony with each other, but this perception no longer holds true. Some are quite frustrated with the term "spiritual" and dismiss it because they seem unable to get a singular definition for what this means. Nor will they. I don't think that there is a singular definition, because people use the term in diverse and often contradictory ways. Rather than seeking a singular definition for "spiritual," we should see it as an umbrella term under which all kinds of ideas and perspectives are gathered. It is a symbolic term—defining the proclaimant as someone who is at the very least neither a raging fundamentalist nor a "boring" church person. I will speak more about this later in the book. The October 15, 2001, edition of the *London Times* included a report on a recent religious survey in which enough people polled about their "religious affiliation" answered "Jedi Knight" (a character from the *Star Wars* movies) that future polls will include this option. This might seem comical at first, but it does point to the fact that a growing number of people do not find their spiritual beliefs compatible with many more-traditional faith expressions. And the use of a fictional character from a Hollywood movie also points us toward another key theme in this book, that popular culture is a prime resource for thinking about issues of faith and belief. People not only "find God" in the movies, they also find new ways of believing and expressing themselves spiritually.

On the one hand, to speak of "religion" now is to imply complicity with static tradition, rigid dogma, and quite often conservative fundamentalism. Spirituality, on the other hand, is perceived as a flowing, vibrant, and meaningful term that describes the religious experience. Accompanying this is a shift away from formal expressions of faith such as public worship, prayer, and other communal rituals; the creation of personalized rituals and practices is a growing trend. At present there is a devaluing of form because form represents dead religious observance. This has led many to dismiss the current state of interest in spirituality as all surface and no depth. While I agree that much of contemporary spirituality lacks substance in its many forms, it is too easy to dismiss the entire state of things in the contemporary situation as lacking depth because it does not meet the criteria of religious expressions as they have been traditionally understood.

It is often difficult for those engaged in more-formal religious expressions to cope with the shift in both attitude and practice. How can we take seriously someone who really believes that a Jedi Knight offers spiritual guidance and insight to the questions of ultimate meaning in human existence?! How can all of these seemingly trendy and often vapid personal beliefs really point toward a meaningful shift in the state of religious affairs? Surely it is not possible, so why waste energy discussing it? Fair enough, it is certainly true that in more stable[5] times the link between spiritual observance and formal religious practice seems to have been more consistent, but in these rapidly changing times this is no longer the case. My conversations with students at Art Center College of Design, where I teach, have affirmed my own intuitions about this shift. In six semesters of teaching a particular class on advertising I have polled a total of seventy-two students on their spiritual and religious interests. Of those seventy-two students, fewer than ten associated themselves with any particular religious tradition, but fifty-four regarded themselves as actively embracing the spiritual in their lives. I am certainly not building the entire case for my thoughts on a straw poll of a few students, but it does reflect larger dynamics I see within the culture. Spirituality *is* the new dynamic, and it is an often surprising, multifaceted, multidimensional expression of faith. As Sandra Schneiders says:

> Spirituality has rarely enjoyed such a high profile, positive evaluation, and even economic success as it does among Americans today. If religion is in trouble, spirituality is in the ascendancy and the irony of this situation evokes puzzlement and anxiety in the religious establishment, scrutiny among theologians, and justification among those who have traded the religion of their past for the spirituality of their present.[6]

Researchers David Hay and Kate Hunt offer this comment from a United Kingdom perspective:

> Something extraordinary seems to be happening to the spiritual life of Britain. At least that's what we think, after a look at the findings of the "Soul of Britain" survey recently completed by the BBC. The results show that more than 76 percent of the population would admit to having had a spiritual experience. In hardly more than a decade, there has been a 59 percent rise in the positive response rate to questions about this subject. Compared with 25 years ago, the rise is greater than 110 percent.[7]

Within this new dynamic the traditional faiths, particularly the monotheistic faiths—Christianity, Islam, and Judaism—tend to function as a subset of the overall religious environment and form a kind of well from which elements of their tradition are appropriated and refashioned into new expressions. They are often viewed as simply another resource for funding new permutations of faith. A pinch of Buddhism, a dash of Zen, mixed with the Sermon on the Mount, and served up with a heavy layer of karma or some "teachings" from the *Matrix* movies. While much of this inclination can be quickly dismissed as little more than trendy and shallow, and thus perhaps not worth serious reflection, there are larger dynamics at work that offer some challenges for Christian faith in the twenty-first century.

This book reflects on a major issue that characterizes much of our contemporary cultural life—democratization, particularly a democratization of spirit[8]—that is sweeping through religion today. Democratization is a key dynamic of our times. I do not mean democratization in a political sense, although that also seems to be a current obsession. The democratization I refer to is linked to new technologies, computers, the Internet, the continuing evolution of capitalism, the dynamics of globalization, the continuing rise and influence of popular culture, and a host of other seemingly unrelated issues that combine to forge a new reality. The collapse or loss of faith in traditional forms of leadership and structure combined with virtually unlimited access to information has resulted in an empowering of the masses that is transforming the culture. Spirit, though closely guarded by religious institutions, is not immune to this democratization process. After the modern age, in which spirit was privatized and banished to the margins of culture, becoming a matter of private faith rather than public discourse,[9] new possibilities have emerged in the search for the spiritual. Spirit in this time of democratization is *liquid*. It is not simply represented symbolically by water, as spirit often has been; it *is* water, it is liquid, flowing freely, barely contained, carving new channels in the culture.

This is occurring not only in the realm of belief, for virtually every area of life is undergoing dynamic change and much of it can be traced back to the process of democratization. Pop music, for instance, has experienced radical transformation over the last twenty years because of new technologies and an anti-establishment attitude. Inventions such as computer-based recording and CD-burning technologies have transformed the recording process and given more people access to the creation and dissemination of popular music. What once required the resources and technological equipment available only through large record companies can now be produced at home. File-sharing technologies have allowed for the transferring of downloadable music files and have forced the recording industry to rethink the control and dissemination of their product.

On another front, the breakdown in social structures combined with a loss of faith in institutions has led to a reconfiguring of family and social life. The question, "What is family?" is no longer easily answered by reference to bloodline or traditional male/female parental roles. Changes in adoption law and new scientific advances in embryonic research allow for different permutations of what constitutes family. Graham Cray, Bishop of Maidstone and key architect of the Anglican Church Fresh Expressions project, said, "What is taking place is . . . the death of the culture that formerly conferred Christian identity upon the British people."[10]

Admittedly this quote is a more direct reference to British society, but given the high level of cultural and social exchange between the two nations and the similar cultural developments over the past forty years, this statement can easily apply to the United States.

The new dynamics in belief today are populist; they reflect what is largely a collection of broad-based people movements rather than a mediated set of practices derived from a professional religious hierarchy or clergy. As a populist movement or mood, it is informed and shaped by popular culture. Thus, I use the term "entertainment theology" to point to the relationship between the contemporary religious climate and the popular consumer culture. A key focus of all this is related to media culture of all kinds. Entertainment theology is both a disseminating point and a central dynamic of the new conversations about all things God, derived largely from the intersection of public interest and media creativity.

Entertainment theology highlights the evolution of theology from a didactic or studied approach to the question of God to a more global *communal conversation* about the sacred in general. Of course, many will argue that this is far from an evolution, but I hope to tantalize the reader and generate enough interest for them to consider a new opinion, and hopefully, a new energized engagement.

These developments in the contemporary religious conversation are driven by a host of developments in media in the late twentieth century: Internet technology, which allows the flow of information and interaction with that material in unprecedented and uncontrolled ways; film, which as a reflector of social values brought the contemporary search for spirituality to the big screen throughout the nineties with films such as *Fight Club*, *The Truman Show*, *Magnolia*, and perhaps most importantly *The Matrix* and *The Sixth Sense*; books, which are often dismissed as the relic of another more text-driven time but which remain important to contemporary religion as they have become the primary means of continuing study of one's spiritual interests in this age of democratization of spirit, whether it be *The Celestine Prophecy* or *The Purpose-Driven Life*; television, that most intimate of technologies, which in reconfiguring the layout of family living rooms opened us up to ideas and issues that were once discussed only in public spaces. The debut of the CBS television show *Touched by an Angel* in 1995—a show with an explicitly religious theme—signaled the emergence of entertainment theology in America's living rooms and launched the conversation into the stratosphere. The success of that show has been duplicated in shows like *Joan of Arcadia* and the HBO channel's *Carnivale*, which have fashioned the continuing interest in questions of ultimate reality into moderately successful television shows. More recently, *Brotherhood*, a crime-family drama on the Showtime Network, explored sibling rivalry and family tensions, using a scriptural reference as a title for each episode.[11]

This new dynamic is also all about fashion. Everything in the twenty-first century is, whether we realize it or not. Religion and spirituality are a matter of design, as is much of contemporary life. Bruce Mau, a leading figure in the world of graphic design, has recently launched an organization called Institute without Borders and a traveling, ever-evolving art exhibition called *Massive Change*. The simple goal of this venture is to gather together people from virtually every area of study and investigate ways in which design can both help and shape ongoing human existence. It is not simply performance art but rather an attempt to shape a new metanarrative for society built around principles of design!

> What we see over the last hundred and fifty years, and in a dramatically accelerated pace over the last fifty, is that design is changing its place in the order of things. Design is evolving from its position of relative insignificance within business (and the larger envelope of nature), to become the biggest project of all. Even life itself has fallen (or is falling) to the power and possibility of design. Empowered as such, we have a responsibility to address the new set of questions that go along with that power.[12]

Developments in design have followed the shifting climate of cultural change and have emerged as a culture-shaping force. We live in a design age. Virtually everything we consume is the product of fashion and design. We speak of designer homes, clothes, vacations, and even babies. Religion is not exempt; the rise of entertainment theology is a testament to this. It is guided by trends in consumer culture and it is consumer driven. "Shopping for faith" and "cafeteria religion" are terms used to describe the current situation. They reflect an awareness that religion and the consumer experience are inextricably linked. This is not completely new; there has always been an intersection between religious expression, material culture, and the arts:

> People build religion into the landscape, they make and buy pious images for their homes, and they wear special reminders of faith next to their bodies. Religion is more than a type of knowledge learned through reading holy books and listening to holy men. . . . Throughout American history, Christians have explored the meaning of the divine, the nature of death, the power of healing, and the experience of the body by interacting with a created world of images and shapes.[13]

What makes this aspect of contemporary religion different is that rather than employing material culture to give visual support to internal belief, it is itself a *product of consumer culture*. It is informed not from without, by institution or tradition, but from *within consumer culture*. It is, as Graham

Ward argues in his book *True Religion*,[14] the commodification (the commercialization) of religion in the postsecular age. It is the redefining of the relationship between the sacred and the profane. Hence there is little issue in the larger culture with a pop singer like Britney Spears, who, before entering into a series of questionable public efforts at self-humiliation and eventual marriage, presents herself as a committed Christian and virgin yet dresses immodestly and presents a stage show replete with images and representations of rampant sexuality.

> The religious experience is inseparable from a consumer experience. The consumer experience (consumer therapy) and the religious experience are both desire-driven and aim at immediate satisfaction.[15]

The topics explored in this book stand then as testament to the cultural and social shifts that have occurred in Western culture since the late 1970s and that now represent a significant challenge to the primacy of traditional faith practices. The emergence of new faith expressions thrusts us into a new social and missiological situation. There is increasing evidence that the locus of contemporary religion is not found in the churches or synagogues or mosques, which give little credence to it, or in the largely materialist culture in which we all find ourselves, but it is found in the lives of those who are fashioning vibrant, new permutations of religious belief and practice in our time, in spite of what seem to be tough obstacles to such a dynamic.

There are tremendous implications of all this on the future of Christian faith. Like other ancient faiths, Christianity has shown itself able to stand the test of time and has proven itself to be a viable contribution to the ongoing human search for God. While I am positive about Christianity's ability to meet the changing cultural contexts of the past, I am concerned that at the present moment Christian faith is losing ground. The Church of England's report issued in 2004, titled "The Mission-Shaped Church," notes that people do not come to church because they consider it "peripheral, obscure, confusing or irrelevant."[16] If this perception is not changed, the gap between a burgeoning spiritual culture and the potential for missional engagement will continue to widen. The purpose of the present book is to explore the shapes and contexts of the contemporary situation and offer a mission-shaped theological response to meet the present challenge.

On a more personal note, I must say that I wrestle with my thoughts and feelings about what is written in these pages on virtually a daily basis. It is complex and often complicated, and there is no "clear" picture, no one answer to what is happening in the realm of all things spirit and spiritual. There are only shades, glimpses, and occasional patches of light in an otherwise opaque situation.

Some of what I discuss in these pages will be quickly and easily dismissed by those for whom these questions are still easily answered by their own religious and theological perspectives. In fact, there is a good chance that some will think I am a little nuts to talk about how a movement toward something like Asian-inspired home furnishings could possibly relate to "real" spirituality, that it somehow must constitute more than that. But for me, these things do matter, and when they are taken as part of a whole, they point to significant issues that affect the way in which faith is approached in our times.

There are people I respect on these matters who dismiss the current fascination with spirituality as nothing more than an attempt by many to placate their otherwise soulless existences with a veneer, a sheen, of meaning. While I disagree wholeheartedly, I can understand why they think this. In my own explorations of these issues, I have come across people I think just need to get a grip on reality and stop playing around—there are a lot of kooky people out there!

As I write, I am holding a couple of things in tension. What I write about in these pages is largely concentrated on what I think is the next religious horizon—new-edge spirituality—but I also think that much of the locus of religious thought and reflection over the next couple of decades will be concerned with the challenges of mainstream theological issues. The current debates and schisms in the Anglican Church over issues of gender and sexuality, as well as the turmoil in Islam, are issues that will capture and demand our attention as these, and other mainstream faiths, work out their own new relationships and identities in and with the new cultural situations. These issues are probably the subject of a very good book, but they will not be the focus of this one. I believe that the other stuff, the alternative expressions, warrants our attention, particularly if we hold any sort of belief in the missional dynamics of Christian faith.

On a more practical note, the book is divided into three sections. Rather than calling them chapters, I am calling them thoughts because I think it helps to set a different tone when it comes to processing what one finds here—I am thinking out loud, attempting to integrate various thoughts and ideas in some kind of cohesive manner.

The first section is largely foundational, attempting to explore some of the necessary social and philosophical issues that have led to the present situation. For many this will be quite familiar territory and will include topics they probably will not wish to explore again, so feel free to jump in elsewhere! Much has been written about this sort of thing, and I realize that it could be unnecessary for many readers who are well ahead of me in this area of study. I have tried not to burden the reader with too much preamble, but in order to make sense of what is going on for readers for whom this topic is newer, I will address a number of peripheral issues.

The second section deals with some key rubrics under which I have collected various manifestations of the new spiritual impulses and have attempted to put them into some scheme of vague categorization. This demonstrates how I process much of what is going on for my own sanity. It was born out of a desire to give more clarity to both students and peers about how I "read" the present moment, how I analyze and process what is happening around me in the world of the spiritual. It covers a lot of territory but is by no means meant to be a complete accounting. As I describe in more detail throughout the book, I am trying to capture a "mood" as much as anything else. What does spirituality look and feel like in the twenty-first century? All this talk of alternative beliefs, how does it manifest, where do I look for it?

The final section addresses the present situation from a decidedly Christian perspective. Or rather, I address Christianity from the present perspective, offering a challenge to one particular faith about how it might respond to the times and become a vital part of the cultural conversation about faith. What I write about is predicated on a belief that things need to change. I have done this principally because Christian faith is where I have hung my own spiritual hat for more than twenty years, and it is from there that my forays into the wider world of religious belief of all kinds began and continue.

My relationship with Christianity is admittedly in a state of flux these days, and I find myself increasingly uncomfortable, and not necessarily in agreement, with where much of the church seems to be heading, and this has prompted much of the final section. I believe there is a different way to process and manifest Christian faith, but it will take some stretching on our part. Christianity has enjoyed a privileged position in the Western cultural imagination, but that does not guarantee it a special place in the new spiritual environment that I am convinced is emerging around us. I humbly offer a few ways I think things could be different. Many will disagree, I am sure, and I lay no claim to being right. I am simply trying to respond to the world I live in.

Theology is a great love of mine—it's rather arcane, I know, but there you have it. And for me, theology, or God-talk, as Phyllis Tickle puts it, is all about dialogue and conversation between our lives and our concepts and constructs of the divine.

The prophet Ezekiel once had a vision in which he was led into water. As he followed the direction of his guide he found himself going through stages of increasing immersion: water to his ankles, then to his knees, and then to his waist, all the while going deeper and deeper into the currents of the river until he reached a point where he could no longer touch the bottom and had to swim in order not to drown (Ezek. 47:1–6). I think it is easy to play with God in the shallows where we can feel the current of the river but do not really face the current as it seeks to carry us away. It is much more difficult to move out into the force of the water and feel its almost relentless challenge, its invitation to be carried away by its current.

Interestingly, in the Bible story I just mentioned, when the prophet left the shore to enter the waters, the ground around him was barren and desert-like, but when he returned after his deepwater experience, the land along the river had become lush and verdant. Sometimes what we hold on to prevents us from experiencing the blossoming of new life. I think there is new life for a faith like Christianity, but in order to discover it we may have to let go of other things first and venture into the deep and feel the current of the twenty-first century river. That is the invitation extended through this book.

Part I

New Horizons

Religion, it has been said, is a social production and as such can be understood only in context. For me, the contexts for understanding religion in our culture have changed dramatically:

> [If] in modernity, contexts for understanding religion included our reliance upon science and technology, the presence of industrial development and the growth of urbanism, of the nation state, and of bureaucratic organization, along with an outlook generally framed by the notion of progress, then what has changed?[1]

In light of this change in understandings about religion, we must discuss the philosophical, cultural, and social dynamics that combine to lay the foundation for the emergence of renewed interest in religion: the contemporary "return to god." I believe there are three key and interwoven dynamics that need to be explored: the reenchantment of Western culture,[2] the rise of postsecular society,[3] and the democratization of spirit. These three are not distinct and separate but form an ever-expanding context into which ideas and reflections from many disciplines and fields of study converge to create new contexts. The three elements explored in this section give rise to certain *characteristics* that make up the postsecular condition. These characteristics include:

- a renewed interest in the spiritual life that reflects a relaxation of the suspicion toward spiritual issues that marked much of the modern era;
- a recognition that secular rights and freedoms of expression are a prerequisite to the renewal of spiritual interest and exploration;
- an embrace of spiritual and intellectual pluralism: "east and west";

- the emergence of a global culture linked by media, technology, and shared experiences.

Key dynamics at work to produce the new religious permutations are:

- the collapse of modern political ideologies that compete with Western democratic capitalism;
- the implosion of modernity via postmodernity;
- the manifest failure of secularism as a totalizing theory;
- the emergence and advance of post-Newtonian chaotic-observer aware science;
- information and communication technology;
- spiritually aware art, music, film, literature, and philosophy.

To chart this rise is complex; finding figures and statistics to prove the rise of alternative faith expressions is difficult, particularly when what is occurring is as much a *mood* as it is a movement, and whatever kind of movement it might be it is certainly not a unified movement with particular and universal tendencies. The entire way people think about life is changing, and how we think about faith is changing just as radically. It is much easier to chart the decline of traditional faiths, which has been done quite often. To chart the emergence of new expressions of religion, we must turn to alternative sites for information and perspective.

Magical, Mystical Polish
The Reenchantment of Western Culture

The emergence of the postmodern has fostered postsecular thinking.

Graham Ward, *Blackwell Companion to Postmodern Theology*

In spite of the predictions of many over the past two hundred years, religion is back and once again at the forefront of Western imagination. The many theories and philosophies decrying our need of and the place for religion in our culture (even our world) have begun to crumble even as the very foundation on which they were built—secularism—itself implodes. According to William Connolly, "The historical *modus vivendi* called secularism is coming apart at the seams."[1] Here I follow Bryan Wilson's definition of secularization: "the process whereby religious thinking, practice, and institutions lose social significance."[2] The last two centuries of Western civilization have been a reflection of this definition. Traditional belief in God has changed and church attendance has declined dramatically; the church has lost its voice in society and is often viewed as marginal and a bit of an anomaly left over from another age. Lonnie Kliever observes:

> This mid-century crisis of faith was partly a side effect of certain changes in the social structures of modern life that were brought about by the scientific revolution. Most telling of all the changes was the loss of the Church's thousand-year monopoly on defining the nature of reality, the order of society, and the destiny of individuals.[3]

Much has been written on the crisis of faith and no time will be taken here to explore it, since the focus of this work is the return of God and religion to the center of social space, not religion's preceding demise. In our "mediated"[4] world we are experiencing a reenchantment of considerable proportion—"God," as they say, has made a comeback. God looks remarkably different in the new context but is back nonetheless. "Religious sentiment is itself a social product," wrote Karl Marx.[5] Marx was deeply influenced by Ludwig Feuerbach's book *The Essence of Christianity*, in which Feuerbach argued that God is a "projection of humanity."[6] Believing that religion had been explained once and for all by Feuerbach, Marx essentially adopted his theory in toto without engaging in any additional reflection of his own. Marx, of course, was attempting to eradicate the religious from the world, and Feuerbach's theories supported and fueled his efforts. "Religion is only the illusory sun which revolves around man so long as he does not revolve around himself," Marx wrote.[7] Marx's anthropocentric view is but one of many reveling in modernity's fascination with itself and focused on humanity.

Regardless of our views of Marx or Marxism, he and Feuerbach were not alone in their theories about religion as a product of society, and today we find that many of those theories have become widely accepted. For instance, commenting on Emile Durkheim's belief in the social functions of religion, Alan Aldridge wrote that Durkheim believed there was indeed a reality behind religion. That reality, however, is not God but society. The religion he spoke of was regarded as fulfilling important social and psychological functions.[8] He also believed that if a society did not have a religion, it would not have a proper consciousness of itself. The heart of religion, according to Durkheim, is that through it society is presented to itself as religion expresses, dramatizes, and symbolizes social relationships.[9] This is but one of many views floating around in the universe today, and all of them contribute in some way to contemporary views about God and religion.

I am inclined to agree with this theory, because I believe that religion is a social production. Having traveled quite extensively to many different cultures, I find it easy to see that different cultural contexts contribute to the ways particular societies manifest their beliefs. What I find really interesting today is that given our movement toward a more global context for the human experience and the fact that few of us live in sociocultural isolation anymore, the production of religion is now not simply a matter of particular cultural expression but is a sort of global mélange or bricolage of ideas that create new and diverse manifestations of the religious impulse that I think beats within the heart of all humans.

The idea that religion is a social production raises the question of what kind of religion is being produced today and *why*. How is Western society and, alongside this, an emerging global society representing itself through religion today? What is being dramatized and symbolized through the contemporary religious experience? The social production of religion in the postmodern era is complex, contradictory, and often confusing. Richard Cimino and Don Lattin note the growing gap between personal spirituality and religious institutions in their book *Shopping for Faith*.[10] Addressing what they see as a divorce between spirituality and traditional religion, they quote a monk, Brother David Steindl-Rast: "There is something happening in our time. . . . The emphasis is moving from the institution to the personal experience . . . the institution has become so rigid and ossified it is collapsing under its own weight."[11] In spite of the authors' best efforts, however, they fail to make a serious distinction between institution and personal experience. They simply highlight the shift in cultural preference for one over the other and the perception that it means something entirely different. But as I argued in my introduction at the risk of added confusion, spirituality *is* the religion of postsecular times. Spirituality, as expressed today, often refers to a belief in faith but a rejection of formalized or institutionalized forms of religious expression. It tends to be a reflection of a highly individuated form of faith.[12] This interest in refashioned faith, devoid of dogma and hierarchical structure, points to a shift toward the reenchantment of society. It is a new form of religious construction.

Max Weber wrote of the "disenchantment of the world" (*die Entzauberung der Welt*), believing that magic and mystery had been driven from the world by the dominance of bureaucracy. Modernity according to Weber can be characterized by rationalization—the rule of experts, the bureaucrats: "Specialists without spirit, sensualists without heart, this nullity imagines that it has attained a level of civilization never before achieved."[13] He argued that rationalization meant the spread of legal-rational systems of domination embodied in bureaucratic systems of administration in which authority is impersonal, top down, and vested in rules rather than the traditional or charismatic forms of authority that were in operation in premodern times. In such a system, rules are followed not because of charismatic leadership or personal authority on the part of the issuer but simply because they have been issued by the appropriate officeholder. Devotion to leadership is replaced with meticulous implementation of regulations in conformity to a chain of command. He went on to declare bureaucracy as the reason for the decline of religious significance in modernity and described it as an "iron cage" in which we are imprisoned.[14]

This dominance of bureaucracy is, for Weber, at the root of the decline of the social significance of religion in the modern world. Weber also declared that modernity's forest was managed, not enchanted.[15] The iron cage of bureaucracy that Weber called one of the defining characteristics of modernity has burst open in the postmodern world, and rationalization and bureaucracy have been largely rejected as a viable means of managing the world. In fact, the postmodernist is not looking to manage his or her world as much as to discover the mystery and magic in it—hello enchantment! What is interesting is that the very technology and rationalism—scientific rationalism, in fact—that Weber identified as the means by which the world was disenchanted has proven to be the tool by which reenchantment has occurred.

In an essay titled "Faith and Knowledge," Jacques Derrida had this to say about the reenchantment of the world: "Because one increasingly *uses* artifacts and prostheses of which one is totally ignorant, in a growing disproportion between knowledge and know-how, the space of such technical experience tends to become more animistic, magical, mystical."[16] The reenchantment of the world is linked to our use of technology. The access to the fruits of modernity, the age of scientific rationalism, is what allows us ultimately to reenchant our lives. Technology, both the written word that perhaps marks the dawning of the modern age and the computer technologies that herald its morphing into a new stage, provides the means by which a bureaucratized culture finds its way back to the mystical. As Ward observes:

> Rather than scientific reasoning and instrumental thinking leading to reductive, positivist and behaviorist accounts of the way things are, such reasoning and thinking has promoted itself through emphasizing its inventive power, its creativity, its imaginative scope. Allied with the glitter of the media and advanced telecommunications, technology has become sexy, seductive and the bearer of messianic possibilities.[17]

Ward goes on to say that science no longer exists simply to provide the means for mastery of the planet or for our personal benefit. Instead it provides the milieu in which we live.[18] We are immersed in technology and we use that technology to investigate and create new possibilities for our lives, leading to a form of techno-transcendence.

My fascination with and interest in the return of the mystical and magical have certainly been fueled by the sheer volume of material that has permeated popular culture since the dawn of the last decade of the twentieth century. Popular culture is another avenue by which reenchantment occurs in postsecular times. Millions of copies of the Harry Potter books have re-acquainted schoolchildren not only with the joy and thrill of reading but also with ideas about magic and mystery and the paranormal.[19]

And not only children. So successful and intergenerational are the stories that new editions have been released with covers and text styles marketed directly to adults.[20] But it is not only Harry Potter books. Blockbuster Hollywood versions of the books were translated into films and found immense, worldwide box-office success. At the same time the runaway success of the film versions of J. R. R. Tolkien's trilogy, *The Lord of the Rings*, has met with similar, if not even greater, box-office success.

This reenchantment of popular culture is not limited to occasional movies or children's novels. For instance, the music video for the song "There There" by the United Kingdom band Radiohead was directed by Chris Hopewell and is based on a series of children's stories called *Bagpuss* by Oliver Postgate. The story takes place in an enchanted forest inhabited by woodland creatures who act like humans; in other words, they have been "civilized"—they live in homes and dress like humans, read newspapers and gather in organized meetings, and are "married" by puritan-like crows. The lead singer, Thom Yorke, is led through the forest to a luminous white coat and magical shoes, which, after he has put them on, completely change the dynamics in the forest! The forest reclaims all the civilization, turning everything, including the singer himself, back into forest. Here is a visual example of the reclamation of magic and mystery and a rejection of the bureaucratized, managed forest/world.[21]

The emergence of spiritually aware art of all kinds and in a broad variety of incarnations—music, film, painting, and literature—mediated to us via popular culture is a key informational source for understanding the present context. Consider, for example, that in the past few years over 150 million books related to spirituality have been sold. Released in 1993, James Redfield's *Celestine Prophecy*,[22] which has sold twelve million copies to date, was one of the first books on spirituality to penetrate deep into supposedly secular contemporary culture. Since that time the various works of Deepak Chopra have sold over twenty million copies; empowerment writer and speaker Wayne Dyer's count is twenty titles with thirty million copies sold. *The Alchemist*,[23] Paolo Coehlo's book of spiritual musings, has sold around twenty-seven million copies and counting. Alongside these books are others, such as Rick Warren's *Purpose-Driven Life*,[24] which has sold fifty million copies so far, and the untold number of the *Left Behind*[25] series by Jerry Jenkins and Tim LaHaye.[26] The bulk of these books inform and help shape contemporary cultural expressions of faith. Actor Matthew Settle, who is playing John Woodson, the main character in *The Celestine Prophecy*, in a film version of the book, had this to say in a recent magazine article about the significance of his character for the contemporary religious quest:

> What I liked about the story is the restoration of wonder to this person's life. John is kind of walking through life with a blasé, meaningless existence, just doesn't feel like he has a sense of purpose. And when he starts recognizing coincidences and trusting his uncertainty, he finds a new certainty in trusting a lack of certainty, you know? He finds confidence in life, confidence in a God-force, and gives himself over to this thing that would otherwise be scary territory. It's a walk in faith.[27]

This "restoration of wonder" is yet another example of the reenchantment of Western culture, a return of magic and mystery to life. Again, this sense of wonder has been aided by advanced media technologies, which are able to produce incredible visual experiences that stretch our horizons of what is conceivable with regard to reality and fill us with a sense of awe about the universe we live in.

As I noted earlier, some of the reenchantment can seem slight when examined alone, but when viewed in the larger cultural context there is evidence of a significant movement afoot in our time.

The Implosion of Modernity
and the Rise of the Postsecular

From the moment that European opinion decided for toleration, it decided
for an eventual free market in opinion.

> Owen Chadwick, *The Secularization of the European*
> *Mind in the Nineteenth Century*

Postmodernism is postsecularism waiting to be born.

> Patrick Glynn, *God: Evidence*

There are many factors that led to the emergence of a postsecular culture.
Postsecular does not mean the end of secularism as much as the transformation of secularism into a new phase. Peter Steinfels, writing in the
August 3, 2002, edition of the *New York Times*, had this to say about
the postsecular shift:

> That the world has indeed become postsecular is now virtually beyond
> debate, though whether this is good or bad is definitely not. Religion is
> booming on several continents, sometimes literally with rockets and artillery
> shells. Resurgent forms of ancient faiths have filled in voids created by the
> collapse of effective state institutions or secular ideologies, whether socialist
> or nationalist. The long running debate about secularization is by no means
> over, but increasingly it focuses on the future of current religious institutions
> rather than religion per se, and on changing ways in which believers—or
> seekers—relate their personal faiths to public engagements.[1]

Steinfels, a senior writer on religion for the *New York Times*, is arguing in
his article for a new discipline—postsecular studies—to replace religious
studies.

> The lesson is obvious. Those who study, articulate or propound the beliefs
> and practices by which most of humanity tries to place itself in relationship

with the transcendent should post themselves. They should simply drop that old-fashioned word "religion." What they are about, they should announce, is "postsecularism."[2]

There is an element of humor in Steinfels's article, but beyond the digs at both traditional religion and the current fascination with adding the word "post" to anything in order to legitimize it in the eyes of contemporary society, he points out that the future of religious studies lies in the broader discipline of postsecular studies, which itself is a marker of the cultural shifts at work in Western culture over the past half century.

On any given day, almost 800 million English-speaking people can be found on-line, according to Global Reach, an Internet-based research company. This figure does not include the hundreds of millions of non-English speakers who also access the web. Logging on, the user is launched into a whole new universe, a new space created by flows of electronic information. Information on any subject is available; contact with other users regardless of geographic location or time zone is immediate. Images and audiovisual tours of the world's great museums and art galleries are all at one's fingertips, twenty-four hours a day.

> Time and space as conceived by empiricists collapse into omnipresence and multilocality. And the ride is continuous, for the electronic tide maintains you on the crest of impending satisfaction, far above any ocean floor, fast forwarding toward endless pleasures yet to be located and bookmarked. Time disappears, boredom is deflated.[3]

Graham Ward uses cyberspace as a cultural metaphor for postmodernism. He links modernism to particular concepts of time, space, and substance and argues that postmodernism succeeds in exploding the myths and ideologies that aided in the construction of modernity.[4]

I would contend that modernity is *imploding* rather than *exploding*. An implosion, in contrast to an explosion, is destruction from within; it highlights the fact that something is corrupt within the very system itself. Forces are rising from within that signal its continuing demise. On one level it will continue to exist in that its creations and contributions to society remain and will continue to live on.[5] The institutional structures, the contributions to architecture and the arts, the systems of education and laws all attest to the continuing modernist project. In fact, a dominant ethos of modernity—the belief in universal human rights—has become a key dynamic of the postsecular age.[6] To declare that modernity is imploding is not to show disdain, it is simply to acknowledge that there is a growing awareness of the intrinsic weakness of the modernist project with its overinflated anthropocentrism and belief in the future. This awareness has come not from without but from within in the form of postmodernity. While Ward argues that postmodern concepts of time and space have exploded the myths and ideologies of modernity, I say that they have been imploded. The very technology that allows for the redefining of time and space in postmodernity is a product of the modern age. Modernity has created the tools of its own demise.

This implosion is linked to four key areas of modernity: time, space, bodies, and governance—or, temporality, spatiality, corporeality, and authority. The implosion of modernity and the rise of the postsecular question assumptions about authority and place issues of identity in the foreground. This is occurring because the very makeup of human social life is undergoing a radical restructuring:

> There are ideologies of space and time and the nature of the entities which construct or fill them. In fact, there are only ideologies of these things, for our experience of spatiality, temporality, and corporeality is caught up with conceptual notions which prescribe an understanding, a nature, to space, time, and bodies. . . . Changes in the understanding of time, space, and the orders of creation have taken place.[7]

Timeless Time

Manuel Castells posited the notion that postmodernity introduces a new concept of time: timeless time. Castells used this term to highlight the transformation of our understanding of time. It refers to "the mixing of tenses to create a forever universe, not self-expanding, but self-maintaining, not cyclical but random, not recursive, but incursive: timeless time, using technology to escape the contexts of its existence, and to appropriate selectively any value each context could offer the ever-present."[8] Living by the clock was a vital ingredient of modernity. The order of life in the modern world revolved around structures of time. Trains departed not by the sun shadowing across a dial or by the shifting of the solar landscape but by the hands on a clock, and, more recently, by the second-fractions of digital clocks. Time as measurable and predictable was the necessary understanding of time in a bureaucratic and managed age like modernity. In our postmodern age the clock is still necessary, but our social understanding of time is transformed. This is what Castells is attempting to illuminate in his writings. "Timeless time" is, for Castells, the dominant form of social time.[9] In modernity, work time, leisure time, and family time were all governed in one sense or another by the clock. One's work time was governed by the time requirements of the employer—gone was the pre-Industrial Age's understanding of time linked to the rising and setting of the sun. The factory whistle signaled the start of work time as well as its ending. And with these shifts we moved into new concepts of past, present, and future.

These dynamics remain within postmodernity, and yet they have been radically altered, particularly in our perceptions of them. For instance, returning to Ward's use of cyberspace as a metaphor for the postmodern condition, we can see that modernity's clock, or concept of time, is devalued. At best it grants awareness of time outside the on-line universe: when we logged on, how long we have been on-line, and what time it is when we complete our on-line journeys. But while we are on-line, modernity's time tools have absolutely no use. We enter a world where time and space mean something else. In the on-line universe, there is no need for traditional senses of time and space because we are, in a sense, in a new dimension of both. It matters not whether it is day or night, because for other users it may be the inverse of our context. This is discontinuous time, which eliminates the need for old-fashioned sequencing of time. It is also compressed time, where past, present, and future come together in continually new possibilities and configurations, allowing us to play with history, ideology, and information and create entirely new conceptions of life and living.

Space—The Final Frontier?

Modernity had a love affair with the idea of space travel. Humans have constantly looked to the heavens and dreamed of what lies beyond the confines of earth, and we have invented numerous tools and technologies, from telescopes to spaceships, to help us connect ourselves to whatever is "out there." The television show *Star Trek* characterized space as the "final frontier" in its weekly adventures of the Starship Enterprise and her crew, led by the inimitable Captain Kirk. Space exploration is a symbol of modernity's anthropocentrism and belief in its own power.[10] Efforts to conquer space fueled the Cold War animosity between East and West. Space remains a frontier in postmodernity, but again it is framed within a different social relationship with concepts of space. In modernity, as we became increasingly tied to the clock, to concepts of and governance by measured time, a separation occurred between time and space. In the premodern context, time and space were linked by a sense of place. But as Anthony Giddens notes, space pulled away from place while time was emptied, facilitating the lifting of social relationships from their traditional locales.[11] Space increasingly came to mean "out there," away from us, and we moved into a world governed more by concepts of time than of space.[12]

Simultaneous with this was a compression of time and space. Technological advancements, such as the telegraph and the telephone, made communication over long distances much more feasible and incredibly faster, and this only accelerated in postmodernity. Geographic space has been compressed by the advent of plane travel, and human contact has been made instant by telephone and Internet. Our temporal worlds have been rapidly compressed:

> The experience of time-space compression is challenging, exciting, stressful, and sometimes deeply troubling, capable of sparking, therefore, a diversity of social, cultural, and political responses.[13]

In cyberspace the only space is virtual space, hence the old categories of time and space that served modernity no longer suffice. Now we must distinguish between real and virtual time and space. Cyberspace is place as "no place." It does not exist geographically, it is not bound by traditional time constructs, and it is increasingly to this environment that we travel to work, play, and be informed. Here, time is transformed—it is accelerated, compressed, and reconfigured:

> Time and space, which in modernity seemed so measurable, so predictable, and which provide the warp and woof of social life, are also in flux. The social fabric is thus patterned in novel ways, with new dimensions. Time-space compression creates a global village, but the village is both everywhere and nowhere. . . . Time also implodes into an endless present. . . . Not only have seasons and day-and-night lost much of their salience for sociality; even the artificial divisions of the nine-to-five and the life cycle culminating in retirement at 65 are subject to rescheduling.[14]

This reconfiguration of time and space has ramifications for the emergence of new religious impulses since there have always been links between concepts of time and space and religious meaning. There is a pop-culture reference to the relationship between time and space and the religious. William Shakespeare's play *Romeo and Juliet*, and its cinematic incarnations directed by Franco Zeffirelli and Baz Luhrmann, gives shape to the time-space implosion.

William Shakespeare wrote his play *Romeo and Juliet* in the years 1594 and 1595.[15] It was a play that drew on an earlier work, a narrative poem by Arthur Brooke, titled "The Tragicall Historye of Romeus and Iuliet." Written in 1562, this poem was an amalgam of two centuries of European folkloric tradition[16] that told the story of two lovers, Romeo and Juliet, whose love is thwarted by family obligations and feuds. The story of the warring Montagues and Capulets in Verona is the context in which Shakespeare sets his tragedy of doomed love. The play begins in an atmosphere of sexual pleasure and violent struggle and is filled with religious references and imagery. Characters bear biblical names, such as Sampson, Abram, and Balthasar. Rosaline, Romeo's first romantic encounter, rejects Romeo's advances because she has taken vows of chastity and will become a nun. Another character, Benvolio, acts as Romeo's confessor and wishes to teach him doctrine (act 1, scene 1).[17] These are metaphorical references, but Shakespeare's metaphors have a habit of mirroring what was happening off-stage in his world;[18] this is what makes his work so enduring. In Shakespeare's time, religious wars were everywhere. These were the early days of the English Reformation, and at the time of writing *Romeo and Juliet*, Shakespeare's England was experiencing an intense time of aggressive persecution of Catholics. Shakespeare's father, John, was rumored to be a recusant, or Catholic sympathizer, and many contemporary writers on Shakespeare cite his father's religious affiliation as a key to deciphering his work.[19] Religion seems to be a subtext of *Romeo and Juliet*, as the two families reflect different religious values and the violence of the two warring houses seems to reflect the religious violence that defined English life during this time period. Erasmus's prayer for the *Peace of the Church* sums up the situation between the warring families: "There is no charity, no fidelity, no bonds of love, no reverence, neither laws nor yet of rulers, no agreement of opinions, but as it were in a misordered choir, every man singeth, a contrary note."[20]

A new cultural sensibility is being defined in *Romeo and Juliet*, and it is related not only to changing religious attitudes and dynamics but also to the shifts in concepts of time and space that accompany these religious changes.[21] The play can be viewed as a reflection of the mounting political and theological confusion attending the times and as a search for a way beyond it. The Capulet family reflects the still dominant Catholic worldview that had been England's part and is now passing away. Juliet's father proposes to hold an "old accustom'd feast" (*Romeo and Juliet* 1.2.20). In a conversation between Lady Capulet and Juliet's nurse, the feast is revealed to be taking place "a fortnight and odd days from Lammas" (1.3.15–20), probably on St. Swithun's Day, which sets the context for my reference to this play. Lammas marked the end of summer and was a harvest festival alternatively called "loaf-mass."[22] This sets the play in mid-July, a time of great importance on the liturgical calendar, which used to govern time in the pre-Reformation era. July was a month of six important feasts: St. Thomas à Becket, St. Swithun, St. Margaret, St. Mary Magdalene, St. James the Apostle, and St. Anne.[23] It was said that if it rained on St. Swithun's day, which traditionally marked the onset of summer storms, it would rain forty days thereafter and could potentially devastate the harvest. It would seem that the summer storms functioned as a metaphor in Shakespeare's play. The calendar of religious holidays and saints' days was an integral part of sixteenth-century English life. However, in 1536, King Henry VIII endorsed Latimer's Act, "for the Abrogation of certain holydays."[24] All the feast days in July, except that of St. James the Apostle, were done away with, including Lammas. This act in effect changed time and space in Shakespeare's England. Life was lived according to liturgical time up until this point, but this act, along with other actions by the Reformers, sought to change the structure of religious life in England,[25] and in so doing led the country into a new understanding of time and space. The play takes place according to the liturgical calendar at a time when the liturgical is being put aside and the new secular age is emerging.

The issuance of the *Book of Common Prayer* in 1552 signaled a major shift away from the old Catholic calendar, which cloaked the living in the mystical world of the saints, into the newly shaped world in which the lives of the saints and the mysteries of the kingdom of God were to play a much less prominent role in shaping daily life. "The calendar of the new book simply bulldozed away most of the main features of the liturgical year, leaving only the great feasts of Christmas, Easter and Whitsun and a handful of biblical saints days."[26]

The new calendar not only reshaped the liturgical calendar but also highlighted a new era in the relationship between church and state. These two realms of authority—ecclesial and civic—clash in *Romeo and Juliet*, which depicts a wrestling between the two and a shift in power as the civic and secular offices claim ultimate and final authority on the matters at hand in the story. In Shakespeare's play, as in his own world, a certain depiction of the experience of life and faith is being portrayed: the church is superseded by the civic. It is the dawn of a new era. Today we find ourselves at a similar junction; the secular, which has been the dominant "authority" in Western culture, is being redefined, replaced even, and a new era is dawning: the postsecular.

What we experience in *Romeo and Juliet* is the tension between the sacramental world and a secular politic regarding governance of the world. This tension signals a new separation between the sacred and the profane. Religion, the sacred, is being pushed out of the center of public life; it will no longer govern life the way it once did. The state, the profane or at least God-diminished, is now gaining ascendancy. The process of restructuring the religious life and landscape of the community of saints in England, begun by the Reformers under Henry VIII and continuing under the reign of Shakespeare's queen, Elizabeth I, was undertaken to purify the faith. What these Reformers also succeeded in doing was changing the liturgical understanding of the world.

To do away with holy days and saint days was to change concepts of time and space as well as the relationship of work, worship, and daily life. Framed by feast days, working life was set in the larger context of the transcendent. To take away church properties and to abolish monasteries, nunneries, processions, pilgrimages, icons, and the acknowledgment of particular saint days, was to change the way space—the relationship between place and sacred space—was understood. To rethink sacraments and ceremonies was to change the nature of materiality itself. The natural world was rendered opaque, not translucent. God was no longer visible in the daily order of things, the new calendar having reduced reference to God, saints, and holy days. Instead, it turned public attention toward the power of men's governance: the power of the throne, the state, or the government—the realm of humanity rather than the heavens. New views of spatiality, temporality, and corporeality were emerging. God's presence was now experienced through the eyes of faith rather than through the calendar. The dawn of modernity was imminent. In 1637, less than fifty years after Shakespeare wrote *Romeo and Juliet*, Rene Descartes offered his famous dictum, "cogito ergo sum,"[27] which is understood to be foundational to the modernist project.

When our concept of time and space changes, everything else changes as well. We live in a world of time and are shaped by our understanding of it. The medieval clock, which had only an hour hand, offers a different understanding of time than the ever-changing numbers on a digital watch.[28] Alternate understandings of the nature of reality accompany those different views. Our understanding of our physical space is linked to our concepts of spiritual space—our perceptions of a space in which our bodies are embedded.[29] The shifts highlighted in Shakespeare's play, and in his own changing cultural and social context, signaled a shift in space-time concepts that affected the whole of life: "In the last five centuries we have mapped the whole of terrestrial space, as continents, ice caps, and even the ocean floors have yielded their secrets to our cartographers' skills. In the present century, we have also mapped the moon. . . . Yet while we have been mapping and mastering physical space, we have lost sight of any kind of spiritual space."[30]

This loss of spiritual space, which characterizes modernity's concepts of space and time, has been reversed and amplified with the implosion of modernity and with the development of cyberspace. In postmodernity, cyberspace signals the shift toward a new understanding of time and space that allows for a reenchanting of the world. In two cinematic versions of Shakespeare's play, one at the height of modernity and the other at the dawn of postmodernity, we see this understanding of time and space as it affects the religious aspect of human life.

Franco Zeffirelli's 1968 version of *Romeo and Juliet* is an attempt to locate Shakespeare's play in its historical context. Typical of the modern age, where religion is a matter of private belief rather than public discourse, the film focuses on other aspects that are deemed more important. Evocation of historicity is paramount and, consequently, great attention is paid to locale and "authentic representation"—the film was shot in a medieval walled city, the actors dressed in High Renaissance style, and the soundtrack is filled with lutes, flutes, and other instruments that, at least if not authentic to the period, create the feel of such times. The focus of the film is the love between Romeo and Juliet, and in this interpretation, the love represented is of a specific kind: it is an idealized and virginal "pure" love.[31] The actors are complete unknowns ("virgins" to the screen and to the audience) and are presented almost as innocent children reveling in a sort of puppy love. There is no reference to Romeo's ardent pursuit of Rosaline, whose rejection of his advances leads to his search for another love in the original play. The "pure" love of Romeo and Juliet is contrasted with the compromised opulence of their warring families and the impure sexual innuendo of their peers. The film moves slowly and lingers over images and settings. It is like a visit to an art gallery. We are given opportunity to savor the opulent costumes and surroundings. The very sound of the words spoken in high Shakespearean style with emphasis on iambic pentameter draws attention to a time when words supposedly carried more weight and meaning.

The film, made during a boom time for Italian cinema (the age of Zeffirelli, Fellini, and Bertolucci), gives a nod to the changing times. The year 1968 was eventful. It was the year of the student uprisings in Paris, the Soviet invasion of Czechoslovakia, and the beginning of the end of the hippie movement, whose defiant dream of peace and love died a vicious death at a Rolling Stones concert at the Altamont Speedway in 1969. But the film attempts to preserve an element of the hippie ethos and presents Romeo and Juliet as a sort of young hippie couple committed to love and peace at all costs while the rest of their clans, the "establishment," continue to practice violence. The film is a critique of its own times, much as Shakespeare's original play was of his. In this version, religion is complicit in the conspiracy against love. Thus, the religious elements in the play are reconfigured. The Franciscan order, with its central vow of poverty and to which Friar Lawrence is joined, is accentuated while simultaneously being undermined by the opulence in which he lives—perhaps a critique of religion's acceptance of materialism and the goals of secular society. The church building in the film is austere, but a very ornate crucifix hangs over the congregation. Overall, however, the film presents religion as subservient to other themes, merely serving as a backdrop for the central story, which the filmmaker determines to be this pure, unadulterated, young love. Zeffirelli wants to make the story authentic by locating it in history and taking us there. The great statement of the film is that these are "not our times"—they are merely a background for a timeless story. This is time and space as past, as history, with which we are not associated except through nostalgic reenactment.

In 1996, almost thirty years later, a new version of the play was released to the cinema-going public. Baz Luhrmann's movie version[32] of the play was nothing like Zeffirelli's. There is no reverence for Shakespeare's love of iambic pentameter, no attempt to be "historically accurate." We find ourselves not in "Fair Verona," the ancient medieval Italian city, but rather in Mexico City, which now functions for Verona. It is not a walled city rising out of pastoral surroundings, as Zeffirelli portrayed it, but an urbanized, congested, polluted, overcrowded, and extremely violent Mexico City, at once riddled with poverty and extreme wealth. There is in the movie no historical dress, no medieval folk music. What we get is jump-cut editing, glaring color, and a vivid sheen to the surface of the film itself, giving a different pace to the narrative. "Breathless" would be the right word to describe the pace of the action, which shifts from locale to locale in blinding, often seemingly disconnected, leaps—the action and pace actually runs over the poetry. There is no pausing to savor

Shakespeare's mastery of the English language, as is often the intent in cinematic renderings of his work. At times it is hard even to hear what is being said, so the viewer must rely on images to give symbolic reference to the events unfolding.

The story itself is recontextualized and presented as a headline story in a television news presentation—presented, if you will, as a "real event." Yet many scenes unfold theatrically, some of them on an old, abandoned theater stage—entertainment as reality, reality as entertainment. The violent actions that frame and color the original play are presented as contemporary racial issues: the dark-skinned Spanish/Italian Capulets versus the light-skinned Montagues. The film also takes issues of sex and sexuality to new heights. Rather than forcing the sexual innuendo that fueled the original play[33] into the background, as Zeffirelli did, Luhrmann heightens it, not only raising issues of sexual innuendo but also expanding this framework to include contemporary debates and shifts in attitudes toward things such as transgender identity, incest, homosexuality, and many other contemporary debates on sexual ambiguity.

The film is a visually stunning event. Where Zeffirelli lingered longingly on ancient artifacts and representations, Luhrmann fills the screen with streams of visual stimulation, or "eye-candy." There is so much to see that one's eyes almost don't know where to focus. The camera keeps bringing forth bright, colorful, and interesting objects for the viewer's eyes to feast on: Juliet's ring, the guns belonging to the two warring families, engraved bullets, vials of colored liquids, tropical fish, interesting cars, clothing covered in slogans and religious imagery that draws attention to itself and the bodies carrying it—everything is overemphasized and alluring. Everything in Luhrmann's created world is a stage prop that undergirds the story. Most of the objects used in the film are given an aesthetic status; nothing is ordinary and nothing is background or incidental. Everything matters.

Catholicism, which featured heavily in Shakespeare's play, makes a return here but in an iconized form. It is the aesthetic of Catholicism that is employed, not the polity or the doctrine but the look—nuns, sacred hearts, Latin words, gothic crosses, statues, icons, candles, incense hanging in the air—religious artifacts, crosses and the like, functioning as jewelry. Luhrmann acknowledges the resacralization of public space in postmodernity but also announces that it is not a return to the old ways but the employ of the old in the service of the new, the different. Luhrmann will not allow his audience to prefocus.[34] We sit in the theater knowing the story, our minds prefocused on certain scenes that have been historicized—

the speeches of Romeo and Juliet that took place in the famous balcony scene—but we are not allowed there in Luhrmann's interpretation. Instead of a medieval city we get a congested urban megacity; instead of an "old accustom'd feast" we get a twenty-first-century rave; instead of the famous balcony scene we get a swimming pool and view the unfolding love between Romeo and Juliet through water (liquid, of course, being a prime symbol of religion in the postsecular, fluid, ever-changing and hard to manage milieu). Zeffirelli's film could almost have been set on a theater stage and captured on camera, but cinema is Luhrmann's context, not theater, and there is no attempt to re-create the staged play. The shift of the famous scene from balcony to swimming pool is perhaps the chief indicator of this: air to water, nighttime to the fluorescence of underwater light, stage to screen, modern to postmodern interpretation.

Luhrmann is intent on the staging of Shakespeare's poetry rather than the *world* of his poetry. If Zeffirelli wished to capture things as they once were by appealing to a certain realism, Luhrmann's intent seems to be the surreal or perhaps the hyperreal. The film certainly assaults the senses and overwhelms one at first. There is both communication and loss of communication when this kind of filmmaking is employed. The movie's reality is forever only "virtual," and yet it has a reality so profound that we are captivated and drawn into a whole new world of experience.

It could be argued that the main character in Luhrmann's version of the play is the Roman Catholic Church and that sacramentalism is the dominant theme, or perhaps I should say "resacramentalism." I say "resacramentalism" because Luhrmann does not seek historical representation as much as he seeks to situate the story and its unfolding dramas in the contemporary context. He resituates the religious in a new situation—postmodernity. The film opens with the image of a huge statue of Christ on a hill split with close-ups of the film's central characters. Two huge skyscrapers, which represent the two households of the Capulets and Montagues, are positioned on either side of the Christ figure; civil strife is focused on the mediating presence of Christ, who welcomes both sides in the quarrel (with a nod perhaps to the pluralism that inhabits postsecular culture). As the film opens, the religious imagery is seized on quickly and remains a central focus of the film's aesthetic, from the tattooed cross on Friar Lawrence's back to the crosses and candles that attend the death and pseudo-death of Romeo and Juliet. But the religion in Luhrmann's film is not simply the recording of acts of devotion. In fact, it is not that at all. Instead, religion is but a cultural production, the content secondary to its staging, or production. The aesthetic of religion—the look, the feel—is what is presented as redemptive. Religion as a word is not used in the film, but it so permeates Luhrmann's version of the film that the cinematic city of "Verona" seems to have no civic space, no secularity. Even its materialism is wrapped up and packaged in the affect of religious iconicity and image.[35] This is the postmodern situation, the reenchanted postsecular experience.

What we experience in Luhrmann's film is again the shift of time and space, not modernity's linear sense of time—past, present, future; yesterday, today, tomorrow—but the reconfiguring of time and space and the relocating of both in a newly resacralized world where the affects of religiosity confer a new idea of holiness to the surface of the contemporary, if not yet to the depths.

In the medieval world picture, the whole of the universe and everything in it was

> linked in a great spiritual hierarchy, sometimes called the Great Chain of Being. . . . When medievals spoke of humans being at the center of the universe, it was not so much our astronomical position they were referring to as our place at the center of this spiritual order. . . . One of the major effects of the scientific revolution was thus to write out of our vision of reality any conception of spiritual space, and along with that any concept of spirit or soul.[36]

Religion and society split in modernity, civic space versus sacred space.[37] But Luhrmann reflects a seismic shift in Western culture toward a reaffirmation of soul space, a remarriage, if you will, of religion and society. There is no doubt in his film that religion informs a sense of place, that conceptions of spatiality and temporality reflect our understandings of the world around us.[38]

Corporeality: The Body Politic

Shifts in conceptions about time and space naturally lead to questions about one's place in life. If we are long separated from the medieval idea of the Great Chain of Being and we are being loosed every day from the tyranny of modernity's regimented clock and finding new spaces to locate ourselves, even if it is the "non-place" of cyberspace, questions about what it means to be human, where we derive identity, and how we locate ourselves in the created order are a natural part of the current quest.

Pahl contends that "many labels, scripts, and narratives that served as boundary markers for identity construction in the past have come to the end of their useful lives. . . . If we cannot be sure of our gender identities, our jobs, our life-course pattern, and how enduring our present set of relationships may be, then evidently, we are alone in constructing our self-identity in our own way."[39]

Included in that list of boundary markers that once served as an aid in the construction of identity is the role of traditional religions. Manuel Castells suggests two kinds of identity that can be distinguished in postmodernity as opposed to the "legitimating identities"[40] conferred by the organizations and locations of modernity that no longer hold power. "Resistant identities," one of Castells's categories, will be taken up later as a key dynamic in postsecular religious expression, as will Castells's other category of the self in postmodernity, "project identity," which is forward looking and refers to a response to the inclinations of the present, be they sexual, feminist, environmental, or whatever. These categories are the means by which Castells denotes our responses to postmodernity. Rather than locating ourselves in the world via the aid of religious faith and devotion as a medieval person might have, or deriving our ideas and a sense of self from the Enlightenment principles that fueled the modern project, such as the static self, or deriving our sense of place in the world from our place in the social order or from our work, identity today is forged in and by a consumerist mentality that drives postmodernity. "Where once we might have identified ourselves in terms of the villages or clans we came from, and located ourselves within a social hierarchy stretching down from prince or president to pauper, now nothing is fixed."[41]

Whence, then, do we derive identity today?[42] I contend that it is largely derived from our imagination. We shop for "ourselves" in the marketplace of ever-expanding ideas brought to us when we enter cyberspace or media culture, or when we engage with the seemingly endless possibilities presented to us by a global consumer culture. By this I mean that the advent of cyberspace, and all the other world-shrinking technologies of the late-twentieth century, serve to fuel the cultural imagination and allow the self to float freely, divorced from any and all legitimizing identities handed to us by the authority structures of both the premodern and modern societies—I don't like gender classification. Then I will be transgendered. As Appadurai points out: "The imagination—expressed in dreams, songs, fantasies, myths, and stories—has always been part of the repertoire of every society, in some *culturally organized way*. But there is a peculiar new force to the imagination in social life today. More persons in more parts of the world consider a wider set of possible lives than they ever did before."[43] Appadurai posits that even the imagination was hierarchically constructed and mediated by the powers that be in former social contexts and that imagination was primarily viewed as a means of escaping from daily experiences. Now, however, the imagination has become accepted as a means of creating social experience. "More persons throughout the world see their lives through the prisms of the possible lives offered by mass media in all their forms. That is, fantasy is now a social practice; it enters, in a host of ways, into the fabrication of social lives for many people in many societies."[44]

David Lyon characterizes this as the "plastic self" and offers the image of the postmodern as "people flitting like butterflies from store to store, and from symbol to symbol, constantly constructing themselves, trying on this fashion, that lifestyle. A sort of pastiche persona results, so the self—and life itself—becomes transient, ephemeral, episodic and apparently insignificant . . . flexible, amenable to infinite reshaping according to mood, whim, desire and imagination."[45] This "plastic self" should not be viewed in a negative light, for it signals that the static sense of self that for centuries shaped Western perspectives on the self has become malleable and shifting, and that the view of the self as static or "concrete" is no longer the shaping idea. This more fluid sense of self reflects a new coming to terms with the postmodern world, a world of multiple options that must be negotiated and processed. As Lyon contends, "A careful sociological listening to contemporary voices reveals a trend towards the general sacralization of the self."[46]

One of the key developments in this area is a growing interest in the sacred[47] and a shift toward understanding the self as connected in some way to a larger whole that may or may not be viewed as God, the divine, the transcendent, or simply something "other." It is not simply the question of interiority and ideas of the self that are in flux, perspectives on the physical body are also in flux. James B. Nelson, in his book *Body Theology*, challenges us to pay attention to the representation of the body in culture: "It is a way of taking sexual/bodily experience seriously in conversation with and in the reshaping of our theological perceptions and categories."[48] Within the culture, the destabilizing of the self that has resulted in the repositioning of the self in relation to others and the ultimate Other, God, demands that we pay attention to the "culturally-mediated body."[49] The culturally mediated body represents a decisive shift away from the privatization of the self in modernity.

In the modern age, two arenas of life in particular, land and body, were subject to privatization. Land, through a series of parliamentary acts in Great Britain, for instance, was fenced off and became the property of the wealthy. "Countryside that had for centuries been open to all, whether for village festivals or the use of smallholders . . . was fenced off and became the inviolable property of wealthy individuals. As a direct result, the landscape changed dramatically, and so did the lives of millions of people who lived upon it."[50] A similar situation arose in the United States with the emergence of the land barons and business magnates of the nineteenth century, such as the Rockefellers, who made deals that allowed them unprecedented access and ownership of vast stretches of the American landscape.

The body, particularly the female body, was a second arena of privatization in the modern era.

> Whatever their other effects, and historians are still debating their impact on agriculture, the Enclosure Acts are regarded as a significant step in the creation of a modern society. What is less frequently remarked upon is the way in which a comparable process of enclosure was acted out in the eighteenth century on bodies, primarily women's bodies. The effect was to divide women into two classes: wives, who were indubitably the property of their husbands, and unmarried or abandoned women who, not belonging to one master, ran the risk of being regarded as the collective property of all.[51]

The anthropocentrism at the center of the modernist project elevated the idea of the autonomous individual to new and dizzying heights. At the same time, however, it succeeded in creating new hierarchies and structures that inhibited individuality under a new layer of laws and social mores. Sexuality in particular was affected by this shift. The rise of feminism in the mid-twentieth century was a movement to liberate women from the enclosing of the female gender that had occurred in modernity's formative years. In postsecular culture we have a new relationship with the body; what was once private is now public.

Consider Madonna, for instance, a pop star whose very public life has ultimately been defined by her flagrant, to some at least, display of her sex and sexuality. She stands as a good test case for the resacralization of both sex and culture in the postsecular age. Alongside her very public sexual exploration she has made no less public her interest in religion and spirituality. From her shocking (particularly to some traditionalists) use of Catholic imagery in the video for her song "Like a Prayer," through her flirtation with Hinduism and paganism on the *Ray of Light* album, to her very public embrace of Kabbalah, a mystical form of Judaism, she has modeled the changing relationships to both sex and religion in our culture. The modern era was characterized by binary oppositions that allowed for delineations—in or out, black or white, and the such. In modernity, what was pure could easily be contrasted with what was impure. For instance, changing social mores and marriage laws in the United Kingdom enclosed the female body within a tightly prescribed "Victorian" worldview and pressed women into binary oppositions; the rise of prostitution in eighteenth- and nineteenth-century Britain concurrent with the enactment of new marriage laws is an example of this.

But all of these oppositions are collapsing in our time. "Like a virgin," sang Madonna, "like" a virgin; not necessarily a true virgin. She performed this song at the 1984 MTV Video Music Awards show dressed in a combination wedding dress/first communion outfit, all lacy and white—the symbolic color of the pure and virginal—and bejeweled with rosaries and other religious affectations, yet coupled with revealed cleavage and other body parts and trashy lingerie reminiscent of a prostitute (collapsing the binary oppositions of the nineteenth-century view of women).[52] The song was performed with an accompanying dance routine that involved her and a number of other dancers moving suggestively and sexually, culminating with all of them writhing around on the floor in a state of pseudo-orgasm while singing the song. The presentation and the song can be read both as a critique of existing social mores and categorization of the female form and as a site for the emergence of some of the dynamics of contemporary religious expression—at once both sacred and profane—collapsing the preexisting ideas and perspectives into a new pastiche.

We live in a body culture, a society with an extremely materialistic worldview. This materialism is not simply a question of possessions and ownership but also of the relationship between humans and the earth. One of the characteristics of contemporary religious expression seems to be an earth-centeredness, a rootedness in *this* world, and a focus on forms of spirituality that aid in navigating the complexities of contemporary life rather than preparing the practitioner for the *next* world, if such a place even exists in their imaginary (i.e., one's capacity to dream, think about, conceptualize, or even rationalize).[53] This is a pendulum swing away from the privatization of self and body in modernity and away from modern religion's—particularly Christianity's—virtual obsession with the afterlife at the expense of life here on earth. Both cinema and science are key sites for the culturally mediated body of the twenty-first century, and often the cinema reflects scientific development and dreams. There is much talk in the world of science about the "post-human" condition. Of this scientific move, Elaine Graham says:

> Perhaps one of the most pressing issues for the twenty-first century will be the impact of new technologies on our experiences and understandings of what it means to be human. For many commentators, this signals the advent of the "post-human condition," in which digital technologies will have the capacity to reconfigure our conceptions of space and time; cybernetic devices will enhance and augment our bodies and minds; and genetic modification will challenge the fixity of "human nature" at its most fundamental level.[54]

Plastic surgery, artificial intelligence, cybernetics, gene therapy, and a host of other scientific and technological developments are enabling contemporary society to press the definitions and horizons of what it means to be human. Graham summarizes the developments in post-human thinking and research into four major categories: *the mechanization of the human and the technologization of the natural; the blurring of species boundaries; the blurring of bodily boundaries; the creation of new personal and social worlds.*[55]

The *mechanization of the human and the technologization of the natural* refers to the medical and scientific advancements that are allowing for the use of self-regulating mechanisms, such as artificial hearts, that mimic physiological functions. Alongside this are more mundane devices, such as pacemakers and hearing aids, that are increasingly employed in contemporary society to replace lost faculties and compensate for debilitations and abnormalities. There are also reproductive technologies, such as in vitro fertilization,[56] and other procedures that allow for the monitoring of neonatal health. This is also the domain of cybernetics and the development of "cyborgs"—creatures[57] who are both human and machine and who are now commonplace on movie screens. "Cyborgs thus inhabit a world simultaneously 'biological' and 'technological.' A living fusion of the human and non-human animal, the human and the mechanical and the organic and the fabricated, the cyborg exposes the collapse of taken-for-granted boundaries between species and categories."[58] Again, the collapse of modern binary oppositions is at work and is changing the way we view ourselves as humans. It is not only the reality of these advancements but also the implications of the shifts that contribute to the ongoing spiritual shift. "For many, however, the cyborg occupies a larger, metaphorical place in social theory, symbolizing the increasing interconnections between humans and technologies, a kind of 'thought experiment' in our understanding of being human in an age of advanced technologies."[59]

The second of Graham's categories, *the blurring of species boundaries,* is a lesser development at this stage and is connected to the creation of hybrids, the grafting of elements of one species onto another in order to create new species. Emerging from this process are species whose genetic composition is "made," not "born."[60] The implications of this for contemporary culture are yet to be fully seen, but the implication and potential of such a procedure factors into changing perspectives on the self and reaffirms the fluid state of the body in postmodernity.

In the 1979 film *Alien,* directed by Ridley Scott, the first in the quadrilogy of films in this series of futuristic horror stories, the audience is introduced to the space creature that possesses the human body as an embryo. This implanted alien embryo incubates in its host until it emerges graphically,[61] stretching the human skin until it finally breaks and destroys all that exists under the skin, resulting in the horrible demise of its victims.

The seemingly impossible act of stretching the human skin beyond the breaking point is the focus of Graham's third category: the *blurring of bodily boundaries.* The "skin has been a boundary for the soul, the self, and simultaneously a beginning to the world. Once technology stretches and pierces the skin, the skin as a barrier is erased."[62] This erasure of the skin as boundary and barrier offers new exploratory horizons for concepts about the limits of the physical body. Graham comments that technologies function as tools, extensions of the boundary of the human body, in much the same way as a hammer or knife did in the past.[63] The difference with the new technologies, however, is that they actually allow for the extension and reshaping of the contours of the body. This works on two fronts: First, as *incorporation*—whether by implant, prostheses, or synthetic drugs—whereby the technology is not extended but incorporated literally into the body. The second feature reflects on the *immersive* aspect of new technologies—the creation of virtual realities would be a recognizable instance of this element wherein new communicative environments are created that provide new space and new configurations for the human. Whether this represents continuation of or flight from embodiment is open to debate, but this arena is yet more evidence of the shifting understanding of corporeality.

The final category Graham outlines considers the ongoing sophistication of digital technology and posits that it will soon be capable of synthesizing an entire virtual environment.[64] The *creation of new personal and social worlds* relates to the creation of cyberspace into which a person can sensorially, if not physically, be assimilated. "In their capacity to engender new immersive worlds that authentically mimic organic reality, digital technologies have become not so much *tools*—extension of the body—as total *environments*. Virtual reality allows the user to project a digitally generated self into cyberspace, synthesizing new spatial and temporal contexts within which alternative subjectivities are constructed."[65]

A rather innocuous form of this can be found in *Suddenly Seminary*, a cyberspace devoted to on-line theological discussion found on the blog site of postmodern missionary Andrew Jones.[66] In this version of cyberspace, attendees pick a *persona*, in this case in the form of a plastic Lego figure, and enter the virtual seminary space, stopping by the virtual coffee shop[67] before joining the live on-line discussion. In this disembodied space, boundaries collapse and modern conceptions of time and space become redundant as conversation shifts among participants joining from different time zones and places around the globe.

Another factor related to the corporeal is the physical body as *a site of personalized ritual and adornment*. The rise of various forms of body modification—from intentional artistic inscription via tattooing and body piercing, to the rise of self-wounding, pain-inducing marks inflicted by individuals on their own flesh—point to the body as a newly contested site. For some it seems to be the last "safe place."[68] The collapse of other social catchalls, such as family, neighborhood, and so forth, have led many to feel isolated and fragmented and without the traditional societal means of marking rites of passage. Although marginalized and largely dismissed by modernity, the resurgence of interest in rituals points to their importance for what it means to be human and in community. In an increasingly mobile society, the body is often the one constant in life—that is, the one thing that can be held on to, that, apart from death, cannot be taken away— and as such is becoming a legitimate site for inscription. The prevalence of tattoos today reflects not only a social acceptance of what was once the domain of pirates, drunken sailors, and a few adventurous souls, but also of its expanded function as a means of marking and ritualizing life.[69] In my research work on tattoo parlors in West Los Angeles, every person I polled commented on the fact that their reason for getting a tattoo or a body piercing was linked to a seminal event in their life that they wished to mark in some permanent way. Tattooing and body piercing are increasingly rituals to which people turn. The inscription of the body is a way of declaring one's uniqueness and is linked to a desire for authenticity and honesty about the pain often involved in the human experience. The more negative side of this is the rise in self-wounding or "cutting"—one person out of every one hundred and thirty is likely to wound themselves in some way in the course of their life, according to one Web site devoted to the subject.[70]

Both the positive aspect of self-inscription, via tattoos or other body marking, and the negative aspect, via self-wounding, seem to point toward an understanding of these practices as attempts to make connections both with oneself and with the newly reconfiguring social orderings. Tattoos and other body modifications are some of the primary means by which we inscribe ourselves into the symbolic order. "Cutters"[71] also are attempting to connect with the social order, but perhaps represent the negative side of a culture increasingly interested in and shaped by the virtual. About them, Slavoj Žižek writes:

> Far from being suicidal, far from indicating a desire for self-annihilation, cutting is a radical attempt to (re)gain a hold on reality, or (another aspect of the same phenomenon) to ground the ego firmly in bodily reality against the unbearable anxiety of perceiving oneself as nonexistent. Cutters usually say that once they see the warm red blood flowing out of the self-inflicted wound, they feel alive again, firmly rooted in reality.[72]

Our bodies are inscribed with certain dominant narratives; we speak of "Victorian attitudes," and we enclose bodies within cultural taboos and sumptuary laws. It was once considered indiscreet for a woman to show her ankles. Today women bare their midriffs and go topless on beaches. It is common to see full-frontal nudity in films today, if the nude is a woman; the same is not true with regard to males. In this there remains a cultural taboo toward certain kinds and presentations of male nakedness. However, this is perhaps changing as we see in recent films, such as *Sideways* and *Kinsey*, in which male nudity is portrayed.

Laws regarding marriage, divorce, and remarriage, as well as other issues related to human sexuality, have been altered quite dramatically in the past century. Homosexuality was illegal in many parts of the United States until late in the twentieth century, and though it is still a contested issue, it is becoming increasingly acceptable in the West. Shifts in attitudes toward sexuality have led to a broadened understanding of human sexuality, including its role not only in the procreation of new life but also in its ability to provide mutual enjoyment. New permutations of sexuality have led to a new "genitality," meaning genital expression of sexuality is no longer exclusively the accepted domain of heterosexuals—male to male and female to female genital activity is increasingly acceptable. As Diarmuid O'Murchu points out, our (Christian, in particular) labels used to address this highlight the difficulty many are having with tackling this subject. "There seems to be an enormous reluctance to acknowledge this new development. Labels such as 'premarital sex,' 'extramarital relations,' and 'sexual acting-out' inhibit rather than encourage a deeper analysis of this new sexual agenda. Culturally, politically and theologically, it has far more serious implications than the so-called sexual revolution of the 1960s."[73]

Not only are the horizons of human sexuality being stretched and at times redrawn, the resacralizing of human sexuality is a key dynamic of cultural and religious expression in the twenty-first century. This is not only reflected in the public performances of someone like Madonna, who seeks to challenge propriety by her overt use of religious imagery in sexualized settings, but also in the rising public interest in forms of sexuality and sexual practice that are linked to religious traditions such as Tantra, a form of Hindu sexual practice. Alternative spiritual journals are full of teachings related to the resacralization of human sexuality. "The breakdown in both spheres is not because of promiscuity . . . it is a much deeper 'revolution,' a quantum transformation, whereby we are invited to reclaim . . . and thus outgrow the mechanization of sex which patriarchy imposed on our world and which has dominated both our attitudes and behaviors since the rise of the Industrial Revolution in the sixteenth century."[74]

Rather than being viewed as an obstacle to spirituality, contemporary corporeality seeks to reconcile spirituality and sexuality. This is part of a larger shift toward holism, the full integration of oneself in the world rather than the fragmentation and compartmentalization characteristic of modernity. It is also indicative of the continuing collapse of dominant binary oppositions that characterized modernity. While this is interesting on many levels, its primary bearing in this context is linked to the role that the body plays in contemporary religious exploration and discovery. This reconfiguring of corporeality presents enormous challenges to traditional faiths and, at the same time, provides potentialities for spiritual permutations. There is new space, namely cyberspace, where religion is practiced. In cyberspace you can go to church from the comfort of your armchair.

Corporeality and Authority

The principles of established order have become questionable and what remains is a "hole, opened by a society which calls itself into question."

Graham Ward, *Blackwell Companion to Postmodern Theology*

Challenge to authority seems to be a key element of the postsecular condition. If Max Weber was correct in defining modernity as a bureaucratic iron cage,[75] then its implosion is defined somewhat by a rejection of the hierarchical structures of modernity. This has specific ramifications for the focus of this book as the emergence of new religious impulses tends to exist largely outside the domain and control of traditional structures of religious authority.

When the tools for the making of meaning are derived from popular books, the Internet, and popular culture in general, and when traditional religion is used as little more than a resource to fuel individualized spiritual journeys, it is difficult to maintain the organizational and power structures of other times. In the 1970s, the revolution in information technology, capitalizing on cultural shifts that arose with the hippie movement, began to unfold new conditions, new times, new structures of power and authority. Information flow began to be the dominant form of influence as society increasingly turned away from hierarchical structures of authority and began to assume a more autonomous anthropocentric authority. Stable meanings and sources of identity, which were once derived from local communities, nation-states, political parties, and even local churches, were no longer helpful.

The network society is at least one way of understanding the new power configuration.[76] In a network society, what flows between the various connections is crucial, and whoever controls those flows controls the power. This power could be in the hands of a multinational corporation, or it could be the two college-dropout creators of Google™, the Internet search engine. There is an increasing suspicion of more-traditional power structures. In fact, in this world of network societies there is little need for political legitimization or dominant values or ideologies. Power has been decentralized and deregulated, the focus shifting from bureaucratic organization to network clusters, which may or may not be connected to older institutions.

What this deregulation means for religion is that the tendency toward syncretism is popularized in practice as well as belief. It is not uncommon to find someone who is a practicing Christian[77] drawing inspiration from Buddhism on a daily basis and combining this with a love of aliens, a daily ritual of prayer at a home altar, and a strong commitment to conservative politics. There is a shift in perspective from "How do I conform?" to "How do I choose?" This reflects the seemingly unlimited possibilities and permutations available in a network of free-flowing information and exchange, in which choice, not conformity, is the dominant mechanism.

A visual example of changing attitudes toward both corporeality and authority is found in the film *Stigmata*. That the film reflects changing attitudes toward both corporeality and authority within the context of a story about religion only serves to underscore this thesis. Director Rupert Wainwright's film, *Stigmata*, presents the body as central to the understanding of the film. The "body" is Frankie, played by Patricia Arquette. In spite of the name, Frankie[78] is female and a particular incarnation of what it means to be female at the dawn of a new era—independent, hedonistic, promiscuous, and in this case, decidedly nonreligious, at least in the traditional meaning of the word. It is in the opening scenes of the film, which are set in a contemporary urban landscape awash in imagery and hedonism, that we meet the main character. We peer into sections of her life and quickly deduce that she is a hairdresser, tattooist, and body piercer who likes to drink, have sex, and generally enjoy life. Her "nontraditional" life is quickly established.

This opening presentation is contrasted with the film's "official" post-credits opening, which finds the viewer transported to a poor village church in rural Brazil where something supernatural is taking place. A statue is weeping blood and a rapt gathering of traditional Catholic worshipers waits in adoration as a representative from the Vatican, an investigator of bogus miraculous claims, joins them to explore the phenomena regularly taking place in their church. Also in the scene is a coffin containing the body of an elderly monk who has recently died. A young boy steals a rosary from the clasped hands of this monk, and this rosary is what becomes the link between this event and the film's central characters. The rosary is sold at a street market to Frankie's vacationing mother, who immediately ships it back to her daughter as a gift. Upon receiving this instrument of religious practice, Frankie thanks her mother for "the necklace," shifting the rosary from an object used in worship to a fashion commodity (something increasingly characteristic of the fashion-driven people's religion). The rosary links two previously disconnected worlds, although each remains somewhat ignorant of the other's understanding of the nature of reality—one person's prayer device is another's piece of jewelry.

The story degenerates fairly quickly into a rather trite Hollywood story about demon possession, although one with a slight twist. The rosary, worn as a necklace, becomes a means by which Frankie receives the stigmata even though she is not a believer per se. She is definitely not a practicing Catholic—the film's message is dependent on this assumption and therefore goes to some length to establish this fact through the dialogue and the visual representation of Frankie's life. Frankie, who wears the rosary as a fashion accessory, is presented in stark contrast to those for whom the wearing of such a thing, the believers in the lower reaches of the Brazilian hinterland, has symbolic and deep religious meaning. The two central characters in the film both come to some kind of faith through Frankie's experience. Father Kiernan (Gabriel Byrne), the Vatican investigator, who, along with the church he serves, has lost his faith and believes only in scientific rationalism, recovers his faith, and Frankie comes to an understanding of the greater realities of life and walks away from her prior hedonism into a newly "spiritualized" understanding of life and her role in it. The demon possession becomes a critique of both trust in scientific rationalism and society's faithful reliance on medical materialism. Frankie keeps going to the hospital after these inexplicable and extremely disturbing bouts of "possession" and their subsequent woundings, but contemporary medicine has no plausible explanation and simply wants to consign the events to psychological problems, explaining that the physical manifestations are extensions of the disturbed psyche. The film places belief in the mysterious and the inexplicable in opposition to science and medicine, thereby exposing the limits of the modernist project. The rosary, which is part of the economy of faith—a tool of prayer—within an ancient tradition, becomes, for Frankie, a trigger to belief but not necessarily of belief in the particular Catholic tradition with which the rosary is connected. In fact, it is used in the movie to dismantle Catholicism itself.

The film can be viewed not only as a critique of modern society's inability to see beyond the rational, but also as a critique of or a ripping away at, if you will, the very fabric of the religion that gives rise to particular views of the spirit. Violence, not beatific devotion, characterizes Frankie's reception of the stigmata. This contrasts greatly with historic artistic portrayals of St. Francis receiving the stigmata, such as Giotto's 1295 painting and Barocci's in 1575, which employ more meditative and devotional poses to show Francis's encounter with the divine and the subsequent stigmata. In these paintings there are angels, light coming down from heaven, and a calm, almost Zen-like Francis, devotedly receiving what could only be the painful marks of his Lord. Frankie's experience is explosively violent; each successive wound increases the wear and tear on Frankie's entire body, not just her physical body but her emotions and her psyche as well. Frankie's coming to belief can only be by violence in some sense as the layers of secular assumption and resistance are torn away. In a bar after one of the episodes, Frankie reflects on her experiences and her embryonic faith: "Hey, do you know what's scarier than not believing in God? Believing in it. I mean, really believing in him is a scary f——ing thought."

This is Hollywood of course, and we are guaranteed a somewhat happy ending. The film ends with Frankie walking in the early morning in a garden with mist still hanging in the air, draped in white and at peace now, attended by a dove, à la St. Francis. But the film insists to the end that old forms of religion are barriers to true religious experience and expression. By including a statement about the *Gospel of Thomas*, which the church regards as apocryphal, as a "way forward" into a new religious future, the film continues to affirm that the church in particular is an enemy of any attempt to reconfigure the divine. This reflects the new access to information available in the computer age and also something of the "conspiracy" theory dynamic that inhabits the postsecular.[79]

But it is the larger issues of corporeality and authority and their working out in the postmodern situation that prompted this reflection. First, there is no dualism at work in the film, no distinction between sacred and secular. The filmmaker seeks to bring the sacred and the secular together and employs the rosary to do so. The authority structures, in this case the Catholic Church and the medical profession, are presented as autocratic, tyrannical, and decidedly out of touch with real life. The medical community can only restrain and medicate, neither of which is powerful enough to address the situation. The church, in a sense, is forced to the sidelines as its obvious secularity, its trust in scientific rationalism, and its refusal to accept the inexplicable and mysterious disallow any real engagement with what is happening to Frankie. It is only as Father Kiernan disengages himself from the church's authority that he can engage in the events unfolding. The institution is rejected because it takes itself too seriously as the mediator of truth, of God, and this is rejected in the end, even by the church's star priest.

The film raises the issue of resistance to a certain doctrinal fundamentalism that arises from power-based interpretations of the relationships with the divine. It is interesting that this anti-institutional posture toward religion does not result in a rejection of the sacred or the presentation of the secular as a viable alternative, because secular society is not presented in a positive light in the film. What is advanced instead is a new understanding of the relationship of the sacred and the profane, the spirit and the secular. The sacred and profane are blended into new configurations. This is achieved by making a well-documented nonbeliever the site of transcendent experience. The church, in the film at least, says this cannot happen, that the stigmata are a sign of special blessing reserved for those with particular and special faith;[80] but the film declares otherwise. The church is presented as maintaining boundaries already rejected by the broader culture, dualities such as saint and sinner, pure and impure, good and evil, and male and female.

Boundaries don't really exist in *Stigmata*; everything is liquid, permeable; the possession happens because there are no boundaries. The first stigmata event occurs while Frankie is in her bathtub, in water, the symbol of the contemporary spiritual dynamic. Even the "other," the evil force that the church assumes is tormenting this girl, is revealed to be none other than the spirit of God himself. This is not possession by negative force but the forceful reassertion of the presence of God in the secular world. Regardless of the church's resistance, faith has been enacted in Frankie's life and she has become the site for a new incarnation of faith, in this case, a decidedly Christian version of faith (although I would argue that culturally this is less likely to be the case, but given the Catholic tone in the story it works in this cinematic context). In a nod to St. Francis, but perhaps with a look forward to contemporary dynamics, this enactment of faith in Frankie leads her to a new relationship with creation—the closing scenes of her with a dove on her arm, walking in a garden, reflect the dominant element of eco-spirituality in contemporary religion. The film ultimately challenges liberal secularism and modern religion and offers a way forward for both sides, should either side be willing to move from its position.

A natural contrast to this film and a way to examine shifting views about corporeality and authority would be another film, *The Exorcist*. In *The Exorcist*, the natural and supernatural are again linked by an object, this time a demonic carving found in the deserts of Iraq (allusions to Babylon?). In this movie, possession is once again the link between two diverse places, the deserts of Iraq and a suburban home in the American capital, Washington, DC. But unlike *Stigmata*, which collapses dualities, *The Exorcist* seeks to maintain them, preserving the existing boundaries between sacred and profane to the end. The possession is demonic—the exorcist is Catholic, resulting in evil versus good, darkness versus light, and body versus soul. Cleanliness and organization versus the vomited filth and demonic chaos—the home of single mother Chris MacNeil is almost puritan (silent but for the ticking of a clock, the symbol of modernity's commitment to bureaucracy and order to which the home reverts after the exorcism is successful), versus the noise and screams of the demonic. The sexual virginity of the possessed child versus the sexual promiscuity and degradation of the demon and, of course, male autonomy and power contrasted with female empathy and sociality.

The possession here, unlike that in *Stigmata*, is not a new incarnation of God's presence but rather evil, in the guise of satanic possession. The violent demonic possession leads to no lasting transformation. When the possession ends, life reverts to its prepossession-secular norm. All the secular institutions continue to exist and govern. In fact, the possessed child's mother, Chris, is depicted as an independent woman committed to liberal Democratic values. She attends antiwar rallies on college campuses and fights for education rights, but she is alone and without love.

There are no father figures in the *Exorcist*, neither human nor divine. There is no permeability in any of the characters; boundaries are strictly enforced. What is presented is secular society's ability to withstand ancient evil, not with the help of the church, for the church plays a passive role in the film, but through and by the hands of a charismatic and renegade priest. It takes "special" faith, not everyday religion, to deal with something like this anomaly. Even the religious keepsake given to the women after the successful exorcism by Father Karras, the exorcist, is handed back to the priests at the end of the film as if to say, "we don't need you anymore, crisis over." Once again, the church is presented as essentially unnecessary. Its role as an instrument of the secular state is to function as a supporter of the secular order, an added maintainer of domestic peace, but the peace it establishes is sterile. As the film ends, the dark-tinted window of the limousine carrying the priests back to their world slowly rises and seals them off from the world of Chris and her recently exorcised child. The car pulls away, and the image of mother and daughter bounces off the tinted window, signaling the return to normality, the return to duality, the sacred and the secular returning to their own worlds, interacting no more.

If in *The Exorcist* the church is viewed as ultimately meaningless in secular life, in *Stigmata* we see yet another change in perspective toward the role religion might play in the affairs of contemporary life. In *Stigmata* the church is portrayed as a fund from which new truth, the "real" truth (because the film is about secret documents that will undermine the spiritual authority of the church), might be drawn. It is presented as basically useless as an ongoing site for religious exploration but not as a resource for new incarnations of the spiritual into once-secular lives, for which it remains a powerful presence. This is a foundational understanding of the nature of contemporary spirituality and the democratization of religion currently underway. As Sulak Sivaraksa stated:

Buddhism, as you know, was founded over 2,500 years ago. And traditionally, it has been a wonderful religion, helping people to be mindful, to be aware of suffering, to transform greed into generosity, to transform hatred into compassion, to transform ignorance into wisdom. But to be honest with you, as it has been traditionally practiced, it won't work anymore. Society has now become much more complex, with urbanization and globalization and the idea of structural violence embedded in the social systems themselves. Unless the Buddhists learn how to tackle these issues, Buddhism will only be good for those who want to have personal happiness.[81]

This is a rare example of someone who practices an ancient faith taking seriously the challenge posited by the present cultural landscape.

When the structures of authority are abandoned, are we then left with lawlessness and madness? Some would say so, but I would argue that what we are abandoning is not authority but authority structures that no longer suffice given the changing social contexts, and thereby we are attempting to develop new means of ordering society. It is a question of whether or not the emperor is wearing clothes. In the fairy tale *The Emperor's New Clothes*, Hans Christian Anderson tells the story of a vain king who loved fine clothes and spent his life in pursuit of elegance. He loved to show off his clothing and wore new clothes every day. Learning of his vanity, two scoundrels resolved to take advantage of him. They introduced themselves at the king's palace as two tailors who had spent years researching the process of weaving a cloth so fine and light that it appears invisible. This cloth was so fine, they told the king's guards, that it would appear invisible to the stupid and incompetent, who would fail to see its quality. The story of the two tailors reached the ears of the king, and he had them brought in for an audience. After they had rehearsed their story, he decided to employ them to make him a suit of the finest, lightest cloth imaginable and gave the two men money, a loom, gold thread, and silk.

A few days later, the king sent his chief minister to see how the work was coming. The two tailors took him to the loom and invited him to "feel" the softness and finery of the fabric they were creating. Not surprisingly, the minister could see and feel nothing, but he remembered the admonition of the tailors that those who were stupid and incompetent would fail to see the finery of the cloth, so he joined them in acknowledging how wonderful the fabric looked. He then reported back to the king that the work was progressing smoothly and that he had seen the fabric and it truly was as the two tailors had said it would be, the finest cloth a man could possess. Finally the king summoned the men to fit him for his suit and they came into his chambers carrying between them what they said was a roll of fabric. The king was taken aback as he could see nothing, but remembering the words of the tailors that the stupid and the incompetent would be unable to appreciate the cloth's quality and thus it would appear to those eyes as invisible, and remembering the report of his wise chief minister, who had seen with his own eyes this fine cloth, the king openly declared his approval of their work and had himself fitted for a new suit of clothes.

Word leaked out of the palace that there was an extraordinary suit of clothes being made for the king, and news reached the palace that the public was eager to see the emperor in his new suit of clothes. The king decided to grant his people their wish and organized a ceremonial parade and called for his carriage to be prepared. The emperor was a little concerned about showing himself naked in public. But since he would appear naked only to those who were stupid and incompetent, he left the palace to parade himself before his expectant public. All the people gathered in the main square to see the king in his new suit of clothes. Everyone wanted to know whether or not his or her neighbor was stupid, but as the crowd pressed in, a murmur rose: "Look at the emperor's new clothes. They're beautiful! What a marvelous train! And look at the colors! The color of that beautiful fabric!" They all tried to conceal their disappointment in not being able to see the clothes, but since no one was willing to admit to stupidity, they all behaved as the two scoundrels thought they would.

But in the crowd was a child who had no important position to uphold, who could see things only as his eyes showed them to him. When the king's carriage passed him he looked in the carriage and said, "The emperor is naked." His father reprimanded the boy and told him not to be stupid and took his son away from the parade. But the boy's remark, which had been heard by bystanders, was repeated over and over until it became the dominant cry of the crowd, "The king is naked! The king is naked!"

In the end, everyone is reprimanded for their complicity in the strange tale of the suit made of invisible fabric. The story works only on the basis of this complicity. As long as everyone "sees" the invisible suit, we can carry on the myth, but as soon as the folly is exposed, the whole thing collapses. Postmodernity, or postsecularity, or whatever one chooses to describe the present condition, is like the little boy with nothing to lose, who exposes the emperor's new clothes, in this case modernity, for what they are: a delicately woven but ultimately flawed set of ideas with which postmodernity no longer wishes to comply.

Rather than continuing to "wear" that particular suit, many today are searching for a new suit of clothes, weaving a new fabric. Secularism and materialism particularly, two of the dominant threads in the modern weave, have been exposed for the invisible and empty promise they ultimately hold.

Evolution Not Revolution

I was initially tempted to describe the emergence of new understandings of and desire for the spiritual as a revolution in spirituality, as others have done, but I have revised my position. Revolution seems to be the choice word when it comes to generating or acknowledging change, but it is a modern word with particular associations that I don't think are characteristic of what is happening now. It is, as I have mentioned, much more of a democratic and evolutionary movement than a revolutionary one. I realize that many revolutions are undertaken in the name of the "people," but the twentieth century would seem to disprove the power of revolution to effect lasting change. Mao Zedong, leader of the communist revolution in China in the mid-twentieth century, wrote that "a revolution is not a dinner party. It cannot be so leisurely and gentle. . . . It is an insurrection, an act of violence by which one class overthrows another." The emergence of new spiritual expression in our time may have revolutionary impact, but I would argue that rather than being a violent insurrection, it is the result of modernity's implosion. It is not the revolutionary imposition of another value system, such as socialism against materialism or totalitarian dictatorship over democratic capitalism, but the almost natural outcome of modernity's implosion and the reemergence of religion from modernity's largely negative view toward it.

The great competing ideologies to Western democratic capitalism, such as communism, all collapsed during the twentieth century, leaving it triumphant. There is a thirty-year gap between the films I discussed above, *Stigmata* and *The Exorcist*, and they are the last thirty years of the twentieth century, a time during which the implosion of modernity occurred. From the ashes of this implosion a new understanding and a new desire for the spiritual have emerged. This is not revolution as much as it is evolution, the gradual development of ideas and thoughts within the broader culture that have coalesced into new configurations rather than a sudden uprising or upheaval. The foundations of the present religious situation were laid long before they developed into something new. It appears revolutionary to many because they were not looking, or because they were looking through the distorted lens of their own particular understanding of religion, and consequently its rise seems to have been immediate and without cause. But this is not the case.

Rather than revolutionary, the emergence of the new spiritual movement can be viewed as evolutionary and as a democratic movement from below. It is a people's movement, evolving as those disenfranchised by society's obvious loss of meaning find alternative ways to fashion meaningful lives. As we saw in the film *Stigmata*, it is a critique and rebellion against scientific rationalism and institutional grips on power. It is not a rejection of science or of power but a rejection of particular incarnations of those ideals.

It is a democratization of the spirit (crowdsourcing) wherein individuals assume responsibility for and take authority over their own lives apart from institutional, "top-down" forms of leadership and authority that characterized other incarnations of the religious. The evolution of spirituality is about finding God everywhere, not in a pantheistic way, but in the sense that prior boundaries and divisions have imploded and religion has been loosed from its previous enclosure. This is one of the main themes of the film *Stigmata*. Communion with the divine, even specific religious figures such as Jesus—once viewed as mediated to us only through the power of the church—is available to all of us anywhere and at any time. The implosion of the dualities that fueled modernity have broken down the walls between sacred and secular. Hence the postsecular world. God is everywhere and not simply where traditional faiths deem God to be! The church in *Stigmata* cannot envision the possibility of someone such as Frankie having a viable spiritual experience or meeting its conventional criteria for what makes a person of faith. Consequently, the church is unable to participate in her spiritual awakening. It can only try to stop this awakening or attempt to force its categories (unsuccessfully in most cases) on the situation.

Traditional religions tend to focus on issues of afterlife and future destination in their modern incarnations. But the new spiritual expressions that are emerging are increasingly related to the direct experience the practitioners and seekers have in their daily lives. Frankie is not a monk like St. Francis and is unlike the other Catholic saints and devotees who have apparently been graced with the stigmata. She is a hairdresser and a body modifier, playing with all the categories of what it means to be human. In her world, very little is fixed and stable; even her hair color is in a constant state of flux. Because this new religious climate is a movement from below, the institutional response, as exhibited in this film, is one of suspicion and disapproval. This remains, for the most part, the response of most traditional faiths to the present state of affairs regarding the new religious environment. As James Twitchell observes, "When we have few things, we make the next world holy. When we have plenty, we enchant the objects around us."[1]

Twitchell's observation about the relationship of material wealth to our spiritual practices has resonance here. The emergence of new expressions of spirituality is closely tied to global capitalism and is the product of a consumer culture. Alongside this, comparative economic wealth in many parts of the world, particularly in the West, has led to a reenchanting of things that once would have been considered worldly or perhaps even unholy. There has been a growing sacralization of sexuality, for instance, in Western culture over the past twenty years. What began as a reaction to traditional social and sexual mores in the form of the free-love expressions of the hippie movement in the late 1960s has transformed into a much broader response to human sexuality. Contemporary religion seeks to be more holistic, encompassing the whole person and the world around them, and less compartmentalized than modern incarnations of traditional religions. Consequently there is a tendency to endow anything with a spiritual glaze, be it sex or nature. In the new context, religion is not a matter of private faith as much as it is public experience and experiment. "God is all of nature. And nature is one big restaurant—everybody's eating everybody; it's a daily menu. It's creation, destruction, life and death happening a gazillion times a second."[2]

There is a tendency by some, in my experience, to view all of this as simply an extension of New Age spirituality. I have used the term "Entertainment Theology" playfully, trying to capture a distinctive that I think is important. For what I write about, what interests me, is religion and spirituality fashioned out of and at the edges of the new cultural conditions in which we find ourselves at the dawn of the twenty-first century. New Age spirituality is but one expression of belief in this new context and is actually a much more modern expression of faith. As such, New Age spirituality is being challenged to redefine itself alongside other more traditional faiths. In fact, New Age spirituality is rather outdated—its basic tenets having been around since the late-nineteenth century—and is frequently viewed as a holdover from the hippie movement's declaration of the dawning of the Age of Aquarius.

The Decline and Rise of God: The Emergence of a Spiritual Society

> Religion belongs to the family of the curious, and often embarrassing concepts, which one perfectly understands until one wants to define them. Postmodern mind, for once, agrees to issue this family, maltreated or sentenced to deportation by the modern scientific reason, with a permanent residence permit.
>
> Zygmunt Bauman, "Postmodern Religion?"

The relaxation of much of the suspicion toward spirituality and questions of ultimate meaning that defined modernity has facilitated, as we have noted, the emergence of renewed interest in spiritual life. Postmodern/postsecular means many things, but without doubt a singular and perhaps most surprising characteristic of the postmodern condition is that it reflects a return to God. In spite of the best efforts of modernity to banish God from the center of human affairs, the shift to postmodern values has dramatically returned God to center stage. Lest we be misled, it is worth remembering again that this renewed interest in spirituality has not marked a return to classic views about God and the nature of reality; the deprivileging of metaphysics and other dynamics discussed earlier precludes this particular perspective.

In his work *Social and Cultural Dynamics*,[3] Pitirim A. Sorokin, founder of the Department of Sociology at Harvard University, developed a complex theory of cultural change that has some important implications for the postmodern situation. Sorokin, a Russian whose life was marked by the upheaval brought about by the communist revolution in his homeland, posited that the crisis all of Western culture found itself in as the twentieth century unfolded was actually the transitioning of the West between two cultural systems he called the Sensate and the Ideational.[4] The Sensate mode is one in which material values dominate. Its focus is on matters of efficiency and bureaucracy. The Ideational is the opposite. Rather than being predominantly sensorially focused, it is more artistically inclined, understanding reality as super sensory. Greek civilization, for instance, would fall into the Ideational mode, given its focus on beauty, truth, and philosophy. The Roman Empire would, by contrast, fall squarely into the Sensate mode, given its commitment to dominance and its gift of organization and construction—the *Pax Romana*. Sorokin believed that the crisis in Western culture would continue until a new mode of civilization emerged that would be markedly different from the Modern Era. He used a third term to describe transitional phases in culture: Idealistic. Each mode of civilization was one in which either the Sensate or Ideational mode was dominant but not exclusive. Both elements were attendant to the culture, but the ascendancy of one over the other was determined by the shape of the culture during a particular time period.

The modern age was Sensate in Sorokin's theory. It was built on material values and given to sensorially derived ideas—scientific rationalism and so forth. But the continuing social and cultural upheavals attending the late modern age of the twentieth century led him to believe that we were, in fact, living through an Idealistic, transitional phase. Research was conducted under Sorokin's commission exploring and researching major social and cultural indicators: the arts, science, philosophy, law, ethics, religion, and so forth. The results, which he felt validated his theory, were published in 1920.[5] There were particular and specific markers that Sorokin used to determine where a culture was, particularly in more transitional times. These markers included events that pointed to social and cultural dislocation and upheaval:[6] wars, revolutions, suicides, crime on the one hand, and times of great artistic output on the other. Sorokin's researchers studied over 100,000 works of art and literature from the Middle Ages to 1930 and charted their relationship to different cultural modes. Shakespeare, for instance, falls into an Idealistic phase between the late sixteenth and early seventeenth centuries. Given the upheaval in the Britain of Shakespeare's day—with its shift away from Catholic liturgical time, the forging of a new church/state relationship by Henry VIII and his ministers, and the wars, upheavals, and social restructuring that attended that time—it would seem there is some substance to Sorokin's theory.

Another perspective on the postmodern as the emergence of a spiritual society is reflected in the writings of Italian philosopher Gianni Vattimo. In *After Christianity*,[7] Vattimo refers to the writings of Joachim of Fiore, a twelfth-century Cistercian monk born in 1135. Often characterized as one of the most important apocalyptic thinkers in the church after John, Joachim's work on the biblical book of Revelation was his magnum opus and life's work. In it he claimed to have been given a spiritual understanding (*spiritualis intelligentsia*)[8] of the symbolism in the book. He divided history into three eras or three stages, if you will, an idea fundamentally rooted in a trinitarian view of God. The first age was the Old Testament period and was the age of the Father. The next age, the age of the Son, was defined as the New Testament period. Fiore looked ahead to another time, the third and final age, the age of the Spirit, a new age, a new era of the church on earth.

Three are the stages of the world indicated by the sacred texts. The first stage is the stage in which we have lived under the law; the second is that in which we live under grace; the third is one in which we shall live in a more perfect state of grace. . . . The first passed in slavery; the second is characterized by filial slavery; the third will unfold in the name of freedom. The first is marked by awe, the second by faith, the third by charity. . . . The first stage is ascribed to the Father, who is author of all things; the second to the Son, who has been esteemed worthy to share our mud; the third to the Holy Spirit, of which the apostle says "Where the spirit of the Lord is, there is freedom."[9]

Vattimo unfolds the implications of Fiore's theory for postmodern culture: "Joachim of Fiore offers us a model for living postmodern religious experience on the basis of the specific content of his teaching on the age of spirit and his general theological tendency to understand salvation history as the story of the transformation in which the Scripture's meaning is spiritualized."[10] Vattimo also notes that Fiore did not think that society had shifted into the third and final phase by the time of his writing;[11] Fiore was merely announcing its future arrival. "Joachim's prophecy remains only a prophecy, namely, a reading of the 'signs of the times' that occur within the historical process."[12] Vattimo then goes on to argue that we are now in the third age prophesied by Fiore, the age of spirit, and heralds its arrival by pointing to the demise of metaphysics as signifier of the event:

So far, the meaning of Joachim's teachings for our discussion seems to lie in the "discovery" that historicity is constitutive of revelation. This historicity, in my view, corresponds to the "event" character of Being discovered by postmetaphysical philosophy. It is useless to stress, once again, that for philosophy this "discovery" has the same character of Joachim's prophecy of the third age. The end of metaphysics is an event that announces itself and demands to be recognized, promoted, and realized, or at least to be explicitly clarified as the guideline for our choices. The signs of the approaching third age, which today we call the end of metaphysics, are obviously not the same ones observed by Joachim.[13]

It is worth noting that Vattimo's own return to faith, and particularly Christian faith,[14] was prompted by his interaction with Heidegger and Nietzsche, both antimodern and both, but particularly Nietzsche, anti-Christian. That Vattimo would come to faith through the most secular of philosophers goes some distance in explaining his conceptualizing of postmodern culture as a decidedly spiritual time. Modernity—the antispiritual, secular age—gives rise, gives birth, to the new postsecular spiritual age. Vattimo states:

> Furthermore, if there is no longer a philosophy (like Hegelian or Marxist historicism or like the various kinds of scientific positivism) claiming to be capable of demonstrating the nonexistence of God, we are free, again, to hear the words of scripture. Moreover, in the postmodern end of absolute philosophies, we become aware that once we discover that the vision of Being as eternal structure of objectivist metaphysics is untenable, we are left with the biblical notion of creation, namely, with the contingency and historicity of our existing. To translate all of this into secular and philosophical terms: it is above all because of the experience of postmodern pluralism that we can think of Being only as event, and of truth not as the reflection of reality's eternal structure but rather as a historical message, that must be heard, and to which we are called to respond.[15]

The deprivileging of metaphysics[16] and the collapse of history, in the modern linear sense, lead not to anarchy or rebellion but to renewed spirituality. Freed from the constraints of modern universals, the potential for a new openness to religious truth is made possible: "We would dare to think of the long process of secularization that separates us from the historical epoch of the abbot from Calabria as the realization of the conditions that are bringing us closer to the advent of the third age."[17] This age of the spirit is not characterized by dogma, for the age of the spirit stresses "not the letter but the spirit of revelation: no longer servants but friends; no longer awe or faith but charity; and perhaps also not action but contemplation."[18] These are at least some of the general dynamics of the postsecular, a time in which, for better or worse, the notion of awe and the idea of fear associated with religion have largely disappeared from the conversation.[19] Charity, interpreted as "belief as practice," takes precedence over doctrinal statements of belief. Vattimo also cites a work by the philosophers Hegel, Schelling, and Holderlein, *The Philosophy of Mythology*, which announces the advent of a "kingdom of freedom" that will be realized only on the basis of a "sensible religion," understood as the "monotheism of the heart, the polytheism of the imagination and of art, and the mythology of reason."[20] It can be argued that these also form part of the contemporary spiritual impulse where individual faith choices are largely generated and mediated via media culture and the social imaginary it affords, and through the reenchanting or remythologizing of our world as we do not turn away from scientific rationalism as much as we turn toward an Einsteinian-driven rational mysticism. As Wallace observes:

> At the threshold of a new century we are witnessing a profound ground shift in the spiritual sensibilities of our culture. There is a sense that we now live in the "age of the spirit," a time in which many and diverse persons and groups are experiencing the immanent reality of a power greater than themselves in their everyday lives. The medieval mystic Joachim of Fiore prophesied that humankind has lived through the periods of the Father and the Son and has now entered the age of the Spirit. Karl Barth mused at the end of his life that the Holy Spirit might well be the best point of departure for a theology that is right for the present situation.[21]

It must be said in conclusion that this age of the spirit is not the age of the Holy Spirit, the third element in trinitarian theologies. It is, rather, the age of "spirit." This is a time in which the notion of spirit is set free from old forms, and new incarnations and new images of the sacred are now possible. And it is fueled by emerging worldviews that offer different configurations of the human condition. Religion in the postsecular is not a collection of doctrinal statements about God, about "bums on seats and if you're living in the West," a critique of religion's colonizing tendencies, as voiced by singer Mark Wallinger in his song "Always on My Mind."[22] Instead it "is indeed the awareness of human insufficiency, it is lived in the admission of weakness . . . the invariable message of religious worship is: 'from the finite to the infinite the distance is always infinite.'"[23] This comment from Leszek Kolakowski reflects the shifting ground on which the new religious impulse is being built. Mystery is a dominant characteristic of all the various incarnations of this new impulse. Awareness that modernity's self-confidence is in fact sinking sand and *not* solid ground, that some things cannot be adequately explained or understood, has led to a new sense of vulnerability that permeates the contemporary religious ethos, a point that will be picked up more specifically in our discussion about the nature of postmodernity. These new visions of spirit—the emerging spirit of the times—are funded in part by the ancient religious traditions, which remain in the cultural mix and in which Christianity in particular (largely, but not exclusively in the West) plays a significant role. But it is more than this.

The Dutch theologian Mieke Bal asserts that:

> The cultural present is unthinkable without an understanding and acceptance of three premises. First, Christianity is there: that is, here (in Europe and the

Americas at least). Second, Christianity is a cultural structure that informs the cultural imaginary, whether one identifies with it in terms of belief and practice or not. Third, Christianity is just that: hence, it is neither the only cultural structure nor the only religious structure around.[24]

The presence of Christianity in the cultural matrix explains, to some degree, the continual employment of distinctly Christian religious affect and affectation, particularly in the arts. Cinema, for example, makes great use of Catholic imagery and iconography in its representations of the religious. But one must also recognize that "spiritual" is a broader and more variegated term than a reference to Christianity exclusively—it encompasses many facets of our engagement with the sacred.

Everything Is Everything

A second dynamic of the postsecular, which has implications for our discussion here, is that not only is postmodernity spiritual but it also has a certain consciousness, a consciousness that can only be defined as the *consciousness of plurality* at every level of human existence. This is one of the chief distinctions between modern and postmodern manifestations of the spiritual. If modernity was characterized by the totalizing attempts in all fields of study, by the commitment to ideologies of universality, then postmodernity is concerned with the particle, the particular, and the specific. It is very difficult and decidedly unhelpful for many people, who find themselves living and interacting in what is an increasingly global environment, to accept that there is one complete and universal answer to anything, specifically to questions of how the spiritual should be addressed. Gianni Vattimo regards Nietzsche as the beginning point for much of this:

> In other words, it is precisely the Babelic world of late modernity that "verifies" the Nietzschean announcement of the death of God and the Heideggerian announcement of the end of metaphysics—which are identical in meaning—by legitimizing them. In a certain sense, which cannot be systematized, this is the world where "the moral God" as metaphysical ground is dead and buried. But the moral God is only what Pascal referred to as the God of the philosophers. There are many indications, therefore, that the death of the moral God has paved the way for the renewal of religious life.[25]

Steve Bruce places the cultural dynamics that have led to the new religious situation even farther back, citing the Protestant Reformation as the starting point of the fragmentation of belief now characteristic of the postsecular era.

> The Reformation did not arise out of nothing. . . . It (the Reformation) inadvertently fragmented the dominant religious culture and created the competition which, in tolerant and egalitarian societies, would lead to relativism and perennialism. By insisting that all people had a responsibility for their own spiritual state, the Reformation also contributed directly to the growth of individualism. It required ordinary people to become better informed about their religion, and in producing the means to service that need (printing, the spread of literacy, and the use of the vernacular), it further encouraged the trend. It also contributed to the rationalization of the world, hence to the growth of modern science and technology, and thus inadvertently to the erosion of religion.[26]

Bruce places a lot at the feet of the Reformers. (Whether he is right in so doing is a subject for debate. He also seems to have a rather low view of the present state of religious life in his essay.) But he does highlight a number of factors that, when put together, go a long way toward explaining the present situation. I am sure that the Reformers had different results in mind for their actions than those that have occurred since the sixteenth century, but it is usually true that we as humans generally underestimate the role and effect that change and new technologies have on us.

Consider electricity. When it was first employed, it had a single use: the provision of light, a monumental use. But in the grand scope of potential uses for electricity we have found today, this represented a myopic view of the potential use of its available power. When homes were first wired for electricity there were no power sockets put in walls, there was simply a light bulb hanging from the center of the ceiling by an electrical cord. It wasn't until the invention of other household appliances, such as the air conditioner and vacuum cleaner and washing machine, that the naïveté was exposed. In order to use one of these new household inventions one had to plug the device into an available power source, which was exclusively in the ceiling, where the light was. This initially led to the development of extra screw-in sockets to be added to ceiling lights, but eventually someone realized that the task of screwing devices into the ceiling and making extremely long electrical cords hang from the ceiling like maypole ribbons was not the best way to approach the use of new devices. This approach, combined with the fact that early household devices did not have on/off switches, led to some precarious situations. Eventually, wall sockets and on/off switches became a natural extension of the use of electricity in our homes. There is a moral to this story: as with technology, so with theology—that which we think is the end is but the beginning.

Things develop in unexpected ways, the broadening of possibilities occurring logarithmically rather than in a linear and neat progression. Bruce writes that the "religion created by the Reformers was extremely vulnerable to fragmentation because it removed the institution of the church as a source of authority between God and man."[27] Again, I am not sure that this is exactly what the Reformers had in mind, but it is certainly the reality today that we find ourselves in a time when a growing number of people are fashioning their spiritual practices and beliefs outside the confines of any mediated structural system of authority.

The form of pluralism at which we have arrived is the perceived reality that there is no overarching framework that encompasses the framework of others. It is the fulfillment of Lyotard's announcement of the end of metanarratives and their replacement with *petit recits* (little stories).[28] I said that this consciousness of pluralism is found at every level of human experience. In the postmodern, it is not simply a question of religious pluralism but of cultural pluralism as well. What I mean by this is that we find ourselves in an increasingly global context in which there is no single totalizing proposition accepted by all. This is why I distinguish the age of the spirit from that of the Holy Spirit. David Tracy has commented that:

> At no other time have people had such a sense of the difference of others, of the pluralism of societies, cultures, and religions, and of the relativity that this entails. One can no longer claim western culture as the center, the higher point of view, or Christianity as the superior religion, or Christ as the absolute center to which all other historical mediations are relative. The world is pluralistic and polycentric in its horizons of interpretations.[29]

Pluralism in the postmodern context is not simply the tense coexistence of competing ideologies, it is also the container, the crucible, where the seeds of the search for the new germinate. All of this to say that in the present spiritual climate, pluralism is a positive and not the negative that modernity held it to be. It is also another example of the democratization process at work in our time. If things are truly flattening out, if the playing fields are level, then surely many ideas can co-exist in equanimity and peace, then there is no need for one idea to gain the ascendancy. Ward contends that "a God is sought who is neither a watchmaker, nor an architect, neither a mathematician nor a bookmaker. God is no longer an omnipotent, omniscient, absolutely perfect person, nor an Archimedean point outside the system. God is all things and more. . . . The divine defines itself beyond abstract rational axioms in a new appeal to the intuition of infinity itself."[30]

The emergence of pluralism in the postsecular context is linked to the emergence of a burgeoning global culture linked by technology and influenced by the global rise of media. The proliferation of technological and democratizing tendencies, which has resulted in access to information and perspective unprecedented in scope, has created a shift in our understanding of the nature of reality. This new approach to pluralism is also fueled by a loss of confidence in Western hegemony among those in the West (it is hard to feel good about your own part of the world and its practices when its global image is generally negative and sometimes even harmful to the common, that is, global, good), the massive loss of faith in modernity's shaping ideologies, and the bankruptcy of materialism (even as we find ourselves becoming more and more materialist!).

Emerging Global Culture and the Symbolic Universe of the Media Generation

The postsecular context has led or, more accurately, is leading to the emergence of a global culture.[1] In employing the term "culture," I am acknowledging that a certain process is at work, a shift in the understanding of culture as the "process of naturalizing a subset of differences that have been mobilized to articulate a group identity" and from "culture as substance to culture as the dimension of difference."[2] In the past, the idea of a single, unified culture was linked to the imperialist and expansionist intents of a particular group that had world domination and subjugation as its focus, be it the Romans or the British.

When I refer to a global culture in the postmodern sense, I do not mean to conjure up the idea of a singular, homogenized culture, nor do I want to define it as a sort of "global Westernization," even though this does form part of the core of what is occurring. Instead, I am referring to a series of cultures linked by certain globalizing tendencies. These tendencies most likely appear in urban centers and create a sort of "culture within a culture." This global culture generally includes the acceptance, assimilation, and use of the technological culture primarily emerging out of the West and elements of Western consumerist tendencies. At the same time and to varying degrees, global culture rejects other aspects of Western modernity, such as its secularizing tendencies and some of its social mores and attitudes, which are often linked with sexuality. Global culture is a web-based idea that is becoming a lived reality for more and more people, especially the wired and connected youth around the globe. Affluence plays a role, but engaging in the technologically driven emerging global culture is not exclusively the experience of the wealthy. Technology is advancing at such a pace that more and more of the globe is finding itself capable of accessing new ways of interacting, expressing, and being in the world.

A key dynamic of global culture, as well as the new religious impulses that accompany it, is the emergence of the imagination as a pivotal means of social production. Appadurai notes:

> It takes only the merest acquaintance with the facts of the modern world to note that it is now an interactive system in a sense that is strikingly new. Historians and sociologists . . . have long been aware that the world has been a congeries of large-scale interactions for many centuries. Yet today's world involves interactions of a new order and intensity. Cultural transactions between social groups in the past have generally been restricted, sometimes by the facts of geography and ecology, and at other times by active resistance to interactions with the Other.[3]

Appadurai argues that the primary forces that sustained cultural interaction before the twentieth century were warfare and religions of conversion[4] but goes on to argue that the role of imagination in social life is reshaping world systems today:

> The crucial point, however, is that the United States is no longer the puppeteer of a world system of images but is only one node of a complex transnational construction of imaginary landscapes. The world we live in today is characterized by a new role for the imagination in social life. . . . The image, the imagined, the imaginary—these are all terms that direct us to something critical and new in global cultural processes: the imagination as social practice.[5]

According to Appadurai, this phase of global culture is the necessary development of earlier forms[6] of global culture that were part of the homogenizing tendencies of colonizing nations: "With what Benedict Anderson has called 'print capitalism,' a new power was unleashed in the world, the power of mass-literacy and its attendant large-scale production of projects of ethnic affinity that were remarkably free of the need for face-to-face or even of direct communication between persons and groups."[7] This version of globalization set the stage for our understanding of global geographies, many of which were dependent on colonial tendencies and their dialectically generated nationalism, that is, constructed ethnicities.[8]

> But the revolution of print capitalism and the cultural affinities and dialogues unleashed by it were only modest precursor to the world we live in now. For in the past century, there has been a technological explosion, largely in the domain of transportation and information, that makes the interactions

New Horizons

of a print-dominated world seem as hard-won and as easily erased as the print revolution made earlier forms of cultural traffic appear.[9]

A recent movie highlights the implications of colonially constructed ethnicities. *Hotel Rwanda* recounts the true story of Paul Rusesabagina, manager of a four-star hotel in the Rwandan capital of Kigali who sheltered more than one thousand Tutsi refugees in his hotel during the genocide that was waged across the country by the Hutu militia. This tribal war had its roots in the Belgian conquest and rule of the country in the nineteenth century, the entire country and its ethnic makeup being largely a product of Western "constructed primordialism."[10]

But is this new configuration an expression of global culture? I argue that it is a global culture in that there is an emerging global imaginary, linked by technology and global media, consumerism and fashion, and the subsequent emergence of a new global consciousness. This consciousness does not express itself in a universal, homogenous form but is discovered as a mood, a shift in attitude and perspective, that is influencing the shaping of postsecular culture. The lack of a universalizing tendency is a marked distinction between modern globalization and the emerging global culture of the postmodern situation. The apparent ascendancy of the West and the continuing view of globalization as merely the continuing process of the Westernizing of the world highlights a significant factor but misses the larger point. The "West" remains a dominant figure on the global scene due to a variety of issues related to the universalizing tendencies of the modernity that laid the framework for its globalizing aspirations. And it is on this framework that the new global culture seeks to emerge. For instance, in *The No-Nonsense Guide to Globalization* we find this statement:

> Globalization is a new word which describes an old process: the integration of the global economy that began in earnest with the launch of the European colonial era five centuries ago. But the process has accelerated over the past quarter century with the explosion of computer technology, the dismantling of trade barriers and the expanding political and economic powers of multinational corporations.[11]

But this is not the full picture of the emerging global culture; other factors are also at work. I have no desire to appear naive and inconsiderate regarding the implications of the continuing dominance of Western ideologies in global affairs. I am acutely aware of the terrible pressure to conform to itself that the West continues to exert on other nations and worldviews. But I am pointing out that those earlier tendencies toward a molding of the world into an expression of Western hegemony are part of the hierarchical structure of modernity that is being rejected virtually wholesale by an increasing number of people, particularly those whose worldview is characterized by a set of symbols different from that of the modern age. It was Western expansionism, democratic capitalist expansion, and Christian missionary enterprise that made the world a laboratory for Western values, particularly in the eighteenth and nineteenth centuries. And while those structures continue to inform and to influence, it is no longer simply the case that globalization and Westernization are one and the same, any more than Western culture and emerging global culture are the same thing. Concerning this, Tomlinson writes:

> These reflections do suggest that what is happening in globalization is not a process firmly in the cultural grip of the West and that, therefore, the global future is much more radically open than the discourses of homogenization and cultural imperialism suggest. We surely need to find new critical models to engage with the emerging "power geometry" of globalization, but we will not find these by rummaging through the theoretical box of tricks labeled "Westernization."[12]

Appadurai agrees with this assessment, stating, "We are now aware that with media, each time we are tempted to speak of the global village, we must be reminded that media creates communities with no sense of place."[13] The world we live in does not fit neatly into earlier attempts to capture the emerging global dynamics.

Appadurai terms this contemporary "no place" as "deterritorialization."[14] Deterritorialization occurs on a number of different levels. The first level involves the geographic relocations prompted by changing flows of peoples, what Appadurai calls "cultural flows."[15] Developments and advancements in transportation and communication have allowed for new configurations of population flows as the world becomes a mix of locals, refugees, immigrants, tourists, and displaced persons.[16]

The second level of deterritorialization is rooted in the involvement of an increasing number of people who interact with available global media and enter environments such as cyberspace and other imaginary worlds created by global communications. This is a new expression of cultural life, one in which geography and location and traditional understandings of time and space are less and less a factor, and other dynamics, such as the effects of global media, are the dominant influence. Rushkoff writes of this phenomenon:

> Welcome to the twenty-first century. We are all immigrants in a new territory. Our world is changing so rapidly that we can hardly track the differences, much less master them. Whether it's caller ID, MTV, digital cash, or chaos math, we are bombarded every day with an increasing number of words, devices, ideas and events which we do not understand. . . . Without having physically migrated an inch, we have, nonetheless, traveled further than any generation in history.[17]

Rushkoff paints a very positive view of the future but notes the significant effect that technology has had on the culture: "The degree of change experienced by the last three generations rivals that of a species undergoing mutation."[18] This process of mutation is caused by the advance of technological development and the explosion of ideas and choices offered to us in its wake. Marshall McLuhan offers a slightly different perspective on the same issue:

> The medium, or process, of our time—electronic technology—is reshaping and restructuring patterns of interdependence and every aspect of our personal life—it is forcing us to reconsider and reevaluate practically every thought, every action, and every institution formerly taken for granted—you, your family, your neighborhood, your education, your job, your government, your relation to the "others"—and they're changing dramatically.[19]

Global communications technology and the proliferation of media have become the site for postsecular self-education. Rushkoff notes the dramatic speed at which this new environment has come to shape the culture:

> When I first wrote this book, in 1995, the kinds of activities and media I explored as examples of youth culture's self-education were considered "fringe" at best. Since that time, however, many of these seemingly esoteric areas of culture—the many unrelated film genres, sports, toys, and television shows—have developed into popular and independent mainstream activities. This is not evidence of my own predictive powers, but an indication of just how much the need for these outlets and experiences has intensified during these last few years before the millennium.[20]

This "need" is related to the implosion of modernity's structures, the institutions that held us—religious institutions, family, neighborhood, society, and the like—and the desire to replace them with alternative forms of socialization and connection. That this self-education is largely linked to developments in communications and technology, such as the Internet and global popular culture, goes a long way toward explaining Appadurai's contention that the imagination is key in shaping social practice:

> In suggesting that the imagination in the post-electronic world plays a newly significant role, I rest my case on three distinctions. First, the imagination has broken out of the special expressive space of art, myth, and ritual and now has become part of the quotidian metal work of ordinary people in many societies. It has entered the logic of ordinary life from which it had largely been successfully sequestered. . . . Ordinary people have now begun to deploy their imaginations in the practice of their everyday lives.[21]

Appadurai interprets this as the growing dream of many people to live and work in places other than where they originated. This is related to his perspective on cultural flows and changing ethnoscapes.[22] It is also the result of a new mythography[23] dependent on mass media and the "images, scripts, models and narratives" it produces. "For migrants, both the politics of adaptation to new environments and the stimulus to move or return are deeply affected by a mass-mediated imaginary that frequently transcends national space."[24]

Appadurai's second distinction of the postmodern imagination rebuts earlier views that the imagination will be stunted by the forces of commodification and industrialization: "There is growing evidence that the consumption of the mass media throughout the world often provokes resistance, irony, selectivity, and in general, agency. . . . T-shirts, billboards, and graffiti as well as rap music, street dancing, and slum housing all show that the images of the media are quickly moved into local repertoires of irony, anger, humor, and resistance."[25] He also comments on the role of religion in this milieu: "there is vast evidence in new religiosities of every sort that religion is not only not dead but that it may be more consequential than ever in today's highly mobile and interconnected global politics."[26]

Appadurai's final distinction regarding the shaping element of imagination is linked to the creation of "communities of 'sentiment,' collective experiences of mass media, especially film and video, which can create solidarities of worship and charisma."[27] These are communities of shared experience, a defining symbol of the media generation, and they may or may not be limited to national boundaries. They are, in fact, more likely to be experienced beyond previous geographical boundaries and limitations, as many of these experiences occur in the deterritorialized spaces of postsecular culture.

There are some dynamics in the emerging global culture that have implications for the shape of religious expression in the postsecular age. First, the global communications revolution is fostering what I can only describe as a new consciousness. The media and technological developments of the past fifty years have completely and irrevocably changed the way we interact. The sheer number of people who are communicating with each other via IT (information technology) is altering our self-perception. This use of the term "Information Age" is prevalent, but such an appellation focuses on the technology and not on the technology's effect on the users. Rushkoff's understanding of a cultural mutation, which I quoted earlier, points to this dynamic.

How is this new global consciousness expressing itself? In at least two ways. First, in our capacity to be self-reflective, to be more detached from the world and our place in it and to be less judging. This detachment from a specific place is linked to the incredible options proffered by technology and mass communication, which allow us to inhabit many worlds at once. Less judgment means more openness, a willingness to accept difference and otherness rather than resorting to colonizing impulses and seeking to process otherness by consuming it.

A second dynamic in the manifestation of global consciousness is what I term a shift toward the "humanizing of humanity." In the West, this appears as a growing rejection of perfectionism and its accompanying concern with morality that has particularly haunted the American social landscape. On a singular cultural level, this shift in consciousness can be seen in public reaction to the Monica Lewinsky affair and former president Bill Clinton's subsequent impeachment: more people than in previous times, had this scandal occurred years ago, seemed able to handle the idea that one could be simultaneously a flawed human and a good leader.

On a broader social scale, all of this is reflected in the dynamics of the postmodern consciousness of pluralism, which is moving toward an increasing acceptance and inclusion of the planet as a whole and away from sectarian homogenizations. This is not to discount the continuing rise of sectarianism and isolation that are also part of the postsecular social imaginary. Not everyone is intent on acceptance and moving toward new understandings of what it means to be human. The rise of fundamentalism is linked to this. It is worth acknowledging that if we all were moving toward the same end, we would probably not be talking about the postsecular situation! Postmodern deterritorialization is at the heart of a "variety of global fundamentalisms, including Islamic and Hindu fundamentalism."[28]

The network nature of contemporary media, be it the World Wide Web or other avenues of collective interaction and communication, has also fostered a growing awareness of interconnectedness. This interconnectedness is tied to a number of events and dynamics: the reality of a true global network as more and more of the planet joins the global culture by cell phone, Internet, and a host of other linking technologies. Alongside this, developments in science, such as chaos theory and quantum physics, have led us to a less hierarchical view of the world and the universe itself. The deprivileging of metaphysics in the West and the embracing of other perspectives drawn from different religious traditions in other parts of the world have led us to view ourselves more as part of a global whole than as isolated individuals, which was the ideal of high modernity.

A dynamic of emerging global culture is a growing ecological awareness and concern. This factor is linked to Wallace's contention about the revalorization of nature.[29] There is a sense in which we—and I use "we" in the global sense—are increasingly aware of the need to find ways of living that honor the earth and preserve it for future generations. The runaway success of former vice president Al Gore's movie *An Inconvenient Truth*, and other films focused on environmental issues such as *Who Killed the Electric Car*, underscore the extent to which ecology and environmental issues are beginning to reshape our lives, both public and private. We are experiencing a "citizens revolution; from all corners of the globe, we are now bearing witness to an emergence of social entrepreneurs with ethics as powerful as their conviction to do the greatest good for all."[30]

Another perspective on this dynamic is found in the children's story titled *The Lorax* by Dr. Seuss, first published in 1971.[31] The Lorax is a creature whose job is to speak for the trees. The nature of his task demands that his voice be sharp and bossy. Since the Truffula Trees (Seuss's term for the particular trees in this story) have no tongues, the Lorax functions as their advocate as well as for all the other creatures and things that inhabit the place where the Grickle-grass grows. But as the story unfolds we learn that the Lorax's voice is no match for those who seek to turn the Truffula Trees into thneeds—the all-purpose items everyone needs. When the last tree is cut down, the Lorax leaves the forest. But it leaves one thing behind; in a small pile of rocks is one emblazoned with the word "Unless." In retelling the story, the narrator, the Once-ler, unlocks the meaning of the puzzling legacy of the Lorax: "Unless someone like you cares a whole awful lot, nothing is going to get better. It's not."

This sentiment reflects the emerging eco-focus of contemporary religious expression.

Alongside this concern for the environment is a burgeoning move toward finding sustainable ways of living. This move could be viewed as a shift away from *Martha Stewart Living*, the lifestyle magazine of choice for the baby-boomer generation, to *Ready-Made*, the magazine devoted to recycling and the reuse of goods for aficionados of the cut-and-paste generation. The difference between the two mindsets—modern and postmodern—is evident in the focus of these magazines. *Martha Stewart Living* is a glossy publication dedicated to the pursuit of perfection and fascinated with the new and the shiny. It is replete with recipes and decorating ideas designed first and foremost to allow the consumer to fashion his or her lifestyle according to the Martha Stewart value system. No expense is spared in presentation, and the magazines are full of photo spreads that demonstrate a commitment to a decidedly upwardly mobile east-coast lifestyle.

Ready Made, by contrast, is a magazine committed to the reuse of discarded items and offers witty and decidedly low-budget home-decorating tips. It is the anti–Martha Stewart lifestyle, defined by its reconfiguring of discarded and recycled items. The "new" things in *Ready Made* are new solely by their reconfiguration. This magazine has a heavy emphasis on global environmental and ecological issues and is produced on recycled paper, thus reflecting the growing concern for the environment and the shift toward more sustainable lifestyle choices that characterize many in the burgeoning global culture.

Two other expressions in the emerging global culture have more direct implications for our understanding of the new religious context.

A Postmodern Ethic

Either no member of the human race has real rights, or else all have the same; he who votes against the rights of another, whatever his religion, colour or sex, thereby abjures his own.

Marquis de Condorcet

First, there is a shift toward the development of a postmodern ethic. The idea of postmodern ethics will probably raise eyebrows in some quarters where all things postmodern are viewed with suspicion. But the emergence of ethics with a postmodern twist reflects the changing dynamics of postmodernity itself. If, as Rushkoff posits,[32] technology is pushing society through massive change, even mutation, and leading to a transformation of social structures, then there has to be some kind of moral structuring to accompany this. The dynamic of global-culture interconnectedness and interdependence demands that we care about those who are far away from us—this caring is the framework for a new moral imagination. Morality has traditionally been handed down either by God via religion or by philosophy. One's moral code was largely grounded in the belief system of one's culture. But the loss of faith, particularly in the West, has created a crisis in that we find ourselves divorced from the instruments of morality within our respective cultural environments. In a recent survey conducted by the Barna Research group, forty-eight percent of people polled replied that they do not know how they make moral choices.[33]

How, then, do we conceive of a postmodern ethic given that the return to God, which has attended the postmodern shift, is neither a return to the premodern God nor a return to premodern moralities? Interestingly, the framework for a postmodern ethic is left over from modernity's universal tendencies. If there remains a single universal idea left over from the modern era that was not rejected with the majority of other totalizing ideologies, it is surely the Universal Declaration of Human Rights. This may or may not be verbalized in the same way the framers of the original idea did, but permeating contemporary postmodern global culture is the idea that we are all on equal ground as human beings: male/female, gay/straight, white/nonwhite, rich/poor. All of us are entitled to freedom and respect for who we are as human beings. The ground of contemporary morality can be understood in reference to the impact of twentieth-century developments such as the civil rights movement, the women's movement, the gay and lesbian movement, and even the environmental and animal activist movements. It doesn't take very long to realize that the early part of the twentieth century was not like this. These liberation movements dramatically changed the moral landscape. We were set free from enclosing and inhibiting prohibitions and were free to be ourselves. Yet with this came not the greater freedom promised but a sense of moral decay and detachment, because the moral ground of the late-modern world had been largely left to the individual. As with other aspects of contemporary social life, it had been a cut-and-paste, pick-and-mix affair that virtually guaranteed the idea that a general ethic would remain a pipe dream.

However, there was a light at the end of the tunnel, which leads me to declare the emergence of a postmodern ethic. "The cure for postmodern narcissism is activism," says Darcy Riddell, a Canadian environmental activist, and activism seems to be the locus of the emerging ethic of the postmodern era.[34] The postmodern ethic remains a fringe issue, but it is on the growing edge of contemporary culture. It is reflected in a number of rising activist movements that range from environmental concerns to human rights issues such as the anti–World Trade Organization movement, the rise of organizations committed to raising AIDS awareness, those groups that campaign for the relief of World Bank debt for third-world nations, and other groups such as Data, Greenpeace, and the like.

It is interesting that spirituality remains, at present, disconnected from ethics and morality. Religion is still not necessarily the place where postmodern ethics is emerging. It will certainly play a role, but it will not comprise the whole moral framework given the general rejection of the authority of traditional faith in matters of social morality. Again, this is the result of the rejection of the totalizing ideologies of modernity.

New-Edge Spirituality

The second characteristic of the emerging global postsecular culture that affects our understanding of the new religious context is the emergence of a new kind of spirituality—the real subject of this book. We have discussed this spirituality's emergence already, but it is important again to reference a few of the defining characteristics before we go on. This expression of religion is an experiential and hands-on expression of belief—post-creedal, post-orthodox, and post-specialist. By this I mean to say that (1) it is not dependent on traditional religious structures for its acts of worship and ritual making, (2) it is not exclusively focused on continuing ancient traditions in the new cultural matrix, and (3) it generally demands no professional clergy to administer truth, instruction, and dogma. However, it is by no means antagonistic toward traditional faith expressions; jaded perhaps, suspicious definitely, but it recognizes the contribution traditional faiths make to the present situation. There is curiosity, even embrace at times, of religious rites and practices, but often at arm's length, and arbitrary in accepting or rejecting certain ideas.

This spirituality tends to be handmade faith, fashioned in the crucible of life in a globally connected world. It is everyone's concern and opportunity and requires no membership in a particular organization or institution—this is the democratization of spirit I alluded to earlier. It is as much informed by popular culture as it is by ancient tradition, hence my use of the phrase "entertainment theology." Entertainment theology does not mean that the subject we are discussing is inconsequential or slight; rather, it points to a source of the impulse (the primary source, as I see it). Everything is being filtered through the media spectrum, everything is entertainment, in that it comes to us via interactive technology and media outlets, whether from a bookstore or from the World Wide Web. Theology, "God-talk," as Phyllis Tickle so aptly puts it, is taking place alongside all the other issues of life, in the mediated environment of a globally connected society. "Life is a sacred adventure. Every day we encounter signs that point to the active presence of Spirit in the world around us. . . . For us, the signs have come most often from books and popular culture."[35]

The role of books in shaping the current imaginary cannot be underestimated. The use of pop-culture artifacts and religion in dialogue together, particularly in book form,[36] is a key dynamic both of the development of new religious expressions and of the continued presence of older faith traditions.[37] Science, no longer the enemy of spirit in the postsecular world, also plays a role. New developments in post-Newtonian science, such as chaos and string theory and the shift in science from certainty to uncertainty,[38] demonstrate our movement past the mechanisms of modernity; but our return to traditional faith expression is severely challenged by the emergence of postsecular culture. The ancient constructs of premodern faiths are viewed as incompatible with the complexities of contemporary urban life. This is the religious expression that shifts the spiritual conversation from designated religious space to work space, play space, cyber space, all space. It is the religious expression of a resacralized, reenchanted postmodern culture. How this expression surfaces within the culture and what it might look like are the subjects of the next section.

Part 2

New Edges

The postmodern mind is altogether less excited than its modern adversary by the prospect (let alone moved by the urge) to enclose the world into a grid of neat categories and clear-cut divisions. We are somewhat less horrified today by the nasty habit things have of spilling over their definitional boundaries, or even by the premonition that the drawing of such boundaries with any degree of lasting reliability defies human resources.

Zygmunt Bauman, "Postmodern Religion?"

I begin this second section with this quote from Zygmunt Bauman to highlight the difficulty of attempting to define what is emerging in totalizing fashions (nor do I have the urge to do so). What I offer instead are some key dynamics that lead me to situate certain dynamics of the postsecular religious expression in broad, but somewhat quantifiable, environments. Rather than presenting neatly packaged and defined categorizations, my desire is to paint a broader picture of the current state of religion and neo-religious practice in the postsecular context, attempting to capture its mood as much as its categories, and then move on to consider what a meaningful missional and theological response might be.

A larger question that emerges from my exploration is the place, or potential place, of an ancient faith like Christianity in a postsecular context. I am aware that it remains a viable and meaningful option for a vast number of people around the globe, but the reality is that in the emerging global culture—the growing edge of the postmodern world, the mass-mediated, populist world of the new urbanity—Christian existence, let alone advancement, remains threatened. Is there a way to reconfigure Christian faith so that it retains its distinctiveness? I believe so, but we will come to that later. First things first.

Before shifting to the manifestations of democratized spirituality in the postsecular, there are three dynamics to explore that affect the general state of affairs in the postsecular context: fetishization, commodification, and popularization. I will address these three issues before moving on to specific incarnations of the spiritual/religious dynamic in the postsecular. These three currents outline something of the "meaning routes"[1] employed in the current situation. They help us see the development of a people's religion not merely through the lens of destabilized conventional religious identity, in an effort to make sense of the residues of their meaning, but by grasping how the present situation is giving rise to particular forms of expression and practice.

Surface as Depth

Faith as Fetishization

There is no lighthouse keeper. There is no lighthouse. There is no dry land. There are only people living on rafts made from their own imaginations. And there is the sea.

John Dominic Crossan

The 1995 Universal Pictures movie *Waterworld* was a box-office dud, in spite of the fact that at the time it was the most expensive movie ever made. It was the product of bad press, bad reviews, bad story, bad weather, bad hair,[1] bad, bad, bad. And yet its story line exemplifies some key elements of the postmodern situation, particularly as they relate to spiritual expression.

Waterworld takes place on earth, albeit a very different earth from the one we are used to seeing. In this futuristic film, the polar ice caps have melted, causing cataclysmic flooding that resulted in the whole earth being submerged under water. The old world remains intact but lies submerged under the new, much as the structures of modernity lie rusting under the new postmodern world. Gerard Kelly notes that the "old civilization has not been destroyed so much as made redundant. . . . A new world has washed over the old, rendering it uninhabitable."[2] Those who survived the deluge live on the surface of the new "waterworld" and seek to fashion a new way of living out of what they can scavenge from the surface of the waters. In his assessment of this film, Kelly wants to retain the past that has been lost in the waters, though I am not sure this is even possible, at least in the way he seeks to. Writing as an evangelical Christian, he offers new models for ecclesiology and leadership in response to the changing circumstances of the shift to postmodernity, but he wants to hold too tightly to a modernist construct of the nature of Christian faith and its expression. Consequently he sees little need for adjusting or recontextualizing the Christian message. As a result, his version of Christian faith will most likely remain "beneath the waves" for those fashioning faith on the surface of a watery new world. Kelly does, however, provide some keen insights into the connections that can be made between this film and some dynamics of the present situation. Especially pertinent to our present discussion are the loss of certainty, the emergence of transitional communities, and the need to remain on the surface in order to be safe.[3]

The loss of certainty is metaphorically linked to the loss of solid, dry ground. In *Waterworld* the driving myth is the fabled existence of a place where dry land still exists. Here, in this world of water, the dominant form of currency is not gold but earth. "Their points of reference, their laws, their notions of civilized behavior, are all called into question by their sea-borne lifestyle . . . there is no fixed point to cling to."[4] Whether those who have known only the waters of postmodern uncertainty still seek solidity and certainty is contestable, but Kelly's comments note the shift in socializing tendencies between the old and new cultures: "New skills are needed for a life, for the time being, without moorings."[5] As the story unfolds, we are introduced to the various incarnations of community in *Waterworld*. Most of them are fashioned together by gathering various bits of salvaged materials from the old world and refashioning them into new habitats. Rust is a dominant visual in the film, as the steel that framed the modern world is better suited to dry land than watery worlds. Nonetheless we find communities of people drawn together and fashioning new floating villages. "Some choose to bolt and buckle together their assorted floating structures to form an outer shell and, within it, to create some semblance of civic life. Others occupy huge abandoned ships, moving together across oceans as mass pilgrims in search of a better future. Others still choose the lone call of the high seas, but live all the same by agreed codes and norms."[6]

There is a transitional nature to all these communities; the constant shifting of the ocean is reflected in the transitory state in which they live, reminiscent again of the shifting world of the postmodern where all is in a continual state of flux, of "global flows."[7] The styles and modes of dress are a strange meeting of old-world styles refashioned into new-world functionality. Some look like pirates, others like street urchins. Everyone is rather shabby, much like early twenty-first century urban fashion, which reflects a laissez-faire attitude toward style and presentation. What we wear expresses the spirit of the times in which we live.[8] The employment of military fabrics, such as camouflage, in the service of civilian fashion reflects the struggle of contemporary urban life. So too does the wearing of sports outfits by those who are spectators, a trend that reflects not only changing attitudes about personal appearance but also the desire of even those who are out of shape physically in our culture to have at least the affectation of being sporty and athletic, even if they do not have the physique to match!

Kelly notes that "in a floating world, deep is dangerous. . . . Preserving life means staying on the surface."[9] This element of the film has particular resonance with the topic at hand, namely, the fetishization of religion in postmodernity/postsecularity. Life exists on the surface in *Waterworld*. What remains under the waves is gone and represents a world no longer functional but submerged under a new social order. The survivors make do by skimming the surface, fashioning new lives and communities out of what they can scrape from the surface of the waves. The old world can be accessed only in short bursts as it requires that one hold one's breath— underwater is no place for a human to be, life must now be lived on the surface. Unless . . . unless one is the Mariner,[10] the main character played by actor Kevin Costner. The Mariner is actually *posthuman* in that he has somehow developed gills, which allow him to navigate the newly reordered world. In this he stands as a symbol for the postsecular human, as a sign for those who seek to inhabit both the world of water and the world of dry land and for those who wish to develop the necessary skills and adapt themselves even physically to their new environment.

Waterworld is essentially a modern tale. The central dream is to get back to dry land, which, when finally discovered by Mariner and his newly fashioned and reconfigured family, is reminiscent of Eden. It is the return to Milton's *Paradise Lost* rather than the discovery of new frontiers. The film represents the modernist's desire to return to the old order, achievable only in the cinematic imaginary, but still a compelling image for many. A key message in the film is that real life and living as humans are possible only on dry land, the utopian tendency of modernity's universalizing binary oppositions. Mariner stands as a testament to the fact that life in other permutations is quite possible, something that is daily being explored in postsecular situations.

But Mariner willingly abandons his waterworld tendencies when dry land is rediscovered. To return to my previous point, the issue of surface living—that it signifies a lack of depth or lack of substance, that it is all veneer—is a central accusation by critics of the postmodern condition. I am arguing here that those are the comments either of persons who do not necessarily understand what it takes to live in a new waterworld or of those who perhaps do not fully understand that the waters of a new spirituality have flooded the dry land of secularism and that secularism will never emerge from those waters to stand as it once did. Even the movie provides not a reversal to the scope of land mass prior to the cataclysm but a simple outcropping. If we continue with the contrast of water world versus dry land, then it follows that what was useful and necessary on dry land might have little usefulness in a wetter environment; "digging is not too valuable a skill in *Waterworld*," Kelly pithily observes.[11]

The use of the phrase "fetishization of religion" might seem to suggest a rather vapid use of religion in the postmodern era, a talismanic approach to religion where the appropriation of faith is nothing more than an affectation. But it is an acknowledgment of something else: the liquidification of religion in postsecular culture. This liquidification is a key characteristic of a society seeking to redefine its relationship with the divine apart from the structures and perceived hindrances of traditional religious doctrines and dogmas. What that new structure or grid might look like will be taken up more specifically later.

Consider the rising use of omamori, a sort of good-luck charm from Japan.[12] Part rabbit foot, part religious relic, part security blanket, an omamori is a centuries-old religious item used to ward off the devil and garner the attention of the gods. Today there are an estimated half billion omamori in use in Japan alone,[13] with a burgeoning market outside that particular culture. Users hang them from school bags, cell phones, and rear-view mirrors. They are an outgrowth of the nation's animistic tradition, but today they can easily symbolize certain aspects of our approach to religion—we incorporate elements of spirituality to help us in hard times, separate from any formalized discipline or dogma.

Much has been written about this approach to religion in contemporary times. Personally, I do not consider the fetish nature of the current situation predominantly a negative. It reflects the realities of postsecularity. Slavoj Žižek, senior researcher at the Institute of Social Studies at the University of Ljubljana, argues that a fetish can play a very constructive role in allowing us to cope with the harsh reality: "fetishists are not dreamers lost in their private worlds, they are thoroughly 'realists,' able to accept the way things effectively are—since they have their fetish to which they can cling in order to cancel the full impact of reality."[14] In other words, the fetishization of postsecular culture is a coping mechanism of the times in which we live. There is an awareness of reality attached to the fetishization process, the opposite of the modern way of dealing with reality, which was often through denial, keeping the harshness of life at arm's length. Employing a fetish is the means by which something continues to live and at the same time a means by which we can negotiate the complexities of postmodern life and living.

Religion seems to play at least two symbiotic roles in the present situation, as Graham Ward has pointed out. First, religion functions as a kind of symbolic capital. With the Japanese charms, their ties to an ancient past, their rootedness in somewhere other than modernity, allows their usage to invest in "places, goods, even people a mystic charge."[15] Adopting a more critical view of this posture, Ward argues that those who are drawn to this mystic charge are "not buying religion, they are not consuming the religion or being consumed by it; they are consuming the illusions or simulations of religion."[16] Alternatively, instead of viewing this fetishization of religion as a mere embrace of simulation, as Ward seeks to do, it should be understood as pointing to the experimental nature of the postsecular era where ideas and practices are explored and embraced on the basis of responses to ongoing shifts and developments in the culture. I have a number of friends who have no particular religious affiliation and yet they employ a series of rituals and practices drawn from a number of environments that are remixed into new personalized configurations infused with an immense amount of belief, commitment, *and* desire.

It is not just those on the edge who have experienced this shift toward the embrace of fetishism, who have experienced the *affects* of a religious life. Many of us have rituals, candles, meditation, contemplation, retreats, ancient religious practices drawn from various religious faiths and expressions in our homes, which are all commonplace today. Magazines such as *Real Life* and *Simple Living* are filled with a sort of "return-to-Eden" attitude toward home and living arrangements and decor. But more to our point here, both magazines regularly feature articles about some form of spiritual practice or ritual that can be undertaken in the home. There are also numerous design and decor books that focus on helping the reader re-create their homes as "sacred spaces." The inside cover of one such book offers this comment: "As more and more people seek meaning in new forms of spiritual practice or renew their commitments to traditional religions, they are creating homes that reflect and enhance the spiritual component of their daily lives. *In a Spiritual Style* offers a range of settings designed for worship and inspiration."[17]

The second point Ward makes about the role of religion today is its use as an *aesthetic diversion* from the uncertainties of life.[18] I have more affinity with his perspective on this point but still argue that rather than simply "creating illusions of transcendence,"[19] there is a genuine search and embrace of the sacred that occurs. But in a postmetaphysical world, spirit has broken free from its former confinement and is now immersed in a much broader realm of human activity. As Ward states: "Religion does not live in and of itself anymore—it lives in commercial business, gothic and sci-fi fantasy, in health clubs, themed bars, and architectural design, among happy-hour drinkers, tattooists, ecologists and cyberpunks. Religion has become a special effect, inseparably bound to an entertainment value."[20] This shift of religion from an isolated function to a broad-based thread that runs through all elements of contemporary culture is something Ward can only see as a demeaning of religion, the reality of being "caught up in the economy of displaced desire (sexual and consumerist); desire without a proper object."[21]

I argue that this new democratization of the spirit is in fact an attempt to put desire in its rightful place, in dialogue and communion with the sacred. But for many people this does not seem to be achievable through traditional religious means at this point in our culture's journey into post-secularity. Instead, this new configuration of spirituality results in a new dynamic, the democratization of religion, the varied and various permutations of highly individualized forms of personal religion all gathered under the rubric of "spirituality," the true religion of our time.

This new configuration of spirituality is the result of any number of social and cultural shifts experienced over the long and painful implosion of modernity in the twentieth century. The dynamic of the democratization of religion is linked to the global communications that connect it:

> Societies have always been shaped by the nature of the media by which they communicate than by the content of the communication. . . . The alphabet and print technology fostered and encouraged a fragmenting process, a process of specialism and detachment. Electronic technology fosters and encourages unification and involvement. It is impossible to understand social and cultural change without a knowledge of the workings of the media.[22]

Ever the prophet, Marshall McLuhan first published these thoughts in 1967, long before the existence of the Internet, cell phone, pager, Blackberry, laptop, and a host of other technologies that now inform the social imaginary. Technology changes us. Interaction and participation with late-twentieth-century technology foster entirely new permutations of human relationships and fundamentally change the way we relate. Consider the humble mobile phone. Since its introduction to the masses in the 1990s it has contributed to the reorganization of daily life. In a report for Nokia, the Finnish-based mobile phone company, author Timo Kopomaa noted that "daily life is no longer necessarily rhythmed into either working or leisure hours but, instead, these two intermingle. People are simultaneously free and under obligation."[23] This one singular development has changed the lives of millions of people around the globe.

I had the experience of seeing a barely clothed goat herder in the rural town of Gannavaram in the Indian state of Andhra Pradesh walking barefoot through the village, guiding his animals. Everything about him was virtually no different from those who had herded goats in this region for centuries, except for the cell phone hanging from his dhoti. "The mobile phone is, in its own way, a meeting place, a popular place for spending time, simultaneously a non-place, a center without physical or geographical boundaries."[24]

The fluidity that defines our lives and that has been reshaped by interaction with certain technologies is reflected in the fluid attitude we now have toward religious expression. Mobile phone technology created a mobile culture in which we do business on the go rather than necessarily in a specific place, and religion has become more mobile, if you will, freed from obligation to a certain place and boundary.

Some will resist the idea that the way we use technology might, in some way, affect something as significant in our lives as religious belief or practice, but I am convinced that Derrida is right on this point. Traditional faiths have not navigated these shifts in the same manner, if at all.[25] They remain, sadly, quite like the characters in *Waterworld*, still dreaming of the day when we can all return to the now mythical "dry land" and get on with the business of living. While I am concerned that the traditional faiths are slow to adapt, the use of traditional faiths as a rich site of resource, tradition, practice, and wisdom seems to reflect a glimmer of hope that if the traditional faiths could recapitulate themselves there might yet be potential for the vibrant remarriage of ancient faith with the spirit of the times.

Shopping for God
Commodifying Faith

The religious experience is inseparable from a consumer experience. The consumer experience (consumer therapy) and the religious experience are both desire-driven and aim at immediate satisfaction.

Graham Ward, *True Religion*

Many have highlighted the connection between religion and consumption in postsecular culture. The shift from production-based culture to consumption-driven society has had dramatic effects on the way we interact with a number of issues, including the religious. In reference to this shift, Bauman writes:

> Consumer conduct (consumer freedom geared to the consumer market) moves steadily into the position of, simultaneously, the cognitive and moral focus of life, the integrative bond of society, and the focus of systematic management. In other words, it moves into the selfsame position which in the past—during the "modern" phase of capitalist society—was occupied by work in the form of wage labor. This means that in our time individuals are engaged first and foremost as consumers rather than as producers.[1]

In Bauman's view, capitalism continues in the postmodern context as consumer choice. In this context "political legitimation, central values, and dominant ideologies are no longer needed."[2] Expanding on his theories of consumer culture and the social shifts they convey, Bauman notes that "consumption is not just a matter of satisfying material greed," it also serves larger cultural purposes, such as the construction of identity, the construction of the self, the sustaining of communal relationships, and the construction of relationships with others.[3] He also notes that the postmodern consumer culture is "dominated by postmodern values of novelty, rapid (preferably inconsequential and episodic) change, of individual enjoyment and consumer choice."[4] The present capitalist system employs the *pleasure principle,*[5] embraced by both producers and consumers. This principle ensures the continuing success of capitalism by viewing consumption as a duty for the consumer—who can forget the urging of Americans to go out shopping as a way to aid in the newly minted "War on Terror" only days after the catastrophic events of September 11 in New York?! And combined with the duty of producers to keep consumers happy, we have the two poles of the present economic situation.[6]

There is a pressure attached to the pleasure principle for the consumer system: a "spend-happy consumer is a necessity and for the individual consumer, spending is a duty." This pressure is unlike earlier forms of capitalism that operated under a production-based model. Those forms were characterized by pressures between labor and capital resulting in the oppressive nature and restlessness of life for many in the Industrial Age. The pressure to spend is a far cry from other pressures that have haunted the human condition. This is not to say that those other pressures have been eradicated, but we have in the shift to a consumer culture a new environment. The surrender to the pressure of spending, for instance, promises mostly joy.[7] This is not the joy of surrendering to something greater—the "object," Ward contends, is missing from the current situation[8]—but a straightforward sensual joy of eating, smelling pleasant aromas, sipping soothing or enticing drinks, taking relaxing drives, or the joy of being surrounded with smart, glittering, eye-caressing objects.[9]

The "special effect" of postmodernity according to Ward is the overwhelming use of glitter, glam, and sensory overload, mediated to us by a media-driven, aestheticized consumer culture where "look and feel" are important.[10] In such an environment, Bauman, referencing Pierre Bourdieu, says that "seduction . . . may now take the place of repression as the paramount vehicle of systemic control and social integration."[11] It is into this world that the reenchantment of society brings about the return of God.

There is a certain pressure attached to the return of God to the center of things in contemporary postmodern life, one that has resulted in an interesting marriage of faith and consumption. The return of God, the emergence of a people's spirituality, sees the return of religion as a resource—as a consumer choice—rather than a matter of private faith, as it was in modernity. The pressure of choice and the dominant pleasure principle now become factors in religious choices and decisions.

This is a long way from traditional ideas of religious obligation, duty, and service. Religion, in the postmodern situation, is often viewed as little more than a commodity, as consumer choice. Richard Cimino and Don

Lattin, writing about marketing in US megachurches, propose that, "In the new millennium, more and more American congregations will take this market-based approach to find new members and keep the ones they have. Megachurches embody the consumerism, eclecticism, and conservatism shaping the religious future. They are the evangelical answer to Home Depot."[12] The megachurch is merely fulfilling its side of the bargain associated with the pleasure principle, namely, keeping consumers happy. This seems a long way from the church's earlier role as moral and spiritual guide for the community. I do not wish to imply that these elements are entirely missing from the new context, but they certainly are manifested in new configurations that can be hard to monitor as they occur in non-systematic and highly individualized ways. Recalling a young couple they interviewed who were seeking some form of religious affiliation, Cimino and Lattin write that "they shopped for a church like they would shop for a car, looking for something comfortable and practical."[13] This is the consumer doing his or her part in this stage of the capitalist enterprise. In a consumer culture, religion is a resource for personal fulfillment rather than communal obligation. This is postsecular religion's strength and limitation.

The *Utne Reader*, an alternative press publication, produced an issue in June of 2000 devoted to this new religious paradigm and focused on the cut-and-paste, cafeteria approach to religion. In this issue, titled "Designer Gods," the magazine explored the contours of a consumer-based religion and its resultant pastiche of religious configurations. Another alternative publication, *Genre*, a magazine devoted to issues facing the gay community, released a "spirituality issue" in May 2000 with a slogan on the cover offering "30 paths to Enlightenment." There are a multitude of examples of this in contemporary culture, where it appears that religion is being embraced as little more than a consumer item, not much different from a bar of soap or a new car or a fetish. However, it is better to see this religious consumerism as only part of the social production of religion in contemporary times, and as such, I would argue, it is not the complete picture. Instead, it should be understood as part of the first pangs of religious reexpression in the reenchantment of our time.

This consumption of the religious, or perhaps even the return of the religious in such a context, is also linked to developments in consumer culture and advertising. One of the significant shifts in the world of advertising in the late twentieth century has been a move away from the direct marketing of products and toward the packaging and selling of lifestyle and identity. Twitchell argues that the distinctive in American culture in the late twentieth century is not "avarice but a surplus of machine-made things." He goes on to say that in and of themselves these "goods do not mean enough so we have employed powerful ways to add meanings to goods."[14] The way we have added meaning to goods is by linking them to identity construction. The destabilized self of the postmodern constructs itself again and again via the medium of consumerism. For Bauman, consumer culture is now the "central register of selfhood"[15] and as such is performing a religious function in the broader culture. To this idea, with which I fully agree, I also add the coda that the employment of religious language in advertising has allowed the religious idea to "remain on the table of ideas." The present return to religion is in this way linked to the maintenance of a religious sentiment within the boundaries of advertising and commercial consumer culture.

To put it another way, advertising has kept religious ideas alive by employing religious rhetoric in its product-selling practices. We are promised salvation through the purchase of automobiles, peace and Zen-like calm through the drinking of a particular tea, and the opportunity to experience life in its fullness through the use of a certain credit card. In light of this, Twitchell comments:

> I am hardly the first to recognize that advertising is the gospel of redemption in the fallen world of capitalism, that advertising has become the vulgate of the secular belief in the redemption of commerce. In a profound sense religion and advertising are part of the same meaning-making process. They attempt to breach the gap between us and objects by providing a systematic order and a promise of salvation. They deliver the goods.[16]

Twitchell goes on to argue that the meaning-making process is achieved by magical promise and says that "the most magical power of magic is that it is so resolutely denied as the major organizer of meaning."[17] This belief in the power of magic, the ability to endow certain inanimate goods with the mystic charge of ultimate meaning, is the unique gift of advertising to postmodern culture. Enchanted goods, magical items, which can transform our appearance, our very lives, are not often considered part of the reenchantment of Western culture, but I would argue that the shift in advertising toward the domain of the philosophical and religious has facilitated part of the reenchantment that then allows for the return of religion to public life, not as philosophy mind you, but as commodity. "Advertising fetishizes objects in exactly the same manner that religion does: it charms objects giving them the aura of added value."[18]

There are at least three perspectives to be offered regarding consumer culture and postmodernity.[19] There is the view that it arises from the "expansion of capitalist commodity production."[20] In this perspective, consumer culture is viewed negatively, and the seduction of consumers away from a more meaningful existence is a prime symptom.[21] A second perspective concentrates on consumer purchasing habits and what this has to say about creating social bonds and distinctions.[22] A third view is characterized by Lyon as "looking at the pleasure it [consumer culture] brings, and at the dreams and desires celebrated within the cultural imaginary."[23] This perspective raises questions about why consumers make certain choices. Lyon also argues that this perspective offers "ways of seeing consumption that neither denigrate it as a capitalist cage nor celebrate it as a cornucopia."[24] How people construct identities and interpret the symbols of consumer culture, how they "assemble their realities," become important questions.

> So shopping skills rise to great prominence in consumer culture. They are central to market dependency. People who know the best deals, who have scrutinized their catalogs, they are truly store-wise. The broader result is that postmoderns constantly "try-on" not only new clothes, new perfumes, but new identities, fresh personalities, different partners. This cognitive and moral cast of consumer conduct also holds good, at least to some extent, in the religious sphere.[25]

If, as Lyon contends, consumers apply their practices to their religious choices, then what emerges is a savvy religious consumer who has done his or her research, who knows what he or she is looking for, and who is willing to experiment and remain mobile, trying on new religious identities and practices. This mobility is often linked to the demands of living in a fluid cultural context.[26] And in this age of rapidly constructed and deconstructed selves, of fashion-driven and consumerist notions of self, much is still invested in the self. "Significance is still sought."[27] In this era, authenticity is important, for "authenticity is now the benchmark against which all brands are now judged."[28] Not all consumption is without merit, however. People simply don't subsist entirely on junk food and plastic lawn chairs.

Religion has also shifted. It is no longer found in the institutions and public locations—the churches, synagogues, mosques, and other buildings of wood and stone that have traditionally housed the sacred. It is now found in the ether of consumer culture, as Ward has noted,[29] in the various sites of a pleasure principle consumer culture. "Religion expands into spheres less visible than the institutional and public ones it occupied in Weber's day. Thus it takes its place alongside other meaning clusters available in the so-called private sphere. There, people are free to choose on their own what to do with their time, their homes, their bodies, and their gods."[30] What surprises some is the ability of religion to manifest itself outside of traditional structures in meaningful ways: "the sacred is able to sustain itself outside of organized religion within consumer culture."[31] But what becomes of religion in such an environment? It becomes democratized and driven by entertainment theology, manifesting itself in surprisingly nontraditional ways and integrating itself into the fabric of society in new configurations. The reenchantment of Western culture sees the deployment of religion for a variety of new purposes, one of which is the constructing of religious identity in a consumer culture.

It is worth remembering that people make some very sound choices in a consumer culture. Lyon notes that consuming may be more dutiful than one imagines and cites Featherstone's research on elements of contemporary culture, such as TV shows, magazines, and even tabloids, that actually promote values consistent with traditional faith practices.[32] This is the age of the researched and empowered consumer. They have been raised in the glow of advertising and exposed to its many claims. They take seriously the construction of identity; much attention is paid to detail. Presentation and packaging are important, as is cultural cache. In this light, the sacred and the consumer approach to religion may be "reduced, in another relocated, in a third redefined."[33] Religion as an instrument of religious identity is one example of its relocation. "It also makes sense to think of religion today more as a cultural resource than as a social institution,"[34] another example of religion's redefinition. What we have, then, in a consumer-driven culture in which religion is a commodity and the object of consumer choice, are some interesting developments on both sides of the religious equation.

For a particular faith tradition, the dizzying decentered manifestations of belief can seem at times trite and inconsequential. They can easily be classified as heretical or unorthodox when placed against more traditional interpretations and practices. This is nothing new of course. The Christian church has a long history of confronting "heresies" within its ranks and a particularly long history of antagonism toward the more mystical of its members. Even St. Francis of Assisi was a victim of this. Such a history does not bode well for church and culture relationships, given the overemphasis on the magical and mystical in today's spiritual marketplace.

The new vitality of religious expression and directions in which this manifests may prove too much for some. But in order to survive, traditional faith must face the pressure of its place in the consumer-culture framework and acknowledge that its role and its success in large part depend on its ability to "corner a piece of the market" (harsh words to attach to sacred entities, perhaps, but a contemporary reality nonetheless), while remaining faithful to its values and purposes.

What should give some hope to religious communities is that the path to at least potentially capturing the imagination of the religious consumer is by investing their "product" with "mystic charge"—give it the aura of added value of which Twitchell speaks. On a broad level, for the Christian church this might mean surrendering bureaucracy and systematized dogmas in favor of more mystery-based practices, but we will return to this later.[35] The challenge for the religious consumer is to make wise and meaningful choices with regard to the sacred.

However, it should also be noted that at the beginning of this book I said that this democratization of belief, this "people's religion," is as much a mood as it is a movement. Movements are much easier to categorize; moods change, and quickly. In the postmodern context, religious moods shift quite dramatically. The limitation of this is that mood-driven, individualized faith permutations can become impulse choices that leave the consumer with regret and dissatisfaction.

A final issue related to consumer choice and religious commodification is the fact that not all consumer purchases and choices are focused on material goods. Consumers choose not only from an immense amount of goods for sale but also from a variety of experiences and fantasies.[36] We live in a carefully constructed and branded world of design and intention. Virtually every experience we have is a carefully planned event in the exchange between producer and shopper in the consumer economy. Why else, for instance, would there be music playing in a supermarket if it were not part of an approach to baptize us into the experience of shopping for groceries? We also increasingly find ourselves in themed environments: theme parks, designer stores, shopping malls, heritage trails, and interactive museums.[37] But nowhere is this effect more prevalent than in the media world of popular culture.

Entertainment Theology

Religion Goes Pop

Poetry will reach a superior dignity, it will become in the end what it was in the beginning—the teacher of humanity.

Friedrich Schelling, *Philosophy of Mythology*

After the seas are all cross'd, (as they seem already cross'd,)
After the great captains and engineers have accomplish'd their work,
After the noble inventors, after the scientists, the chemist, the geologist, ethnologist,
Finally shall come the poet worthy of that name;
The true son of God shall come singing his songs.

Walt Whitman, *Leaves of Grass*

Movies in particular spit out fantasies and themed worlds of all kinds on a continual basis, each of them more realistic, more overwhelming, more fantastic than the one that came before. Religion competes with the transcendent as it is mediated through a host of other avenues: film, TV, music, thrill rides, theme parks. "For the moment we must recognize the complex combination of experience-hungry consumerism and religious simulation."[1] To Ward, this is the development of the new context of the relationship between consumer and religious experience. Ward also argues that the "sacred establishes itself with respect to the profane,"[2] meaning that our understanding of the religious experience is contrasted with that which we consider not religious, or profane. In a resacralized culture in which ideas of the transcendent and the divine are released from their traditional locations, in a world of deprivileged metaphysics and the loss of a "proper object" (as per Ward), where is the profane? I believe that the idea of the profane is to a degree in flux in the present setting. The binary oppositions of sacred versus profane that attended modernity no longer suffice.

In modernity, the godless secular society (at least on the surface), it was easy to establish the sacred with regard to the profane; the sacred was found in everything supposedly untouched by secularity. The lines were neatly drawn, the City of God versus the City of Man.[3] But in the present situation, these dividing lines are no longer viable. The general view is that the sacred is available anywhere, even in the midst of what might have been viewed as profane in other times. The sacred is viewed as part of the very fabric of the world we inhabit, not standing in opposition to it. Hence the transcendental element in popular culture. This idea is, I believe, at the heart of David Lyon's book *Jesus in Disneyland*, often referenced here, which explores the role of Christian faith in a world of theme-park experiences. Understanding the role of fantasy in this context is best captured by Slavoj Žižek:

> The first thing to note is that fantasy does not simply realize a desire in a hallucinatory way: rather, its function is similar to that of Kantian "transcendental schematism": a fantasy constitutes our desire, provides its coordinates; that is, it literally "teaches us how to desire." The role of fantasy is thus in a way analogous to that of the ill-fated pineal gland in Descartes' philosophy, this mediator between *res cogitans* and *res extensa*: fantasy mediates between the formal symbolic structure and the positivity of the objects we encounter in reality—that is to say, it provides a "schema" according to which certain positive objects in reality can function as objects of desire, filling in the empty places opened up by the formal symbolic structure.[4]

If the defining element of the Enlightenment project was reason, namely, Descartes's dictum "I think, therefore I am," then postmodernity's defining element is fantasy, and more generally, the imagination. Fantasy[5] functions as the orientation to the new world we find ourselves in. If reason were the eyes we were given to see the world and structure our desire in modernity, then in postmodernity, in the postsecular, the structure of desire and our orientation to the emerging new order are achieved through fantasy. Petrarch's plague of fantasies,[6] rather than blurring our clear reason, has become our reasoning tool—a principal means of constructing self-identity. "Fantasy is, rather, that little piece of imagination by which we gain access to reality—the frame that guarantees our access to reality, 'our' sense of reality."[7]

Earlier I referred to Appadurai's idea that the imagination is a social organizer in postmodern times. This is evident in the rise of entertainment theology. Entertainment theology is simply ideas about God that emerge outside of previously legitimized environments and structures of mediation. It is the "god-talk" of Phyllis Tickle's book with that expression in the title;[8] the experience of the divine or the transcendent in a sensorially overloaded, special-effects laden, fantasy-world movie; it is the explosion of literature filled with self-help, folk religion, magic, and mystery; it is the emergence of Web sites and chat rooms as locations for further and deeper communal exploration of the sacred; it is the emergence of spiritually aware art forms; it is popular culture as a site for the exchange of ideas, values, and challenges; it is the new philosophical site, the new cultural imaginary. This simulation of the real found in popular culture[9] has become the new real, more real than the real.[10]

> With the ascendance of popular culture, the 1980s gave access to what has been called a culture of simulation. The simulation (or intimation) of reality found in video culture—for example in film, music video, video games— was of a piece with the rise of lip-synching, the Internet, and virtual reality. These latter media were forms of not-quite-real communication, usually measured against "real" communication. Alongside what we used to think of as exclusively "real," its imitation gained prominence.[11]

Ward acknowledges that the implosion of the modern has facilitated a "return to the theological, and a new emphasis on re-enchantment,"[12] but this return was not signaled by theologians in the classic sense of the word. This return was heralded by a new breed of theologian, one who worked primarily in the realm of the arts. The return to the theological, the rise of the postsecular, was signaled by "filmmakers, novelists, poets, philosophers, political theorists, and cultural analysts."[13]

It is in the context of this and the other dynamics, thoughts, and ideas reflected in the first section of this work, that we now attempt the folly of placing a people's religion, beyond truly quantifiable[14] categorization, into some form of collected shapes. With these things in mind I now explore some of the ways democratized spirituality emerges in contemporary culture.

Postsecular Soul Space

The meaning-routes through the postmodern are characterized by the consumer choice in identity construction. The fragments used are drawn from, among other things, new media but these may also refer to older sacred stories. The meaning-routes and varied selves help us understand the novel contexts within which faith is forged and spirituality explored in the new millennium. It would be a mistake, however, to allow the term meaning-routes to suggest anything too closely resembling the clearly defined highways or the precisely timetabled railways and flight corridors of modernity.

David Lyon, *Jesus in Disneyland*

As already noted, the contours of belief in such a democratized space, one that is at once interconnected and highly individualized, are difficult to chart. It would also be a mistake to view the presentation of certain meaning-routes and alternative self-constructions as the exhaustion of all the possibilities.[1] What I offer are a number of rubrics under which we find similar trajectories and focus. Some of these rubrics appear more "religious," in the classic understanding, and seem to bear at least some of the traditional marks of a devotional life. Others may seem to defy the traditional logic. But for me they are all part of the same thing. I have given up trying to categorize people who do supposedly religious things, such as going to church or temple or praying, and those who don't. To me the religious is a part of what it means to be human. John Caputo writes that he does not "confine religion to something confessional or sectarian, like being a Muslim or a Hindu, a Catholic or Protestant."[2] I find myself in similar territory, believing that the religious impulse has in a sense been radically liberated from its traditional environments and has exploded into a million pieces of unique and vibrant expression.

The rubrics as I see them are as follows: (1) Zen Culture, (2) The Next Enlightenment, (3) Retrolution, and (4) Resistant Communities. What I am attempting to do with these categories is plot the contours of what is occurring rather than chart which particular demographic utilizes them. I am more interested in the general shape and apparent contours of religious belief and practice as they move through the social imaginary, largely generated by interaction with entertainment theology, namely, the religious as it is processed through pop culture. Who does this kind of stuff? People of all ages and backgrounds, all around the globe. Some of them do it while maintaining a more formal religious tradition. For others it is the sum of their religiosity.

Zen Culture: The Tao of Postmodernity

> I am neither Christian nor Jew nor Gabr nor Muslim,
> I am neither of the East, nor of the West,
> nor of the land, nor of the sea;
> I am not of India, nor of China, nor of Bulgaria
> nor of Sasquin . . .
>
> > Jalauddin Rumi, "Diwan-i Shamsi Tabriz"

The reenchantment of the West and the emergence of a postsecular environment reveals a unique development. In this time when the competing ideologies to Western democratic capitalism have fallen into the dust of modern history, at a time when largely Western-developed technologies and capitalist consumer culture are becoming a global phenomenon, something strange is occurring. Žižek calls it the "ultimate postmodern irony." "When, at the level of 'economic infrastructure,' 'European' technology and capitalism are triumphing worldwide, at the level of 'ideological superstructure,' the Judeo-Christian legacy is threatened in the European space itself by the onslaught of the New Age 'Asiatic' thought, which in its different guises . . . is establishing itself as the hegemonic ideology of global capitalism."[3] I part company with Žižek in calling this a New Age phenomenon, which will be explained in the next section. There are links to New Age thinking to be sure, but what is emerging is something other, something new, something decidedly a product of the postmodern situation (whereas the dominant ideologies, including the New Age movement, are more often rooted in modernist constructs). However, the rise of the influence of Buddhism is pervasive. Žižek names this "Western Buddhism,"[4] but I would use the term "Westernized Asian thought" because it envelops something larger than Buddhist philosophy and reflects greater interaction with various elements of Asian cultures from ancient wisdom to anime cartoons and manga magazines.

The use of this broader term allows for the fact that what is being re-contextualized is not simply Eastern Buddhist teachings and practice. In the West we find ethnic Buddhism generally linked to immigrant cultures alongside the new incarnations of Asian thought. Žižek writes that were Max Weber alive today he would "definitely write a second, supplementary, volume to his *Protestant Ethic*, titled, *The Taoist Ethic and the Spirit of Global Capitalism.*"[5] This highlights the situation.

It has been argued that there is an indelible link between Western democratic capitalism and Christianity, the Protestant version in particular. Yet in the ongoing capitalist adventure, the Protestant ethos seems to have fallen by the wayside. In their book *Funky Business*, writers Ridderstråle and Nordström invoke Luther's maxim, *ora et labora*—prayer and work—as the link, the combination, that connects capitalism and Christianity.[6] This ties in with Bauman's view of the relationship between labor and capital in the production era of modern capitalism. On the other side of the world, the writers claim, the East embraced its own Luther: Confucius. Luther venerated work; Confucius venerated wisdom.[7] It is perhaps easy to understand the Western embrace of Eastern thought in the shift toward a consumer culture.

When production is the dominant expression of capitalism, work is a paramount virtue. But when that production shifts to consumption, then work becomes less important as a social defining value. And given the sheer number of choices demanded of us in this world awash with technology and goods, it is wisdom we seek to help us manage our lives in the new situation.

Žižek advances a rather more negative perspective on the rise of the East in the postmodern. For him it is the perfect remedy to the stressful tendencies of capitalist dynamics, "allowing us to uncouple and retain inner peace . . . a perfect ideological supplement." Žižek views the West's embrace of the East as a renunciation of control over what happens as a result of the global capitalist situation. He invokes his charge of fetishization again, claiming that the mystic charge of "Zen-like calm" aids in achieving some kind of inner calm while allowing us to retain full participation in the "capitalist dynamic."[8]

This turn toward the East is, as I have noted, not merely the appropriation of Eastern philosophy and religion but primarily a Westernizing of those beliefs into new configurations. Take the worship event, for example. Buddhist practice in the West is quite different from the Buddhism practiced in its more familiar contexts in non-Western nations. It is not merely the use of practices that look and feel like Western-church experiences: quasi-

Christian worship practices, forms, and structures—including choruses in tandem with more traditional Buddhist chanting—the use of sermons and lectures, and women priests. It is also the content and the focus of those teachings and practices that differ.

Buddhism in its newly Westernized forms reorients its focus on detachment and antimaterialism to focus instead on issues of control and power; that is, it is perfectly acceptable to seek wealth and fame, just hold all things lightly—hold them, don't let them hold you. This is a twist on the Dalai Lama's own teachings on the beginning of wisdom, which is "to realize that all living beings are equal in not wanting unhappiness and suffering and equal in the right to rid themselves of suffering." In the East this translates into the more traditionally recognized Buddhist principles of detachment; in the West this becomes the pursuit of happiness and wealth as a means of liberation from unhappiness and suffering. Even though there are sermons and teachings, there is also an emphasis on praxis (*dharma*).[9] As a quote from the Buddha that a friend gave me reads, "Free from the domination of words you will be able to establish yourselves where there will be a 'turning about' in the deepest seat of consciousness by means of which you will attain self-realization of Noble Wisdom." This lack of focus on words not only fits with the postmodern shift toward more symbolic and visual language signs but also reflects the continuing rejection of the word-based focus of Christian faith and religion.

The rise of Westernized Asian thought is also linked to *anatta*, or the erasure of the self posited by Mark Wallace as a key element of the postmodern shift and a dynamic of postsecular culture. The loss of the idea of a stable self fits well with the Buddhist view on the nature of the self. The Buddhist concept of the self is called *anatta*, often translated as the concept of "no self." This is, in some ways, a little misleading. The idea of there being no self seems inconsistent with a religion that includes ideas such as karma and rebirth. A broader explanation of *anatta* is that it is "the doctrine that denies the existence of a constant, stable and discreet personality."[10] In other words, fluidity of self is a dynamic of Buddhism just as it is in postsecularity: "The Buddhist provenance of no-self does not undermine its appeal in the late capitalist West because the credibility of such non-Western ideas rises in inverse proportion to the decline of the intellectual and plausibility structures that once supported the traditional model."[11]

Lyotard's proclamation of the end of ideologies and the end of metanarratives[12] is directed at those ideologies attached to scientific rationalism. The abandonment of those ideologies has not signaled the loss of desire for shaping stories, and this shift toward Buddhism reflects the belief that Buddhism's metanarrative is one of the most significant of the post-secular age so far. "Disillusionment with the Platonic and Augustinian orientation (to this I would add Lutheran) has set in motion the 'Pacific shift' toward more non-substantive and less atomistic understandings of personhood."[13]

> The Buddhist *anatta* doctrine and corollary idea that the "self" is always interdependently "arising" have deep resonances with postmodern notions of intersubjectivity and its criticisms of the entitative Cartesian subject. The eclectic affinitives between these two positions—Buddhism and postmodernism—deepen the appeal of both thought currents and widen their distinct but related credibility bases. The conclusion of both perspectives is the same: there is no essential "self" that underlies all humankind; selfhood, rather, is an ongoing task that requires the active construction of a life by each individual.[14]

According to the Buddha, *anatta* is characterized by five constituents of the human personality known as *khanda* (heaps, bundles, lumps). The five *khanda* are body, feeling, perception, volition, and consciousness. These five personality traits are helpful signposts in a culture where *personality* rather than *character* is key. Having the right kind of personality is important in postsecular culture, in which a sense of self is constantly under investigation, exploration, and construction. "The virtues of personality, rather than those of character, become significant."[15]

Alongside the notion of *anatta* is the lack of a God figure at the center of Buddhist philosophy. This also has resonance in a postmetaphysical culture in which the idea of god as being is increasingly dismissed (Ward's "lack of proper object"?).[16] Of all the world's major religions, Buddhism is the "godless" religion. The Buddha proclaimed that the ultimate nature of everything, seen and unseen, is emptiness: "Form is emptiness, and emptiness is form." This foundational emptiness is one of the distinctives of Buddhism.

Not surprisingly, there are different views of what exactly this nothingness is. In Tibetan Buddhism alone there are different schools of thought, some of which teach that there is an ultimate, transcendent reality that inherently exists while others teach that emptiness is just nothingness.[17] Thus, there are diverse avenues of engagement with Buddhism that require neither dogmatic acceptance of a rigid set of principles nor a definite acceptance of the idea of godhead, which, given the failure of theodicy in the twentieth century to adequately address the tumultuous events experienced in that time, is a promising turn of events for some. It is important to note that we are speaking of Westernized Asian thought here—a potpourri of various snippets of Eastern wisdom, style, and cultural affectations—and not necessarily the acceptance or embrace of the whole of the Buddhist construct.

Another issue related to the West's embrace of Buddhist thought is the idea of deeds and activism. *Dharma*, which originally meant the natural condition of things, was revised to mean "doctrines and practices that make up the religious system," and has come to mean acts of kindness and compassion in the postsecular West. The focus on *dharma* has led to the belief that Buddhism is more about how you live with others than what you believe. This is largely because *dharma* is wrapped up in other Eastern concepts such as *karma*. *Karma* is another idea prevalent in pop culture. "Instant *karma*'s gonna get ya," sang John Lennon, signaling the detachment of *karma* from notions of continual reincarnations, life after life. Instead, *karma* has become a sort of instant payback for behavior. *Karma* is also translated in some Buddhist circles as "action."

The "Pacific shift," the recontextualization of Eastern thought and practice noted by Wallace, is reflected very heavily in popular culture. I initially toyed with the idea of titling this book "Everybody Is Kung-Fu Fighting" in an attempt to capture something of the current cultural imagination. It is not only the religious aspects of the East that are filtering into the postsecular religious imaginary. Along with these aspects are all the affects of Asian lifestyle, which, with its focus on minimalism, is seen as an antidote to the pressures of our cluttered worlds. The operative word for this is "Zen." In the East, Zen is a Japanese form of strict Buddhist practice. In the West, it is more of an attitude and fashion style, particularly in homes. Zen is everywhere. I was given a book titled *Zen Guitar*, which claims that "Zen guitar begins with a single premise: We carry a song inside—the song that makes us human. . . . Zen offers the key to unlock this song."[18]

I have a number of friends whose lives have demonstrated this Pacific shift. Many of them never exhibited any religious tendencies until recently, and what has been remarkable is the number of them who have quietly appropriated aspects of Asian thought into their lives. A couple of them have stopped attending twelve-step groups and started practicing various forms of Buddhism to help with their addictions. Beyond the overtly religious aspects, there are also the cultural affectations of the Pacific shift present in their lives. It's not just a question of sushi and Thai food, noodle bars and green tea emporiums. It is the wholesale Asianizing of elements of the postsecular world.

A friend of mine who is a well-known jewelry designer is a vivid example of this. Her company, now called LRG, was once called Loree Rodkin Gothic and featured an array of expensive jewelry that was reminiscent of the medieval period. She made "Pope" rings, rings with gothic crosses, and skull rings and necklaces. Entering her design studio was like walking into a medieval church: furniture made of old pews shipped in from Europe, statues, icons, skulls, altar crosses, crucifixes, and velvet brocaded religious wall hangings. Her home, which has been featured in a number of interior design magazines, was a similar feast of religious imagery, like walking into a candlelit Benedictine monastery in the twelfth century. She has a worldwide celebrity clientele, including major rock stars such as Elton John, Rod Stewart, and Cher as well as a host of rock bands, Hollywood actors, and the like. Her fascination with crosses was interesting given her decidedly nonreligious outlook on life and her Jewish upbringing! However, over the last two or three years she has completely transformed her home, company, and life and has shifted toward the "Pacific." She gutted her home and work studio of all the affects of Christian religious imagery. First to go were the dark velvet curtains and heavy, wooden bishops thrones. The statues, angels, skulls, and crosses went next. She eventually sold her home and spent almost a year redecorating her new one. Now one is greeted by a huge golden Buddha on entering her gates, and the house is nearly empty, decorated with muted colors and soft furnishings. Outside, there are a number of Asian statues; and, in the garden, Japanese plants and fountains complete the picture. Her work soon followed suit. Suddenly she was adding Buddha charms to delicate chains and making her jewelry more minimal and less obtrusive. When I asked her about all of this change she replied, "Zen is the future. I needed some kind of peace in my life. It was too cluttered and this new space helps me relax."

Perhaps this is not the most concise theological response but it is one I find echoed quite frequently. Another friend, a yoga devotee, likens his exercise to the experience of what he wishes church could be like: "a place where you can go to find peace of mind and chill, not be talked at and given a bunch of rules."

Part of the allure of the East and a reason for its current acceptance is its "otherness," its difference. Even in high modernity, the Victorians were fascinated with what they called "Orientalism." The height of Victorian elegance was the creation of rooms and houses that echoed and replicated (in a decidedly Western fashion, still using table and chairs for example) the East, the mysterious Orient. This fascination with the "otherness" of the East has not dissipated with the removal of geographic barriers that now permit increased travel and access to previously unreachable places. Moreover, almost from its beginning Hollywood has been a location for the perpetuation of this idea of the mysterious East. And if there is a center for the emergence of all things Buddhist in the Western imaginary, it is not China or Japan or India, the birthplace of the Buddha, but Tibet.

Tibet, with its particular form of Buddhism, is filled with "tales of amazing spiritual feats, demons, and tales of magic and mystery, that continues to hold special fascination." Tibet is "still imagined as the cure for an ever-ailing Western civilization, a tonic to restore its spirit."[19] The Dalai Lama is the leader-in-exile of Tibet and spiritual leader of Tibetan Buddhists scattered around the globe. Hollywood first jumped on the Tibet wagon in 1937 with the release of director Frank Capra's film version of James Hilton's 1937 book *Lost Horizon*, a huge success and the world's first paperback novel. The story concerned a plane crash in the Himalayas and conjured up images of a place called Shangri-La, far removed from the complexities of life in the West that was still struggling with the Great Depression and facing the growing threat of Nazism.

Through most of the middle decades of the twentieth century, however, Hollywood was fairly silent with respect to religion. But beginning with a comedy called *Golden Child*, released in 1986, the floodgates seemed to open and a revival of interest in the mysterious East began and has not stopped. Not only is Hollywood making comedies about the East, three films in the 1990s explored Buddhism and the Dalai Lama in depth, but at the same time the new religious dynamic began its first murmurings. In 1994, Italian filmmaker Bernardo Bertolucci made *Little Buddha*, starring Keanu Reeves as the young Gautama, the future Lord Buddha, whose journey to nirvana was chronicled in the midst of a secondary story about the son of a young Seattle couple who was invited to be considered as a candidate for the reincarnation of a dead Buddhist religious leader. This film was one of the first to bring the exotic "other" into direct interaction with the lives of Westerners here in the West. It was closely followed by two films that explored the early life of the Dalai Lama: Martin Scorsese's *Kundun* and *Seven Years in Tibet*. Scorsese, a renowned Catholic filmmaker and the director of one of the most controversial religious films, *The Last Temptation of Christ*, made *Kundun* in conjunction with Walt Disney Studios. This film was quickly followed by *Seven Years in Tibet*, another film about the Dalai Lama, starring Brad Pitt.

Around the same time a series of protest and awareness-raising musical events called the Tibetan Freedom Concerts was inaugurated and organized by Adam Yauch. Yauch, a member of the Beastie Boys, a rap group, was himself a practicing Buddhist. He had this to say about Tibet and Buddhism:

> Tibetans have been refining what it means to be human and then, by a miracle, dispensing this around the world. Tibet is a model of what a society can be when people start to realize that we are dependent upon one another. The animal, plant, and insect kingdoms all keep us alive, not just water and oxygen. Tibetan culture represents a people truly living in balance with themselves and the world.[20]

"What it means to be human," a model of interdependent society, a "people truly living in balance with themselves and the world"—these are elements of the postsecular desire briefly stated. Whether or not Tibet truly models these things is almost irrelevant, the illusion is more real than the real.[21]

Other leading music figures, from Paul McCartney to REM to Pearl Jam and a host of others, lent their support to this musical endeavor. The events were attended by thousands of young people and Buddhist teachers alike. At these events, the audiences were exposed to Buddhist thought, invited to join in Buddhist prayers, and treated to a visit from the Dalai Lama himself.

Pop music remains an important venue for Westernized Asian thought. Once again, this emerges in surprising ways. Take, for instance, the Dharma Punx,[22] a loose federation of punk musicians and fans who seek to blend their love of a particular musical genre—punk—with Buddhist and other religious practices. Punk music, which burst onto an otherwise complacent music scene in England in the summer of 1976, would seem to be an unlikely place for the emergence of spirituality. Built on socialist ideology, influenced by Guy Debord's Situationiste Internationale, and fueled by British working class frustration, the punk movement is exemplified by its first and perhaps most famous band, the Sex Pistols.[23] Their first single, "Anarchy in the U.K.," saw them denounced by the British Parliament as a threat to the British way of life. Interestingly, their album cover was designed by Jamie Reid and is now regarded as symbolic of the first foray of graphic design into the postmodern world.[24] The first three singles released by the Sex Pistols were a critique of every aspect of life. "Anarchy in the U.K." was a rage against the present, "God Save the Queen" was a diatribe on Britain's past, and "No Future" was an inspired critique of modernity's love of progress. The notion that a movement framed by bands like the Sex Pistols and other equally angry songwriters and musicians could inspire any kind of spiritual stirrings would seem unlikely in any other context. "Damning God and the state, work and leisure, home and family, sex and play, the audience and itself, the music briefly made it possible to experience all those things as if they were not natural facts but ideological constructs: things that had been made and therefore could be altered, or done away with altogether."[25]

Of course those things *were* constructs, and the music of the punk movement was just one of pop-culture's attempts to voice the growing cultural dissatisfaction with the status quo. Cultural change was never going to happen through the music. Music was merely an attempt to voice the discontent, and an attempt to wake up a sleeping populace— medicated by the intoxication of impossibility—that seemed to fill the streets of Britain at that time, which was a period riddled with three- and four-day workweeks, oil shortages, power outages, gross unemployment, and massive disputes between labor and management. The death throes of modernity were felt everywhere, and Britons lived on the edge of the shift into a new form of capitalist relationship, a shift from production to consumer culture with all its necessary hardships and pressures.

Punk was not nihilism, as is commonly assumed. Nihilism is a belief in nothing; punk was actually about finding belief in something, anything, but something or anything that was "not of the old order." Punk was rage against the machine, a shaking of Weber's iron cage of bureaucracy, which had drained the mystery from Western cultural life. Punk was the sound of the music business imploding and deconstructing. This was pop culture reorienting itself as a site for postmodern discourse. This was not the protest music of the sixties calling for a little peace and love, this was a seething rage against the systems that kept people marginalized and held down with invisible hands, anger directed against the modern that had birthed it. But it is interesting how this connects with Buddhist theology, or at least some interpretations of Buddhist ideology and practice. As Brad Warner states:

> My definition of Buddhist has nothing at all to do with the social institutions all over the world that call themselves by that name. Zen Buddhism is direct pointing to the truth. It's cutting through the crap and getting to the ground of things as they really are. It's getting rid of all pretense and seeing what's actually here right now . . . the rest of what people call "Buddhism"— the temples, the rituals, the funny outfits, and the ceremonies—it isn't the

important stuff. It's just decoration . . . it's hardly necessary for seeing the reality that the Buddha's teachings point to.[26]

The link, then, between punk and a Westernized form of Buddhism is the perception that it allows one to see things for what they are and offers no illusions. This is but one form of Westernized Asian thought. Another reason this form of expression is taking root in the postsecular can be found in a quote about the East made by Lord Curzon: "The East is a university in which the scholar never takes his degree. It is a temple where the supplicant adores but never catches sight of the object of his devotion. It is a journey the goal of which is always in sight but is never attained."[27]

As I said earlier, this is not simply about Buddhism, it is about the Westernizing of much of the East, both religion and culture, into new permutations. The presence of the "East" in various forms is rampant in pop culture. The dominant form of combat in action movies today draws heavily from Asian martial arts, whether the movie is set in the past, as with *The Musketeer*—a remake of Alexander Dumas's classic tale of *The Three Musketeers*—or set in the future, as in the Matrix trilogy. It could be argued that no movie is untainted by these issues today. Even the latest installment of the Batman movies—*Batman Begins* (2005)—finds the young Bruce Wayne learning martial arts and Asian wisdom high in the Himalayas, which is a long, long way from Gotham!

In a subtle shift in the locus of moviemaking we see Asian-made movies emerging alongside Western counterparts. Audiences clamored to see *Crouching Tiger, Hidden Dragon, Hero*, and *House of the Flying Daggers*. Quentin Tarantino's recent films *Kill Bill, Volumes One* and *Two*, displayed a decidedly Eastern flavor, employing anime, martial arts, samurai sword fights, and Asian actors and locations to tell his "western"[28] story of revenge. Japanese anime cartoons, such as *Ghost in the Shell* and *Spirited Away*,[29] generate huge followings in the West, with their focus on magical worlds of cyborgs, half humans, ancient spirits, and technology. Cartoons such as Powerpuff girls and children's adventure shows such as Yu-Gi-Oh and the Power Rangers expose younger children to Japanese characters and sentiments in story lines that feature a great deal of martial arts and Asian wisdom.

The recent homage to Tokyo, Sofia Coppola's *Lost in Translation*, seems to capture the essence of what is occurring in the realm of the spirit at present. The film is ostensibly about an American actor, Bob Harris (played with immense pathos by Bill Murray), who is going through a mid-career, midlife crisis and has journeyed to Tokyo to film a Japanese whiskey commercial. He forges a relationship with a newly married, younger woman, Charlotte (Scarlet Johannson), who has plenty of time on her hands and who is processing her own existential crisis in the form of insecurity about her role and purpose in life. These two are drawn together by shared jet-lag and common struggle: "Charlotte is having that early 20s 'what do I do with my life' crisis. She and Bob are two people at opposite ends of something comparable: she's just going into a marriage and he's on the other end, having been in one for years. There is camaraderie between them at the moment in time that they're at. It's two characters going through similar personal crises."[30] Together they break out of the isolating and extremely Western-looking environment of their luxury hotel and take to the streets of Tokyo.

The city of Tokyo provides the exotic and quirky background for working out their problems and finding new belief in life's possibilities. Tokyo looks like the West, but clearly it is not. It is a blend of futuristic, high-tech, and ancient culture. Scenes in the film take place on the busy and crowded streets, filled with wildly dressed and happy people. Jumbotron video screens are on the corners of every building, filling the sky with advertising and adding to the disjointedness of the environment. Juxtaposed to this are scenes showing the serenity of a group of women practicing a very stylized form of flower arranging in a calm Zen-like state. The obvious happiness on the faces of the locals they meet and the calm of others stand in stark contrast to the existential angst both of the Westerners are experiencing. There is a faint nod to the role of religion in this culture when the young woman goes on a sightseeing tour of the beautiful and ancient city of Kyoto, the heart of Japan's Shinto faith.

The two lead characters must journey to the other side of the world to work out issues in their lives. This is reminiscent of the Westernizing of Asian thought, which is a metaphorical journey to the "other" in order to discover more about oneself. It is also an acknowledgment that this particular journey, the spiritual one, is largely "foreign" to our culture given its recent reenchantment. The journey East reflects the foreign aspect of the current return to God: in the implosion of modernity, the opening of the spiritual is a journey so foreign to us that we must travel to the other side of the world, even if it is metaphoric, in order to process it.

Another film that captures this trend (and that could, in fact, be viewed as an example of almost everything I address in this book) is the film *The Fountain* (2006), from writer/director Darren Aronovsky. *The Fountain* is a science-fiction fantasy film about the Tree of Life, a source of healing and wisdom. The movie follows the search for enlightenment and for answers to the mysteries of life through three interwoven stories that take us on a cyclical journey from the sixteenth to the twenty-sixth centuries. The lead character(s), played by actor Hugh Jackman, is a research scientist in search of a cure for death—his wife is dying of brain cancer and he desperately wants to save her.

As the movie unfolds, we are introduced to neuro-scientific thought, existentialism, science-fiction, Mayan theology, and ultimately spirituality. Time is parallel and linked; at one moment in the film the viewer looks through a doorway in the sixteenth century that opens into the twenty-first and beyond into the future. There is no linearity to the story. It revolves and evolves, each story completely independent and yet interdependent on the other two for its meaning and context. The final portion of the film takes place in the future. Jackman's character now appears with a shaved head, is dressed in monk-like garb (more Buddhist than Western monastic), and is living in a sort of bubble floating in space at the base of the Tree of Life he has been seeking. The movie ends in an explosion of light as he surrenders to the unanswered questions about life, love, and death that have haunted him, and becomes enlightened. As the movie closes, he is floating in space in a yogic pose, having embraced uncertainty, mystery, and chaos. Much like *Lost in Translation*, this film tells the story of the disoriented Westerner who reorients his life by embracing the "other," the wisdom of the East. Interestingly, both films subtly critique the West by highlighting its seeming inability to aid its citizens in the development and healing of their souls.

Beyond the Westernizing of Asian thought and the recontextualizing of Eastern religious practices, there is another expression of people's religion specifically emerging out of this realm of the postsecular. I am here referring to the marriage of West and East to yield new religious configurations. "People and societies progress by building more spacious cognitive worlds, expanding their boundaries, and moving beyond the limited perspectives of the past."[31] Because of the glut of available information, technological interconnectedness, and a broad sense that traditional approaches to religion and belief no longer suffice, more and more people are experimenting with entirely new permutations of the sacred, and the boundaries of how we understand religion and/or spirituality are being redefined. Here, Eastern philosophy meets Western science, and art and psychotherapeutic principles are merged to present new options for belief and a new synthesis.

Within this particular realm of the postsecular the boundaries of how we understand religion and/or spirituality are being redefined. Here Eastern philosophy meets Western science. Art and psychotherapeutic principles are merged to present new options for belief and a new synthesis. These new approaches are focused on dismantling the old dualisms of mind/body, science/spirituality, and self/system and embracing and integrating these dualities in a larger theory of human evolution and development. Much of the nature of faith is based on an acknowledgment that the whole arena of identity and cosmology is changing.

The theoretical formulations of self and identity have been challenged for a long time. "Under postmodern conditions, persons exist in a state of continuous construction and reconstruction; it is a world where anything goes that can be negotiated," says Kenneth Gergen.[32] This renegotiating of the self is shaped by a desire to move beyond the boundaries and notions of the modern constructed self, as we discussed earlier. This also reflects the emergence of a new cosmology (the way we think about the universe). The universe is growing exponentially. As science continues to advance, ideas and theories about the universe—quantum physics, chaos theory, quarks, black holes, and so forth—frequently change.[33] There seems to be another shift that parallels these new scientific discoveries and that is manifested in a change in perspective about the universe—a new cosmology—away from an objective (read "transcendent"), that is, "it's-out-there," view toward a more immanent view—"we are all part of the universe and it is here as well as there." Changing views in cosmology and identity are also attended by new views on the nature of truth. Remnants of postmodern deconstruction of a singular metanarrative or view of truth, which shaped modernity, are complemented by new ideas about the very nature of truth itself. The plurality of postsecular society has brought most of us to the place where we no longer are willing to recognize that a single truth exists, that there is a singular answer for anything—no one truth or one right belief. Those exploring these issues within the new horizons of religious expression are doing so in part because of an increasing awareness that older views on religion and spirituality are simply not sufficient to address the changing context and that a new paradigm for belief must either emerge or be facilitated.

Traditional religion, as it is examined in this rubric, is commonly viewed as a yoking system that, rather than fostering a common sense of humanity, ties us to a system of belief that often is in conflict with other peoples and forms of belief. Spirituality, that all-encompassing, catchall word used to describe religious intentions, sentiments, and desires not bounded by traditional religious forms, is also viewed in a largely negative light because there exists within "spirituality," particularly of the "New

Age" kind, a tendency toward narcissism and a romanticized view of enlightenment and discovering one's true "inner self." On the surface, at least, some of this new focus seems to be emerging from what were once termed "New Age" forms of religion. But this is not the "old" New Age. A growing awareness that the New Age impulses are falling behind the curve in today's global, pluralistic societies has led some to reconsider or abandon the framework of New Age beliefs and produce new iterations of the religious impulse, the "god-effect." This will be taken up next as we explore the "Next Enlightenment."

The Next Enlightenment: Rational Mystics

> The new forms of spirituality that will likely emerge from the ongoing collision of the ancient, modern, and postmodern worlds will be unlike any that this planet has ever seen before.
>
> Carter Phipps, in *What Is Enlightenment?*

I became aware of the monumental shifts in views on religion in my own world when a friend of mine, Robin, a guitar player in a rock band and a lover of "good times," asked me whether I had read *The Celestine Prophecy* by James Redfield. I was a little taken back that this particular friend would have read what I, at the time, had simply dismissed as yet another book on New Age views of the world. "No, I haven't," I replied. "Well, you should," he said. "Don't worry, it's not a New Age book." He went on to tell me in great detail how the book had given him confidence to explore a part of his life formerly closed off—the spiritual part—and how it had helped him see that one could be, in his words, "religious without going to church and stuff." Growing up in the shadow of a largely ineffectual church presence in England, Robin, like many of my generation, including myself for a long time, simply dismissed the viability of something so staid, stuffy, uptight, and obviously pointless as the church. The church was a place for grannies and Luddites, offering no real spiritual insights to those of us for whom the world had opened up in ways our parents could never have imagined. Some things about his comments surprised me. First, that he thought I would dismiss a book simply because of its association with the New Age movement (I would have at that time, but I didn't think it showed!). Second, that he would not consider this particular book a New Age publication. The third, and perhaps most important, point was that, in my own blindness at the time,

I thought his rejection of formal religion meant that he wasn't interested in spirituality at all when in fact he was. He just needed to find a way to unlock his own spirituality.

The Celestine Prophecy is about finding ways to connect with God, and trusting yourself to do so, without the traditional support structures of formalized religion. After reading it I understood why it had such a potent influence on my friend's life and on countless others. When it comes to this new phase of religious expression, especially among those associated with more formal expressions, there is a tendency to gather it all, place it under the broad umbrella of "New Age" spirituality, and dismiss it as inconsequential to the larger purposes of more formal expressions of faith.

Highly individualized faith expressions are quite troubling to formal religions (although given the fact that Christianity revolves around "personal decisions for Christ"—that people should make other choices based on personal decisions—should not come as a surprise to us). It is partly linked to formal religions' failure to see the viability of other faith expressions and a blindness to the realities of heightened individuality and freedom of choice in a consumer society. In other, more stable times, spirituality was an extension of the religious impulse and was the mark of rare and extreme devotion and exemplary religious character, as expressed within the boundaries and horizons of a formal faith. The "form," if you will, gave rise to the spiritual. But in a time like ours, marked by uncertainty and instability, the rigidity, or perceived rigidity, of the formal structures results in a split between those who remain faithful to the formal—the "form"—and those who seek to express their spiritual desire in new and creative ways.

Spirit can give life to form if it is given enough room for creative expression. This sometimes presents a challenge to many formal religions. Within traditional faiths there is generally a link to certain expression, usually to a past time and space, that is, another age. Formal/traditional faiths tend to view their function as the recitation and repetition of the past. When I raise the issue of radical change, I repeatedly hear from Christians, "God is the same yesterday, today, and tomorrow." The implication of this statement is that the culture needs to revise its expression rather than the church. My response is that while God may be the same unchanging, eternal force, culture is not. God in heaven may be unchanging and eternal, but on earth God's work accommodates itself to the spirit of the times. Because a religion's God is eternal does not mean that the institution is. It is a product of historic interaction with the divine, but its task is not merely to repeat and rehearse the past; it also needs to stay in touch with the unfolding of human history and adapt to meet the needs of a changing world. I realize this sets off alarm bells for some, but Jung wrote that "all true things must change and only that which changes remains true." The "truth" of God is manifested in the presence of God in the new cultural process.

The challenge for the adherents of more traditional faiths is to discover how to change with the times and address their situation's needs without sacrificing their own doctrinal orthodoxy. Is this achievable? Of course, but we must be open to the world around us and God's hand in it and not close ourselves off from what is occurring in the culture in a vain attempt at self-preservation. The great challenge for traditional religions at present is that the shifts in postmodernity—the compression of time and space, the loss of the notion of a stable self, the rejection of history, and so forth—are the result of the implosion of the old order that has been rejected and replaced with a new social ordering. All too often traditional religion wants to take us back to "what was" rather than help to root us in "what is." It is quite remarkable that what the press constantly tells the public about more traditional religions, and that means specifically Christianity in the West, are all the scandals, failings, and sexual improprieties; seldom do we hear the church positively portrayed. This also tends to extend to other media representations of traditional faith.

Those who hold more traditional views and forms of faith are usually portrayed in a somewhat negative light in pop culture, and their institutions are usually presented as ineffectual and corrupt, man-made edifices that are artificial vehicles of man-made dogma. Even a television show such as *7th Heaven*, which is fairly sympathetic to formal religion and unfolds a weekly drama of a family growing through life together, generally portrays the father, who is a minister, as the one who struggles most to understand and accept the changes going on among his teenage brood. Elsewhere the pop cultural mediations of formal faith traditions seem to take every opportunity to destabilize those institutions in the public's eye.[34]

Is this really an attack on religion? A cultural war between sacred and secular? I don't think so. I suggest that it is a manifestation of a different kind of battle being waged, the battle between the new impulse of religion in the emerging postsecular culture and old ways of reaching the divine: a battle between spirit and religion. A good example of this is the recent NBC television drama *Studio 60 on the Sunset Strip*, a show about a weekly comedy-sketch show, much like NBC's own *Saturday Night Live*. The show features a lead character, Harriett, who is a practicing, and very vocal, evangelical Christian. Barely an episode goes by without some challenge to Harriett's beliefs, but it is not her overall belief in God that is being challenged as much as it is some of her views and opinions that clash with the various situations in which she finds herself. Small-mindedness and judgmentalism are constantly addressed in the conversations between Harriett and her cast mates, many of whom seem to play the role of devil's advocate, offering Harriett a different perspective and thus an opportunity to reassess her own views.

The balance of power has shifted in the postsecular—spirit is in the ascendancy, religion is in the decline. Hence my assertion that spirituality *is* the religion of postsecular times. And it is *personal* religion, not dependent on institution or clergy—outer guidance—but dependent instead on inner conscience. Such spirituality is rooted in self-education and reflection rather than the acceptance of mediated information. There is a desire for communication with peers, strangers, and media culture of all forms rather than clergy or spiritual guides, at least in a hierarchical sense in which such persons would be acknowledged as having some kind of "inside track to God."[35] Ward writes that the roots of the word "religion" are found in the Roman word *religare* ("to reread") and then asserts that religion is "worship of the true."[36] While in other times this idea has been linked to community, formal liturgy or worship, and the practice of an established faith tradition, in the postsecular age religion is the worship of the true outside the confines of traditional ideas of community, liturgy, and the practice of a particular faith.

The word "spirituality" seems increasingly hard to define. Ask one hundred people and you will probably get one hundred different answers. I asked someone sitting next to me in Starbucks to define spirituality and she said that it is a "way of connecting with God but not in a religious way. It's a moral code you find for yourself by exploring life."[37] She went on to say that she also thought that religious people could be "spiritual, but spiritual people wouldn't be religious because it's the imposition of a belief system from outside." She told me that she was raised with a heavy dose of what she termed "puritanical religion" and now considers herself a "puritanical existentialist spiritual person." She described most of her friends in a similar light, commenting on their various appropriations of elements of a wide variety of religious and psychological influences.

We are able to define spirituality less and less because in postsecularity it is coming to mean more and more. As the new religious dynamic in postmodernity continues to expand, spirituality becomes a bigger catchall for the various incarnations of the spirit in these times. It could be said that virtually anyone can bring himself or herself under the general banner of spirituality, and in a myriad of ways. The inclination toward spirit seems to be communal and collective, a general characteristic of the age, but the experience remains intensely personal. Hence the attempt in this book to make general observations about certain inclinations rather than to formally declare highly specified categories.

But back to the New Age. There are some obvious connections with the New Age movement as we have experienced it over the past forty or so years. Emerging on the cultural scene about the same time as the hippie movement of the 1960s, it heralded the cultural shifts beginning to occur as the rise of the Age of Aquarius. The Age of Aquarius is taken from an ancient astrological timetable related to signs of the zodiac, according to which the Age of Aries would be followed by the Age of Pisces, and finally a new age, the Age of Aquarius (the Water-bearer).[38] There are obvious connections between the idea of a new age of spirit and the Aquarian concept of water poured out on a thirsty earth, the function of the water-bearer of the zodiac. There are also links to the theories of Joachim of Fiore,[39] whose theories seem to be getting a lot of mileage these many years later. The Age of Aquarius was to usher in a time of peace, harmony, wholeness, and restoration for people and ultimately the entire universe. During this age there could be a reunification of God and people and a rediscovery of the "oneness of all things."[40] As a result of this pouring forth of the waters of the spirit, the subsequent time could be one of human cooperation rather than one characterized by domination or competition.[41]

The emergence of social and cultural unrest in the 1960s, charged by antiwar sentiment among Western youth, and a cry for a new era of peace and love seemed to validate the call of the prophets of this new age. It is perhaps no wonder that many see the democratization of spirit as mere New Age spirituality. Given its rise during a time of popular culture's ascendancy as a shaping cultural force, it should not come as a surprise that the first public intimations of this new spiritual dynamic emerged in the lyrics of a rock song.

The 1967 musical *Hair*, which was dedicated to the public celebration of hippie culture, was perhaps best remembered for its hit song "The Age of Aquarius." The marriage of a new philosophical idea with music was a perfect match at a time in the history of Western culture when trust in institutions and other forms of social ordering to shape the social imaginary were being rejected as inadequate to address the needs of a restless generation of people wearied by war and worn down by the failed promise of a better future. Pop culture became the site of legitimate philosophical, moral, and ethical debate and discussion. Bob Dylan could sing, "The times they are a-changin'," and a whole generation knew it was true—they *felt* it. They wanted change and were prepared to sing it into existence. This was a viable option, at least as viable as the failed attempts of the proponents of the old order, whose proclamations of a better future for all of humanity were laid waste in the settling dust of over a half century of world wars, genocides, and totalitarian regimes.

For the advocates of the existing structures, the heralding of a new and better future involved escaping the confines of this world, quite literally, in the form of a spaceship. The race to the moon, an expensive competition between two modernist ideologies—capitalism and communism—was viewed as the continued validation for the modernist project. Back on earth the answer to the problem of modernity, according to the youth of the West, was a new social order, the Age of Aquarius. In other words, they were advocating a paradigm shift, which "is a distinctly new way of thinking about old problems."[42] Ferguson describes the paradigm shift heralded by the Aquarian Age as "seeing humanity embedded in nature. It promotes the autonomous individual in a decentralized society. It sees us as stewards of all our resources, inner and outer. It says that we are not victims, not pawns, not limited by conditions or conditioning. Heirs to evolutionary riches, we are capable of imagination, invention, and experiences we have only glimpsed."[43]

In direct opposition to the dominant order's commitment to the continuation of the Enlightenment project, many people began to search for a different kind of enlightenment, one that came from within rather than from without, one found within the systems of human beings. In spite of the "evolutionary riches," which Ferguson claims were part of the impetus for the heralding of the Aquarian age, the initial murmurings of this new age movement were attached to the revolutionary desires of disaffected youth.

Despite the frustration with the larger societal way of doing business, change by revolution was still viewed as viable. The hippie generation merely changed the weaponry from guns and bullets to peace and love. "Make love, not war," was a classic slogan of the time. Student protests on many university campuses around the globe in 1968 and 1969 featured confrontations between student advocates of peace and love, armed with passivity and flowers, and soldiers, police, and National Guardsmen, armed with the conventional instruments of combat: guns, clubs, and guard dogs.

For a moment it seemed that a capitulation would occur and that the old order could actually be overthrown, but this was short lived. The error of

New Age spirituality was its assumption that revolution was the answer. When the promised revolution of peace and love failed to materialize, the newly voiced form of New Age philosophy slowly morphed into New Age spirituality and virtually disappeared into the fabric of the newly minted alternative culture that now began to live alongside the dominant culture in something of a standoff. Areas of cities became devoted to alternative lifestyles. The appearance of *head shops* (purveyors of drug paraphernalia), music stores, cafes and organic restaurants, markets and alternative bookstores in communities such as Haight-Ashbury in San Francisco, Greenwich Village in New York, and Venice Beach in California became the new locales for the continuation of the Aquarian dream.

But this was largely lost on mainstream culture until the 1980s, when suddenly there was widespread interest in all things New Age. Once again this move came through a populist source: actress Shirley MacLaine, whose autobiographical books on her encounters with New Age philosophy became best sellers. Marilyn Ferguson's book *The Aquarian Conspiracy* was a best seller then and remains so today. It became an instant classic for those searching for forms of spirituality and religion that would meet the more diverse tastes of an emerging globalized culture used to a diet of fusion foods, world music, foreign films, and the consciousness of pluralities at the very core of its destabilized psyche.

You want a little Native American religion? The New Age is your destination. How about mixing in a little yoga with that? How about a pinch of past-life therapy, deep-tissue massage, Tantric sex, and authentic ayurvedic incense from India? A company called Inner Traditions[44] offers courses in Zulu shamanism, Taoist cosmic healing, and Tantra, to name just a few of its products and courses. The New Age will market all of this to you. In this, New Age spirituality is a parody of the present situation, not the sum. It parallels some elements of the democratization of the spirit in its desires and manifestations, but it is not the same. It is the fetishization, the mystic charge, of the new impulse in the postsecular age.

Given its appearance on the cultural imaginary at a time when the Enlightenment project was both at its height and on the precipice of decline and implosion, it is no wonder that a central tenet of New Age philosophy was an alternative enlightenment. Being enlightened—or conscious—and becoming cosmically aware are key understandings that permeate broad-based New Age spiritualities. In contrast to the Kantian motto of the Enlightenment, *Sapere Aude!* ("Have the courage to use your own intelligence"),[45] the New Age version was the promise of entry into a "new era of man in which humanity will transform itself into a Global

Mind, leaving behind petty individualism."[46] The current age of spirit is anything *but* a cohesive global mind. Having abandoned individualism for a collective awareness, it is now quite the opposite. Again this points to the parodic tendencies of New Age spirituality that, in its philosophical roots, is at odds with the current situation. But I do want to address another "enlightenment," one that emerges from some of the dynamics of Westernized Asian thought and developments in Western science. It is the "new" new age, the age of the rational mystic.

The December 2002 issue of *Wired* magazine, the "Bible" of tech freaks, geeks, and computer and technology enthusiasts, featured a picture of a silvery robotic human figure whose legs dissolved into a symbolic representation of the DNA strand placed over an oversized red heart, both of which were laid upon a crucifix that featured a pair of outstretched cyborg arms crucifixion style. The cross itself was constructed in classic Catholic style but was made up of elements of technology, such as metal, switches, screws. Surrounding the cross, in iconic style, were all the elements of the scientific age: Newton's apple, a satellite, the printed page, an embryo, a dinosaur, a microscope, a test tube. Over this was the headline "Science Gets Religion." One could also invert that expression and say that "Religion Gets Science," in a whole new configuration. The magazine carried articles with titles such as "The Pope's Astrophysicist" and "God and the Computer." This magazine exposes another arena in which we find some general characteristics that comprise part of the religion of the resacralized West.

This theme is taken up by Walter Truett Anderson in his book *The Next Enlightenment*. Here, Anderson argues that the next phase in human evolution will marry science and religion, the study of the physical universe and human consciousness, as two sides of the same coin. Anderson wants to shift the conversation about enlightenment out of the hands of those who make it the reserve of a select few individuals[47] and present it primarily as a self-help tool, arguing that it is not the domain of a few but something better understood as an "evolutionary project."[48] In this, Anderson wants to marry Eastern religious philosophy to Western scientific concepts, particularly evolution. Anderson isolates five "evolutionary" movements from within Western culture: the Enlightenment, the Darwinian movement, psychoanalysis, existentialism, and the human potential movements.[49] He seeks to blend these with more classic enlightenment perspectives drawn from such Eastern religions as Buddhism and Hinduism.

For Anderson, the Enlightenment represents three important elements: the notion of progress, the encouragement to think for oneself, and the encouragement to question all dogmas, including those of established religions. The Darwinian movement offers two ideas: we live in an ever-changing universe, and we are integrally and inseparably a part of all life on earth. Psychoanalysis, in Anderson's view, is a kind of sequel to Darwinism in which "connections are made between the human mind and its biological origins." Here the conscious mind is viewed as a fragment of the self rather than a fragment of the whole. Existentialism led to "new psychological theories and therapies based on the proposition that we repress not only thoughts of sex and violence but also our sense of being." Finally, the human potential movement of the 1960s and 1970s offered the first blending of East and West and proffered the vision of a transformation of the human species.[50] These five foundational ideas are still in play in postsecular culture and provide the framework for the future evolution of the human into a new self-understanding and a new relationship with the world.[51]

There have been a number of recent films that posit variations of this perspective. Two of them, *What the Bleep Do We Know?* and *I Heart Huckabees*, seek to blend science and religion in new ways. *What the Bleep*, a sort of spiritual infomercial documentary, adopts a science-meets-New-Age attitude and emphasizes the human potential movement. The main character is in existential crisis and is urged to find liberation by coming to terms with who she really is. Echoes of Nietzsche's dictum to "become who you are"[52] reverberate throughout the film, as do references to new scientific advancements. *I Heart Huckabees*, the story of a man in existential angst, is more oblique with its spiritual references, and given that the film is a comedy, plays lightly with complex theories. The film was, in the words of its writer and director, David O. Russell, a film about the "meaning of the universe. A film that would synthesize religion and philosophy and mathematics—Buddhism, string theory, nihilism, psychoanalysis."[53]

Another series of films that captures much of this movement is *The Matrix Trilogy*, created by the Wachowski brothers. Today, the worldwide grosses for these films are approaching $2 billion. The films are an exploration of the nature of reality and present the inhabitants of the world as caught between two realities—one real, one false. Driven by groundbreaking cinematic style and featuring effects-laden visuals and state-of-the-art martial-arts fighting, these movies are a futuristic and inspiring meeting of East and West. The first film was well received by the Christian community, especially youth groups, which was surprising given the level of cinematic violence but unsurprising given that the film

New Edges

was apparently influenced by Christianity. That Zion was the name of the human city of the "real" world, hidden from a population blinded by the matrix—a computer-generated world of illusion—and given that the hero of the film was the messianic Neo, an anagram for "the One," it was quickly adopted as a metaphor and used as a means to insinuate Christianity back into mainstream cultural conversation. This intention was greatly undermined by the second and third installments, which exposed the more complex influences of the films. Buddhists claim the film as their own, as do gnostics, atheists, scientists, and other philosophical groups.

> *The Matrix* is a postmodern philosophical movie in which fragments of philosophy do the *Casablanca* cliché dance. There's Christian exegesis, a Redeemer myth, a death and a rebirth, a hero in self-discovery, the Odyssey, Jean Beaudrillard (lots of Beaudrillard, the best parts of the film), science-fiction ontological riffs of the Phillip K. Dick school, Nebuchadnezzer, the Buddha, Taoism, martial-arts, mysticism, oracular prophecy, spoon-bending telekinesis, Houdini stage-school magic, Joseph Campbell, and Godelian mathematical metaphysics.[54]

In December 2004, a boxed-set special edition of the films was released along with hours of commentary on the nature of reality and consciousness featuring Ken Wilber and philosopher David Chalmers, director of the Center for Consciousness Studies at the University of Arizona. In a press conference, Larry Wachowski, one of the film's co-creators, both of whom have chosen not to speak publicly about the film's influences, used Wilber as the prime spokesman about the roots of the film and declared that "Ken Wilber is Neo."[55] Wilber's most widely known work is *A Theory of Everything*.[56] It is an attempt to provide an "integral" vision for what he terms the Kosmos, which in his translation is what the Greeks understood as the "patterned Whole of all existence, including the physical, emotional, mental and spiritual realms." Expanding on the Greek idea, Wilber advances his own vision of the Kosmos with his own theory of the integral:

> "An integral vision"—or a genuine Theory of Everything—attempts to include matter, body, mind, soul, and spirit as they appear in self, culture and nature. A vision that attempts to be comprehensive, balanced, inclusive. A vision that therefore embraces science, art, and morals; that equally includes disciplines from physics to spirituality, biology to aesthetics, sociology to contemplative prayer; that shows up in integral politics, integral medicine, integral business, integral spirituality.[57]

The list goes on. Again, what is occurring here is an attempt at a holistic view of life, a collapsing of the binary oppositions that structured modernity and compartmentalized life. Wilber derives his use of "integral" from the work of sociologist Paul Ray and in particular research from *The Cultural Creatives*.[58] The cultural creatives are identified as a previously unnoticed segment of the American adult population that number about fifty million and are called the *integral culture*. Ray believes this group is at the creative leading edge of the culture and is characterized by a "serious concern for their inner lives with a strong penchant for social activism, including a commitment to a sustainable future."[59] He notes that this group is committed to spirituality, altruism, and self-actualization, and that its members value authenticity, are careful consumers, buy more books and magazines and listen to more radio than other segments of the population, are aggressive consumers of arts and culture, are into "whole process"—they want the whole story of whatever they are into—are innovators, are experiential consumers, and are prototypical innovators in the search for holism.[60] Their dislikes are equally important and include social inequality, intolerance, and the Religious Right. They are critical of every big institution in modern society. They reject narrow analyses and fragmentary and superficial glosses of what passes for reality. Instead they want a reality that encompasses heart and mind, personal and public, and individual and community.[61]

Wilber wants to offer a different version of *integral* and argues that those surveyed by Ray are still locked in a "flatland holism," reflected in their lack of second-tier consciousness, mature vision-logic, and seeking of a universal monological holism.[62] They have yet to "further the transformation of their consciousness."[63] Integral, for Wilber, means a new understanding of the human condition less rooted in the binary dynamics of the old order. He further argues that there is now a "cultural readiness for a more integral embrace."[64]

This is a framework for the "new" new age, one not characterized by an embrace of alternative and obscure religious practices snatched from around the globe and contextualized into a world of designer gods and designer religious lifestyles, but one that is characterized by a dominant ideology at its core—the commitment to a holistic marriage of East and West into a new "rational mysticism." Rational mysticism is a good term to describe this aspect of the postsecular world. Wilber, for instance, posits that his integral vision—taking in all of life and seeking to integrate all aspects, including science and religion—will eventually lead to the highest form of mystical experience: divine mysticism, the next enlightenment, and

New Edges

fully realized integration. In this, Wilber seems to be employing Evelyn Underhill's levels of mystical experience but reinterpreting them for his own schema, which for him means that divine mysticism is the state of nondual union.[65] It is not simply that this group relies on science to validate its religious experiences. It is more a matter of seeking to integrate disparities and acknowledge the widespread desire afloat in the culture, a desire to reconcile the fragmentation of the human psyche created by modernity's binary oppositions and its dismissal of religion from the center of human life, social order, and cultural affairs.

Scientific developments over the past 150 years have increased the potential for human evolution. These developments emerged in the shift from Newtonian-based physics to the new sciences, which have opened up a space for mystery in the field. In turn, this space for mystery in science has the potential to create new configurations of religion and science—the rational and the mystic, the knowledge of the West with the wisdom of the East.[66]

> Numerous other areas of contemporary science sound like supernaturalism dressed up. Researchers studying the motions of galaxies have found that the stars and gas clouds within them behave as though they're subject to 20 times more force than can be explained by the gravity from observed matter. This has led to the assumption—now close to a scientific consensus—that much of the cosmos is bound up in an undetectable substance provisionally called dark matter.[67]

Dark matter. It all sounds very mysterious, which leads us into the next rubric: the rise of the gothic.

Retrolution: Postmodern Gothic

> Life is something unfathomable, ever-changing, mysterious, and every attempt to confine it within an artificial, abstract structure inevitably ends up homogenizing, regimenting, standardizing and destroying life, as well as curtailing everything that projects beyond, overflows, or falls outside the abstract project. What is a concentration camp, after all, but an attempt by utopians to dispose of those elements which do not fit in?
>
> Vaclav Havel, *On Evasive Thinking*

> God is nowhere, God is now here.
> God is now here, God is nowhere.
>
> Douglas Coupland, *Hey Nostradamus*

Darkness has more Divinity for me,
It strikes thought inward, it drives back the soul
To settle on Herself, our Point supreme.

Edward Young, *Night Thoughts*

Seventeen million people have read Dan Brown's *The Da Vinci Code*,[68] a tale of murder, mystery, and intrigue, in the first two years of its publication and millions more have seen the movie. It is the story of an American symbologist, Robert Langdon, who while on holiday in Paris is summoned to the Louvre late at night for a meeting with the curator of the museum. Upon arrival, Langdon is shocked to discover the death of the curator, whom he finds clutching a baffling cypher. Langdon begins to solve the complex riddles contained in the code, discovering a trail of hidden clues in the works of Leonardo da Vinci. As a symbologist, Langdon sees things differently, and the clues that lay dormant in Leonardo's most famous paintings, right before the public's very eyes, are revealed by this new form of detective.

The Da Vinci Code is a spiritual story disguised as a murder mystery. The heart of the story is the discovery of a secret society, the Priory of Sion, whose past members, along with Leonardo, included Newton, Botticelli, Victor Hugo, and other key figures of European history. This society is engaged in a secret mission, which, if revealed, would threaten the very existence of Christianity. As the story unfolds, there are notes and fact pages alongside the narrative that contain verifiable historical information on the works of art, the existence of certain societies, and other "secrets hidden before our very eyes." To say more would ruin the enjoyment of anyone who has not yet read it, and the telling of the story is not the ultimate point here. A veritable cottage industry of books seeking to refute many of the claims of *The Da Vinci Code*, from a number of upset Christians who see in this yet another attempt to destabilize the Christian faith and its claims to spiritual ascendancy, has arisen in the wake of the book's phenomenal success.

There is also something reflected in the success of this book other than its dubious historical claims, which along with a number of other developments leads us into a discussion of another dynamic of a people's religion. This dynamic falls into two groupings, both of which fall under the same rubric. I will use the terms: the rise of the gothic, and the new medievalism. They are two distinct versions of a similar response to the present situation. As Umberto Eco, the semiotician, has said, it seems that many of us in the twenty-first century are "dreaming the Middle Ages."[69]

If the last category considered those who are pushing forward into new futures with regard to the religious impulse, this category refers to those who deal with the present by practicing *retrolution*, "a way of presenting aspects of the future through terms set by the past, in order to make it seem palatable."[70] Further, not only is it an effort to make the present palatable, it is also a way of navigating the present situation by using instruments readily available in the premodern and early-modern periods, before the corruption of modernity set in.

I will attempt to explore the rise of the gothic and the turn toward a new medievalism independently of each other, but they are not that neatly divided categorically. So there will be some "bleeding" (apropos for a discussion of the gothic perhaps).

Writing about the immensely, and globally, successful Harry Potter novels, themselves a rather benign manifestation of the gothic with their tales of alchemy, magic, wizards, and flying broomsticks, Andrew Blake notes that the "stories explore the old, and a little under the surface deal with the new; past literary forms and present concerns exist side by side."[71] From the first, let me say that the primary embrace of gothic sensibility and effect is quite simply related to one concern, one dominant characteristic of the contemporary cultural context—uncertainty. The problem may be mediated through what appear to be otherworldly means, but the focus in its present manifestation is decidedly contemporary. This uncertainty about contemporary life is threaded throughout various expressions of both the rise of gothic and the new medievalism. Eco argues that the interest in all things medieval is indicative of our quest for roots, and that we are, in a sense, looking for "reliable Middle Ages."[72] This idea fits nicely with the desire to navigate and negotiate the minefield of uncertainty and unpredictability that characterizes our lives today.

How the employ of the gothic actually aids in the processing of the uncertainty and other more troubling aspects that attend the human psyche at present is somewhat abstract. Let us return for a minute to Robert Langdon, the riddle-solving hero of *The Da Vinci Code*. He is a symbologist, an interpreter of symbols. The dictionary definition of a symbol is: "something that represents something else by association, resemblance, or convention, especially a material object used to represent something invisible."[73] Langdon moves through the story interpreting the visual clues laced in Leonardo's paintings in order to discover some truth about faith that has meaning for the present context. The story attempts to lift Christian faith out of a certain box and place it in another, which, at least to the author, seems a better fit for the times. But the larger issue is that

Langdon moves us into a world of symbolism, and this is how we must approach the gothic.

The gothic—one aspect of a turn away from modernity and toward premodern perspectives on life—stands as the symbolic representation of that which is invisible, namely, the desire of some to process their anxiety, uncertainty, and confusion in ways that will aid them in navigating life in the new matrix stripped of traditional support structures and flooded with options, choices, and decisions. In its initial incarnation in the eighteenth century, the terror and excess that attended the gothic was intended to warn the reader of the potential for their extinction.[74] Today, the potential for extinction remains, but now the prime objective is learning to deal with this potentiality rather than fearing one's demise. Employing the gothic is how we learn to live and cope in a world of chaos.[75] We must "read" it symbolically, looking beneath its surface for the meaning of what is being shown to us:

> In Gothic productions, imagination and emotional effects exceed reason. Passion, excitement and sensation transgress social proprieties and moral laws. Ambivalence and uncertainty obscure single meaning. . . . Gothic conjures up magical worlds . . . associated with wildness, Gothic signified an over-abundance of imaginative frenzy, untamed by reason and unrestrained by conventional eighteenth century demands for simplicity, realism, or probability.[76]

Reading Botting's description of the gothic, it is not difficult to make connections with the present condition and see how accessible and appealing the idea of the gothic would be and how easy it is to spot the sensibilities at work in the culture. Appadurai directs us to the "imagination as social practice" and contends that imagination is no longer mere fantasy or escape but is a "form of work, and a form of negotiation between sites of agency and globally defined fields of possibility."[77]

Adopting this view helps us to see the rise of the gothic as a tool of imagination used by some to negotiate specific situations in the global present. This may be the most pervasive of the rubrics at work at present. I hesitate to make such claims, but the sheer presence of the gothic effect at work in virtually every arena of the contemporary arts as expressed through pop culture, from fashion to film, as well as in the realm of religious exploration and practice, makes a strong case for such a claim.

The gothic bestows its wisdom through the celebration of mystery and the mysterious, the grotesque and the desolate. The ultimate wisdom it grants is that it teaches us to live with mystery, and this is accomplished by attuning us to the unexpected, sharpening our instincts, and nurturing our creativity. As Botting wrote, imagination and emotions exceed reason—the "whys" of the gothic are not explained as much as they are presented to be engaged.[78]

We will now consider several elements of the gothic as it manifests in the postsecular: the aesthetics as the specific focus of the gothic imaginary; the contours of uncertainty that the gothic addresses and the symbolic cures it offers; the new medievalism and its religious manifestations; and mystical codes.

Gothic Aesthetics: Seeing in the Dark

The gothic signifies a trend toward an aesthetics based on feeling and emotion and associated primarily with the sublime.[79] "Be Afraid of the Dark." This was the slogan that accompanied a film released in October 2001 called *Donnie Darko*. The film was not very successful when first released. To a country still reeling from the events of September 11, a movie about a deeply troubled young man who was off his medication, was receiving apocalyptic messages from outer space about the imminent destruction of the world, and was haunted by a grotesque human-size rabbit named Frank, was too much for most people to stomach. Added to the mix was the destruction of Donnie's bedroom by an airplane engine that mysteriously fell from the sky, which, considering that planes were involved in the terrorist attack, was too close for comfort for many.

It was not until a strange turn of events in England that the film began to generate interest. Since then it has become something of a cult classic, often cited as a favorite among young people. The closing song of the film was called "Mad World," a song originally written and recorded by the band Tears for Fears and performed in the movie by Gary Jules. This song was a plaintive and melancholy critique of the contemporary culture, and in the winter of 2002 it became a huge, and surprising, Christmas radio hit in England.[80] The accompanying music video, which featured abstract elements of the film, was played incessantly on MTV in both Europe and America. With this song spreading its melancholy over the music network, the film finally claimed an audience.

In the film, Donnie Darko (Jake Gyllenhaal) doesn't want to be medicated. He rejects his enforced therapy sessions and proves an unwilling patient. What he really wants is to be awake, even if being awake means that he has to be haunted by visions of the apocalypse and strange creatures.

The film is set on election night 1988, near the end of the Reagan political era, and it opens with the classic American sitcom version of family—the tense mother, supercilious dad, irritating little sister, and Donnie, who avoids eye contact with everyone at the table. In fact, he avoids eye contact with virtually everyone in the film as well as the audience via the camera. The film is a critique of 1980s American culture with its commitment to overmedication and therapy as means of shutting out anxiety about the future. But Darko would rather not be medicated, or undergo therapy, or listen to his high-school motivational speaker, who spews litanies of trite, neatly packaged self-empowerment messages to a largely uninterested and blank-faced audience of teens. In this light, we can see the appeal of the gothic. It seeks to awaken the public to things as they are in all their sublime forms, exposing the veneer, the underbelly.

The gothic first arose in the late eighteenth century as the other side of the Romantic era. It was everything that Romanticism detested and avoided. In the postmodern situation it functions in a similar fashion. Hollywood has produced this genre of films for decades, from the 1937 movie *Jekyll and Hyde* to last year's *The Ring*, but the sheer number of movies dedicated to this overarching gothic sensibility seems to increase exponentially as we move into the latter decades of the twentieth century and on into the twenty-first. Ward observes that "Since the 'slasher' movies of the 1970s there has been a cultural reaffirmation of the gothic expressing itself on a number of social levels: the 'goth' look; the mass international consumption of the Harry Potter series; the fascination with psychopathy; and the lurid world of cybergames."[81] The breadth of incarnations of the gothic extends to virtually all forms of popular culture, even to television. *Buffy the Vampire Slayer*, *Angel*, and HBO's *Carnivale* are just a few of the shows that ply the gothic trade. Fox Television debuted a show titled *Point Pleasant* in January 2005. It is the story of a teenage girl with dark powers who goes to live in a suburban community, plunging the community into disturbing and challenging scenarios. The advertising for the show is laden with gothic imagery and text that make full use of gothic sensibility.

Central to the gothic is its portrayal of evil. Ward makes an interesting comment about the understanding of the nature of evil as a contributor to the postmodern condition: "Whereas evil in modernity was understood as social and anthropological (corruption, violence, tyranny being exercised by human beings), evil in postmodernity is concerned with the unknown and the indeterminate: forces that render human defenses inadequate."[82] To this I add only that I am not sure that it is a question of binary opposition, an "either-or" situation regarding evil. In postsecularity, our understanding of evil includes the modern understanding of the nature of evil, as outlined by Ward, coupled with additions created by the postmodern condition. A key point here is that the existence of evil is not, and cannot be, avoided in the present situation. No effort is made to nullify or deny its existence; instead, it is often elevated and amplified. Evil permeates and haunts the world of the gothic and is often presented in stark, merciless, and brutal ways.

The seven deadly sins of the Catholic Church, for instance, are shockingly utilized in David Fincher's movie *Se7en*. Fincher always creates gothic landscape in his films,[83] employing decaying buildings, lots of shadows and fractured light, and often an abundance of rain to add to the gloom of the dark worlds he creates. A series of shocking and gruesome murders, each representing one of the seven sins, haunts the lives of two detectives as they seek to interpret the symbols and capture the killer. The gothic tone of the story is heightened by director Fincher's[84] use of dimmed lighting, rain, and run-down and decaying locations for the enactments of the crimes. The darkness is supported by a film score by composer Howard Shore that features dark, disturbing strings that generate and heighten the ugliness of what is occurring on screen.

The resacralization of society makes this gothic use of the magical and mysterious work. The religious in inverted forms becomes a viable tool for exploring the forces of evil and good in the postsecular by functioning artistically in the realm of the sublime. Botting offers two views on the sublime:

> In contrast to beauty, the proportioned contours of which could be taken in by the eye of the beholder, the sublime was associated with grandeur and magnificence. Craggy, mountainous landscapes, the Alps in particular, stimulated powerful emotions of terror and wonder in the viewer. Their immense scale offered a glimpse of infinite and awful power, intimations of a metaphysical force beyond rational knowledge and human comprehension. In the expansive domain opened up by the sublime, all sorts of imaginative objects and fears situated in or beyond nature could proliferate in a marvelous profusion of the supernatural and the ridiculous, the magical and the nightmarish, the fantastic and the absurd.[85]

The manifestation of the gothic today plies this same territory, employing darkness in the service of the social imaginary as a means of gaining sight—seeing in the dark, if you will. The world of the gothic is the world of the sublime, not the beautiful, manifesting in the horrific, the terrifying, the scary. In its postmodern version, it is home to sweeping hordes of alien creatures, monsters from the deep or monsters from space. It is the world of terminators and barbarians, aliens and borgs, robots and mutants, vampires and werewolves.

Today, this sublime landscape is mediated mostly through the visual realm of cinema, where the vast potential of the marriage of creativity, vision, and technological capability expands the landscape possibilities from European Alps to literally other worlds—the sheer vastness of their scale almost overwhelming. To consider the hordes of grotesque warriors who pour out of the dark lands of Mordor to attack Frodo Baggins and his friends in the *Lord of the Rings*—the sheer spectacle of such a fully realized world blended the New Zealand landscape with computer-generated images to create in stunning detail J. R. R. Tolkien's Middle-earth—is mind boggling. Such created worlds tend to focus on the gloomy and the dark, in spite of their sheer visual spectacle. Consider *Bladerunner*'s gloomy and ever rainy Asianized Los Angeles of the future, or the dark reaches of space where hordes of faceless stormtroopers threaten the future of the Federation in the *Star Wars* films. The dark is also expressed in the apocalyptic landscape of the *Terminator* movies, where robots, which look so human, rise up against the real humans and destroy civilization. The world is often threatened by nature itself in these films—earth-destroying meteors, huge storms, melting polar ice caps. It is everyday apocalypse. As Botting states, "Through its presentations of supernatural, sensational and terrifying incidents, imagined or not, Gothic produced emotional effects on its readers rather than developing a rational or properly cultivated response. Exciting rather than informing, it chilled their blood, delighted their superstitious fantasies, and fed unified appetites for marvelous and strange events."[86]

If we wish to understand the appeal of horror movies among teenagers or the continued hunger for rock music filled with apocalyptic emotion, whether it be through the music of Ozzy Osbourne and Marilyn Manson or of Radiohead and Linkin Park, we should look no further than the gothic imaginary. The continuing desire to be "scared out of one's wits" by a two-hour horror movie is linked to a deeper cultural anxiety about the future, as is the anger and frustration expressed in heavy metal music.[87]

The *pleasure* of such experiences is linked to two dynamics. First, the awesome and often terrifying landscapes in which the gothic manifests itself function as a stimulus to the imagination:[88] the screen is filled with imagery too hard for the gaze to take in. If beauty is in the eye of the beholder, then the sublime nature of gothic artistry is a world too big for the eye to behold, the images being beyond the scope of the single gaze, beyond the scope of comprehension by the rational mind. The gothic represents a shift in the way we understand both the nature of beauty[89] and the beauty of nature—the contrast between conventional notions of beauty and the sublime. It is the expansion of the postsecular universe into a multiverse more resonant with the pluralities that drive the postmodern consciousness. Second, the terror that is created has an epiphanic effect akin to the sense of wonderment that accompanies religious experience. The shocking sights, the supernatural incidents, the quickening pulse of the viewer, and the atmosphere of inexplicable gloom and mystery promote a combination of fear and awe. Sublimity offers intimations of a great power, if not a divine one: "If I were pressed to submit one reason for the contemporary proliferation of the Gothic, that reason would in a certain sense be religious. . . . With the contemporary return to the Gothic . . . we recover a horizon of ultimate meaning. We recover something of what is lost with the withdrawal of God from the day to day world."[90]

The rise of the gothic is part of the process of reenchantment of Western culture, an effort to recover a horizon of ultimate meaning. Ward reads this as a religion about the "absence of God."[91] I read it as an effort to reconfigure the horizon of ultimate meaning in a world where the narrow universe of the gods of traditional religions seems insufficient to address the multiversal potentialities of the postmodern world. This is summed up in the achingly sublime and reflective song "The Day after Tomorrow," by American gothic folksinger Tom Waits. A story of the tensions faced by a young US soldier in Iraq, this song reveals heartfelt uncertainties about the God of modernity during the rise of postsecular pluralism. It contains these compelling lyrics:

> You can't deny the other side, don't wanna die anymore than we do
> what I'm tryin' to say is don't they pray to the same God that we do?
> Tell me how does God choose? Whose prayers does he refuse?
> Who turns the wheel, who rolls the dice on the day after tomorrow?[92]

Postmodern gothic expands the category of the gothic from its earlier constraints and fills the social imaginary with an ever-increasing number of characters, scenarios, and persona "lying utterly outside the moral universe of Christianity."[93] It is about the search for a *God big enough* to meet the needs of an expanding universe and about the shift beyond metaphysical understandings of God, which are both reflections of the ongoing attempt to process anxiety and uncertainty in the meantime by employing the gothic as a coping mechanism—learning to stay cool in disturbing times. "The groundrule of that (Newtonian) universe, upon which so much of our western world is built, has dissolved."[94]

The recitation of the gothic in our time is about fashioning redemption through one's own effort in a world still waiting for something to arise on the horizon of ultimate meaning. To return for a moment to the movie *Se7en*, the use of the church's categories of sins as a template for murder is a critique of religion's inability, at least in traditional forms, to do anything about the nature of human and social sin. It is not enough to categorize its sins. The film offers a visual representation of Wallace's "failure of theodicy." The world is too complex, too smart, to respond to mere religious categorization. It needs more. This is the focus, the reach, of the gothic impulse.

What Would Buffy Do?[95] is an obvious play on the *What Would Jesus Do?* craze that captured American Christian youth in the late 1990s and bubbled over into the pop culture psyche. Using this as her book title, Jana Riess explores how the gothic-influenced television show *Buffy the Vampire Slayer*, which ran for seven seasons from March 1997 to May 2003 and followed the exploits of Buffy, a teenage vampire slayer, can address the spiritual needs of people. Rather than interpreting the show as simply mindless entertainment, Riess offers a serious exploration of how the television show—driven by Christian symbolism, Buddhist teaching, Wiccan ethics, teenage angst, and shopping malls, all immersed in a gothic overtone—addresses personal spiritual needs and helps frame one's spiritual journey.

The show is entertainment theology at its best. In this one television show we find many of the characteristics of the contemporary religious and spiritual impulses converging, serving, and interweaving in continually shifting permutations, highlighting the nonlinear approach to faith in the postsecular era. The absence of God is a dominant theme in *Buffy*, alongside the obvious spiritual references. What is interesting, as is well noted by Riess, is that "despite their unanswered questions about God, they (Buffy et al.) never fail to do their job: saving the world at whatever personal cost."[96] This lack of "proper object" does not result in complacency toward the world as others claimed it would; rather, they "care passionately about right and wrong, good and evil. So although the show demonstrates a lot of ambivalence about the existence of God, it offers a deep spiritual core that is based in ethical behavior."[97] Here is a postmodern ethic emerging in the split between traditional religion and postsecular culture.

Taming the Darkness: What Would Buffy Do?

As to the second issue involving the kind of uncertainty addressed by the gothic, the focus is not simply the existential, which concerns questions of existence and ultimate meaning, but also the uncertainty of the everyday. "Uncertainties about the nature of power, law, society, family and sexuality dominate Gothic fiction."[98] These are the uncertainties of postmodern life, experienced as it is, in the collapse of the supporting structures of modernity, in the loss of traditional social orderings. The postmodern gothic explores all of these issues. Increasingly, particularly in movies, reconfigurations of what constitutes family and community are explored. For instance, in the *Fellowship of the Ring*, those who are compelled into mission by a desire to protect the world from those who seek to do it harm are drawn into new community relations. Consider also the strange amalgam of robots, space royalty, and adventurers of the *Star Wars* series: C-3PO, R2-D2, Princess Leia, Luke Skywalker, and the Wookiee Chewbacca. All of these reflect negotiations with the established order, negotiations of issues that emerged with the arrival of the gothic in modernity and that continue in the disestablished order of the postmodern gothic.

In the gothic world, as in the broader culture, all is in a state of flux. Family and society in the gothic imaginary appear transitory; filled with temporary alliances, groups unite to confront a particular issue and then morph into something else. Community is mobile, as is family. It is not blood that unites, but common cause, and common cause allows for strange bedfellows.

Changing attitudes toward sexuality are also a large part of the post-modern gothic.[99] The loss of stable social constructs has raised questions about gender and identity and has given rise to mainstream pornography and sexual exploration. Sexuality is extremely fluid in the gothic imaginary, and increasingly so in the culture as well, it is surely a "dominant discourse of power in the West." Loosed from traditional categorization, sexuality is a floating signifier.[100] Issues of gender are collapsed, and horizons and potential for new permutations of gender and sexuality are made possible. This in part seems to explain both the rise in public displays of cross-dressing, transgender, pansexual, and homoerotic imagery and the broad public acceptance of it all.

In the gothic imaginary, from the sexualized robots of *Bladerunner* to the potential for interspecies relations in Tim Burton's recent remake of *The Planet of the Apes*, the possibilities of sexuality are endless. The sexualizing of cartoon characters in Japanese anime is a reflection of both the different moral coding of Japanese life and the revelation of the gothic in the East. The transgressing nature of the gothic[101]—the crossing of social limits and boundaries—is made all the more potent by the loss of definition concerning these boundaries and limits within the culture. There are also links to issues of power and control. The rise of fetish sexuality and sadomasochism, with its very gothic black leather and rubber clothing, and the linking of sexuality and pain in many forms in the culture point to this. When a major Hollywood film (*Exit to Eden*) revolves around the comedic tale of two bumbling cops (played by popular comedians Rosie O'Donnell and Dan Aykroyd) who go undercover to an island resort devoted to bondage and sadomasochistic sex, you know times have changed. That deviant sex could be used as a comedic device demonstrates a widespread understanding (the comedic device depends on self-knowledge on the part of both the performer and the audience) of changing values toward sexuality.

Slavoj Žižek links this rise of new forms of sexuality, and particularly those that include domination, with the desire to "counterbalance the loss of official authority by invoking private laws or relationships of dominance or subjection. . . . When everyone has free choice, denying yourself that free choice becomes transgressive."[102] The transgressive nature of the gothic makes it a natural site for this experimentation and exploration.

How embracing the gothic in social relationships and sexuality allows for coping with uncertainty is not explicitly revealed. Given that the gothic functions beyond the domain of rational comprehension and works in the imagination through heightened feelings and emotions, the coping mechanisms must lie and remain buried there.

The dominant message attained through the gothic is "learn to live with mystery," and this is accomplished by sharpening one's instincts. Living with mystery is not simple resignation or passivity. Rather than seeking to restrain passion, the gothic finds in the wild embrace of passions and negative emotions a strength for dealing with the times. The negative emotions of fear, terror, horror, and sadness and the more fiery passions of anger and rage become means by which we learn to "fight back."

This impulse is revealed quite graphically in Chuck Palahniuk's novel *Fight Club*[103] and made even more visually explicit in the film of the same name, directed by David Fincher and starring Brad Pitt and Edward Norton. The film explores the life of men in a consumer society who come to epiphanic awakening through the formation of a secret "fight club" in which they are able to rediscover their ability to react and fight against a system that is draining the life from their souls. Through graphic and brutal bare-knuckle fights, they come to terms with the world around them and discover a renewed sense of themselves through their commitment to a new code of living based around the club they form.

The hero of the postmodern gothic is more often than not an ordinary person, who in moments of extreme danger or threat taps a heretofore unrealized set of skills. Wisdom seems to emerge commensurate with the escalating systems arrayed against that individual. It is in the realm of the imagination, the world of art and magic, that the tools to deal with postmodern uncertainty and postsecular complexity emerge. "This instinctive response to circumstance could be defined as 'creativity.'"[104] Here is a strategy for coping. Creativity is the weapon of choice in the postmodern world. A common sentiment seems to be that the more creatively we can interact with what life presents us, the better off we will be. In the gothic, this creative giftedness is not imparted or encouraged from without but is "drawn out from within" by the shock tactics and multiple layers of supernaturalism, alchemy, magic, and alternative sources of power for life that come from the complex and multidimensional space of the postmodern gothic imaginary.

Getting into the Habit: Neomedievalism

The ideal condition would be, I admit, that men should be right by instinct;
But since we are all likely to go astray, the reasonable thing is to learn from those who teach.

Sophocles, *Antigone*

A final element of this rubric is the new medievalism. Neomedievalism was a term first used in 1978 by French historian Alain Minc in his work *Le Nouveau Moyen Age*.[105] But to begin this section and give some overarching shape to this element of the postmodern gothic, I turn our attention to Umberto Eco, the popularizer of neomedievalism, and in particular his book *The Name of the Rose*, a gothic crime novel much like *The Da Vinci Code*. It concerns the story of a monk, William of Baskerville (a nod to Sherlock Holmes, and played in the movie version by Sean Connery), and his novice, Asdo (who narrates the story), whose arrival at a monastery is preceded and accompanied by a series of enigmatic murders. The monastery is, in fact, a scriptorium, dominated by a huge library where the monks work, translating and creating books.

Among the monks of the monastery, who are steeped in superstitious literalism, the murders are viewed in an apocalyptic light. Only Baskerville, who applies rationality to the events (à la Sherlock Holmes), sees other things afoot. At the heart of the story is a mysterious book (the novel being ultimately about texts) containing knowledge that is perceived as a threat by some but is greatly desired by others. The book is Aristotle's *Poetics*, a book on comedy. Baskerville's foil is Jorge, keeper of the library and orchestrator of the events behind the murders. Jorge's view is that if the book should fall into the wrong hands it would undermine the power and authority of the church and, in celebrating comedy, would turn the country lawless and disrespectful to authority. For Jorge, laughter is the enemy of truth and power. For Baskerville, the real horror is Jorge's perspective of superstitious and tyrannical oppression (linked to the injustice and cruelty of the Catholic Inquisition) that comes, in his view, from reading this and other texts in a singularly restricted and politically motivated manner. In contrast to this, Baskerville offers a different approach to texts, a rational one; but the rationality he offers is a different kind, one in which truth and reason are not seen as tools of the establishment and therefore subject to political and power motivations, but one that offers an approach to texts that leaves them open and plural, their meaning not limited to a single, homogenized interpretation.[106]

Baskerville, like his creator, is a semiotician, an interpreter of the signs and symbols in language. Much like Robert Langdon in *The Da Vinci Code*, Baskerville is not interested in taking things at face value. He wants to dig beneath the surface, read between the lines, and open up the meaning of the text, not to minimize its meaning but to maximize it. At the end of the story the great library is largely destroyed in a fire, as is much of the gloomy monastery. Before Baskerville and Asdo leave for the next leg of their pilgrimage, Asdo rummages through the library's ruins and collects some of the remains of the books: "I had before me a kind of lesser library; a symbol of the greater, vanished one; a library made up of fragments, quotations, unfinished sentences, amputated stumps of books."[107]

I rehearse this gothic tale of intrigue and end with this quote to highlight the nature of the new medievalism: it is a fragmentary view, comprised of a quote here, a book there, a clue, an intimation. More than anything it is the re-embodying of what is perceived as a defining element of medievalism—mystery. It is as if in looking to navigate the postsecular, attention is focused on the last place, at least in Western cultural history, that mystery seemed to play any part. I include this in the gothic rubric largely because the gothic emerged at a time when the Middle Ages were looked down on and carried the sentiments of that period within it. "The dominance of classical values produced a national past that was distinct from the cultivation, rationality and maturity of an enlightenment age. This past was called 'Gothic,' a general and derogatory term for the Middle Ages which conjured up ideas of barbarous customs and practice, of superstition, ignorance, extravagant fancies and natural wildness."[108] The revival of the gothic points to the inversion of values at work in contemporary culture. The enlightenment project has been rejected and in its place a resacralized environment has emerged. This has led to a resurgence of interest in a period of history largely rejected by the Enlightenment. The world of Dante, of Leonardo da Vinci, of St. Francis. These are the figures who had religious experiences before the Protestant Reformation, the Enlightenment, and the Age of Science. Their religion was lived out in an age of magic and alchemy, of spells and potions and astrology. This is the age of stigmata. Some claim that St. Francis was the first to carry these unexplained physical manifestations of the wounds of Christ celebrated in the film *Stigmata*. This was the age when religion was perceived to be less dogmatic and more open to the larger mysteries of the universe.

The new medievalism is found in books such as *The Da Vinci Code* and in the BBC's new version of Chaucer's *Canterbury Tales*, which lifts the stories from their historic setting and places them in the landscape of twenty-first century Britain. It is also found in Mel Gibson's film *The Passion of the Christ*, with its violent and bloody, and distinctly gothic, retelling of the Passion of Christ. The film's visual style was drawn from paintings from the pre-Reformation period, and its story line was drawn from the Bible and a host of apocryphal myths that grew up around the truth, such as Veronica's veil, upon which, according to legend, Christ left his image. This is the Christ Passion of medievalism; its resonance with Reformation Protestants is the result of shrewd marketing, temporary alliances (all Christians surrendering infighting to fight together to make Christ's story in the culture a success), and the turn toward the medieval (exhibited in the Protestant embrace of elements of Celtic Christianity, monasticism, labyrinths, contemplative prayer, and spiritual guides, much of it gathered under their own rubric of Ancient-Future).

Ancient-Future has a number of different locations within Christian circles, both Catholic and Protestant. That Catholics would explore the medieval is not as new of a dynamic as it is among the Protestant community. Chief among these developments is the rise of neomedievalism in decidedly evangelical communities. Robert Webber's book, *Ancient-Future Faith: Rethinking Evangelicalism for the Postmodern World*,[109] is a prime example of this shift, containing sections dealing with monasticism and medieval spiritual luminaries such as Bernard of Clairvaux. Apparently the future of evangelicalism lies firmly in the domain of the neo-gothic, embracing what the early Reformers reacted against on some levels. This is not surprising. For an arm of the Christian faith that is uniquely modern, the postmodern shift comes as something of a shock. Resources for dealing with the nonrational, the plural, and the mysterious are in short supply in evangelicalism, given its rationalizing tendencies.

This desire for the monastic is also reflected in the Emergent churches, particularly through the work of Andrew Jones,[110] who presently is in the process of developing a postmodern monastery on Stromness, one of the Orkney Islands and a former cradle of Celtic Christianity and Benedictine monasticism. Alongside Jones and others we find Karen Ward of the Church of the Apostles in Seattle, who is but one of a growing number of "urban-abbesses" who view their pastoral and missional roles much more in the light of monastic style and organization than in the more familiar hierarchies of traditionally pastor-led church groups. This neomedieval monasticism is emerging in even more charismatic evangelical communities, such as the Vineyard Churches of Canada, who have released a plan for "spiritual monasteries" all over the world.[111] These communities would practice ancient disciplines and seek to develop a new monasticism. Quoting Ignatius of Antioch, a significant aim of this new monasticism is demonstrated: "A man who has truly mastered the utterances of Jesus will also be able to apprehend His silence, and thus reach full spiritual maturity, so that his own words have the force of actions and his silences the significance of speech."[112] For a proclamation-based and expressive form of Christian faith, this desire for the power of silence marks a major shift in its theological grid and demonstrates the influence of entertainment theology on the church as much as on other seekers in the postsecular age.

The strains of medievalism are heard as well in the music of the Ancient-Future record label and particularly in the artistry of Loreena McKennitt, Enigma, and Delirium, all of whom produce music that is techno-mystic, a blend of Gregorian chant, medieval instrumentation, Sufism, the aroma of Byzantium, and electronica. This is the music of the new spiritual nightclubs, environments devoted as much to the celebration of mystery as to hedonism. *Spirit*, a club in Dublin,[113] is the first of a multimillion-dollar plan to develop seven clubs that cater to spirituality in major urban centers around the globe.

I began this section with a quote from the closing of Eco's book about the fragments of the library with which Asdo was left. Just as with Asdo, what we are left with is not a revival of full medievalism but an embrace of available fragments and pieces fashioned together in new permutations. This is particularly true of neomedieval monasticism and its disciplines. Much of the information gathered today is derived personally through interaction with books and Web sites rather than through community, at least as it was practiced in the Middle Ages. Today the communal interaction might well be temporary or transitional and there would be little in the way of structural hierarchy or authority at work. This is not to undermine what is occurring as much as it is to observe that this is yet another example of the reconfiguring of the past in the present. In fact, the fragmented nature of the content in this new interest in all things medieval is not as important as the mood—the feel of the medieval—the idea that there is something in the focus and style of the particular rubric that aids in navigating through the postmodern. Its very eclecticism is indicative of the plurality of ideas at work in the postsecular. If we place too much emphasis on refuting the content, we might miss the opportunity to engage with and address those who are obviously seeking to put some kind of framework, however vague, on "the divine."

There are other elements of the medieval reflected in the culture. These come in the form of paganism, particularly Wicca,[114] but also in events such as the Burning Man Festival.[115] All of these are shaped by some, if not all, of the dynamics of medievalism and the postmodern gothic. They all fall rather generally under more than one of the rubrics I have created, demonstrating the difficulty of firm categorization. Generally I would place these expressions here rather than in the New Age, where they are often placed by those of more traditional faith perspectives who tend to lump together all the things they can't define. Before we leave this rubric there remains a high-profile form of the new medievalism that has not yet been addressed. Given its growing interest and appeal in the postsecular dynamic, it warrants some discussion.

Mystical Codes and Modern Methods

Do you have questions about the secrets of the universe you would like answered? No problem, call 1-800-KABBALAH and a willing Kabbalist will be waiting to answer your deepest questions, twenty-four hours a day.

In something of a surprising move, Madonna, one of the most high-profile female celebrities and one of the world's most recognizable figures—pop star, movie actor, sexual explorer, and fashion icon—became a Kabbalist in 1998. The current public interest, no doubt fueled by a certain celebrity factor, is in Kabbalah. Medieval cool. That I place Kabbalah in this rubric might be contested by some who would classify it as New Age or isolate it as a particular form of Judaism. But given its emergence in the twelfth century, a decidedly medieval time, and its focus on mystery, I argue for Kabbalah's inclusion here. Yet, it is a very particular and specific version of Kabbalah that I reference regarding the new gothic and the rise of a people's religion. It is the twenty-first-century version of Kabbalah—pop-Kabbalah, and I mean no disparagement by this term—that I include here.

The first translation of the entire Zohar, the complete teachings of the Kabbalah, into modern Hebrew was not undertaken until the early twentieth century, and it took another hundred years for an English translation to be made available.[116] Kabbalah was a form of Judaism built around secret teachings drawn primarily from the books of Genesis and Ezekiel, and its very secret origins and meanings were long protected by the refusal of its practitioners to translate it into any vernacular language. This was a way to control who had access to the teachings of the Kabbalah, which in its earliest incarnations was an extremely obscure arm of Judaism. Thus the translation of the Kabbalah into the Western vernacular launched a veritable avalanche of interest. Approximately thirty thousand people a month sign up for an on-line class and more than 3.9 million people have gone through the doors of a Kabbalah Center.[117] This tremendous growth has been accomplished by removing the restrictions imposed by Kabbalists for centuries. These included, among others, prohibitions on anyone but married men over forty being able to participate in Kabbalism.

But what is Kabbalah? Zetter defines it as "the mystical, esoteric side of Judaism that delves into a deeper understanding of the Hebrew Bible beyond its literal interpretation to provide us with information about the soul; the nature of God, Creation, and the spiritual world; and about our individual relationship to God and each other."[118] An older interpretation of Kabbalah, dating from the mid-eighteenth century, says that it is like salt; it is not a food but rather something that adds flavor to other foods, bringing out their tastes. The emphasis in Kabbalah is on the mystical nature of the Hebrew Bible and involves a code found in Judaism.[119] It is about symbolism as much as anything else; for instance, the sip of wine tasted by faithful Jews on the Sabbath, according to Kabbalists, is meant to alert one to the nonvisible spirit world that lurks beyond the surface of the physical realm. In this it appeals to another aspect of the wider culture's ongoing fascination with secret messages, hidden meanings, and mysterious codes.

A perfect example of this fascination is the movie *National Treasure*, starring Nicolas Cage. It tells the story of a vast treasure amassed by the Knights Templar—a thirteenth-century military/monastic order who fought in the First Crusade—that has been hidden for centuries. The final location of the treasure is apparently in the United States. Members of a secret society were involved in the transportation of the treasure to this country, and they left a secret map, not visible to the naked eye, on the back side of a most hallowed American artifact: the Declaration of Independence. Crazy stuff, but it reflects a continuing cultural fascination with the deeper meaning in things. Seeking to go beyond the literal and factual, this fascination reflects a revival of mystery, the postmodern mythic. That this dynamic is expressed in both popular culture and contemporary religious formulations is again indicative of the symbiotic relationship between the two.

Kabbalah in the twenty-first century presents itself as both an ancient and a mysterious faith, but also as a nonreligion. "Kabbalah predates any religion or secular organization. It is the heritage and birthright of all humanity."[120] Madonna has frequently said that she is not religious and that Kabbalah is not a religion. In fact, the central tenet of the newest incarnation of Kabbalah is quite simple, according to its adherents: sharing. Kabbalists believe that there are two polarities for humans to live by: the will to receive and the will to bestow.[121] Fulfillment and joy in life are found by shifting from the egocentric "will to receive" to the communal "will to bestow," a posture of giving and learning to share, or of becoming a "being of sharing," to quote Philip Berg, founder of the Kabbalah Center in Los Angeles and pop-Kabbalah's chief architect.

Celebrating Celebrity

I introduce this form of people's religion under this rubric, not only to demonstrate the continuing development and use of premodern constructs as aids in the present context, but also to highlight an additional issue with regard to contemporary religious expression: the power of celebrity and the relationship between current religious expression and what could be termed the "cool factor." That interest in various religious ideas is often celebrity driven is evident in the role the entertainment industry, and media culture in general, plays in fashioning the cultural imaginary.

We have discussed Madonna and Kabbalah—one could also reference John Travolta or Tom Cruise and Scientology. But beyond such particular examples is a more general pattern in media culture that provides the various environments: cinematic, video, cyber, and literary in which information and ideas can be shared and explored. This is the philosophical domain of the contemporary religious; ideas reach the culture through "entertainment theology," which is defined as that which is disseminated through the various avenues of the media. The contemporary religious landscape is largely mediated through the various elements and avenues of popular culture, a populist movement (a "people's religion"), with populist methods of engagement and access. Entertainment theology arises from popular culture, which contains those things pertinent to the conversation: it reflects and shapes the cultural imaginary, it is the main site for the exchange of ideas in contemporary culture, and it serves as the lingua franca of the postmodern world—if you can't speak pop, there is a chance your ideas won't be heard.[122] Pop is the democratized space where classic philosophy and Japanese cartoons live side by side. The new media, and new medium, do the work of the old.[123]

Within this environment, celebrity is a legitimizing element. In the world of popular culture and entertainment theology, celebrity functions iconographically as the "communion of saints." In religious practices that employ icons, the faithful bow before the icon and "see beyond" the representation to the divine it represents. In popular culture, celebrity functions in a similar manner. Access to ideas and feelings about life (remember, the people's religion is a mood as much as it is a movement) are mediated via the celebrity gaze. This is because "celebrity is the main currency of our economy, the prime value in our news and the main impetus in our charitable works. It is the predominant means of the giving and receiving of ideas, information and entertainment. Nothing moves in our universe without the imprint of celebrity."[124]

The dynamics of celebrity are complex.[125] Celebrity is manufactured, not merited. Created initially as a publicity tool by the early Hollywood film studios, it is dependent for its survival on a veritable industry of behind-the-scenes activity.[126] What makes celebrity significant with regard to the present state of religion is the fact that, while they are persons elevated to some special status, celebrities remain persons. The importance of this dual perception cannot be overlooked, for it also refers to our attitude

New Edges

toward the litany of more iconic figures of traditional religious faith. The saints and martyrs were people like us, but they are also *special* in that they have achieved something extraordinary. Now, of course, a singular difference between the litany of ancient saints and the cult of celebrity is that ancient sainthood is a meritocracy. The elevation to sainthood is the result of a lifetime of singular devotion and self-sacrifice to the cause of the sacred, whereas celebrity is manufactured. But in consumer culture—a world of fantasy—wherein imagination is a function of social process, the manufacturing of celebrity status is not understood as a devaluation. As Twitchell points out, "The celebrity/priest is the central character of the commercial world. He (or she) has one foot in our world and one foot in the magical world of adland. He or she must be recognized as 'one of us' and 'one of them.'"[127]

Like a saint of old, the celebrity is the possession of both its manufacturer and the public. The church would regard itself to some degree as having proprietary rights over saints, since it is the creator of the hierarchy. But in gifting saints to the public, the church offers some possessive rights to those who embrace and employ the saint in their lives. The same is true of celebrity. Producers of consumer culture create the environment in which a particular celebrity emerges, but almost instantly that celebrity becomes the possession of the public.[128] In popular culture, what is produced becomes the possession of the consumers, and the consumers develop their own relationships with the product.

This idea of possession goes a long way toward explaining the meaning people often ascribe to particular songs, which may or may not be the intended meaning of the songwriter. Consider the song "Losing My Religion," written and performed by the rock group R.E.M. For many people this song has come to reflect either their feelings about their personal loss of faith or the broader culture's loss of trust in traditional religions. In reality, the song is about the demise of a relationship, and the title of the song is simply a poetic device to place the loss on a new level of significance. But with pop music, the meaning of a song is not found exclusively in the lyrics; it is also found in the emotional arc the song creates.

Music is a presentational rather than a discursive language.[129] The same process occurs in some sense with our use of saints; we reduce their lives to our own personal interaction with the iconized versions, which contain some elements of the reasons for their elevation to sainthood but hardly the full meaning. We define them by what they have come to represent, "so and so—the patron saint of whatever."

The same dynamic occurs with celebrity—we take them out of their original context and apply other meanings to their lives. In our present circumstance, this extends to celebrity as a viable legitimizer of religious and philosophical ideas. While Marshall McLuhan noted that "the medium is the message," he also noted that the "content of any medium is itself another medium."[130] Or to put it differently, every avenue of communication becomes the source of another one. Celebrity is both medium and message.[131]

Initially the function of celebrity was solely related to the selling of products. First, it was in the selling of the movies that the cult of celebrity emerged, but later this was expanded to include a wide range of consumer items. Attaching a celebrity to a product was viewed as an essential element of an advertising campaign and a guarantee of added sales.[132] The endorsement of a particular product by a celebrity was a means of developing trust between producer and consumer, the celebrity acting as guarantor for the integrity of a product. The function of celebrity in society has expanded greatly from this role as advertising tool. Trust in celebrity endorsement now extends beyond traditional consumer items—films, household products, clothing, etc.—to include the realm of philosophy and religion. If celebrities speak, we see their views as significant, whether or not they actually know much about a particular subject.[133]

Hence, celebrity plays a role in politics; they are actively sought out for their opinions on a broad range of social topics. Their comments legitimize the conversation on the level of popular perception. Consider the galvanizing efforts of pop star Bob Geldof in raising public awareness of the plight of millions starving in Africa. He succeeded in raising millions of dollars for relief efforts. Or consider the charitable group DATA, initiated by Bono, lead singer of the band U2, which brought the issues of third-world debt relief and AIDS relief into the public spotlight. Bono was named "*Time* Person of the Year" in 2005, along with Bill and Melinda Gates, for his considerable achievement in raising awareness and money for AIDS relief and a host of other challenging social issues. Bono has addressed the United Nations, the Davos Foundation, church leadership conferences at Willow Creek, and the campuses of colleges and seminaries, using his powerful celebrity to effect change.

Celebrities, simply by their involvement, make things "cool." To the uninitiated, the idea of "cool" might seem inconsequential, but it is the currency of contemporary culture. When things are cool they have a better chance of capturing the cultural imagination.

Capturing Cool

Barely fifty years old, rising with the emergence of pop culture, "cool" is "destined to become the dominant ethic among the younger generations of the whole developed world."[134] People would rather be perceived as cool than good; it is a postmodern virtue. Cool is first and foremost a dynamic of the psyche. It is something that emerges in people's attitudes to things, not something inherent in the artifacts themselves.[135] Our attitude, our perception of things, determines their value. The reality of all this is that something being cool or not cool can determine its success or appeal to a large degree. Cool is mutable, changing from place to place, time to time, a reflection of the transitory nature of the times. This does not bode well for traditional faiths. At this point in the cultural imaginary, Buddhism is cool and Christianity is not. At least the cultural idea of Christianity is not cool: institutional, hierarchical, right wing,[136] decidedly modern and out of touch.

Surprisingly, or not so perhaps, Jesus remains cool. It's just his official earthly representation—the church—that has been deemed "uncool." This is reflected in the continued cultural interest in Jesus,[137] which extends, for example, even to T-shirts made by Urban Outfitters—purveyors of hip and cool clothing for young people in shopping malls around the world—that are emblazoned with dechurched Jesus slogans, such as "Jesus is my Homeboy" and "Jesus surfs without a board." The perception that in spite of his "religious affiliations" Jesus remains cool and is a subject of interest in the postmodern matrix extends to a continuing number of publications, books, and magazines devoted to wresting Jesus away from the authority and confines of the Christian church.

This trend takes a number of forms. The desire to wrest Jesus away from the institutions deemed by many to have too strong a claim on Jesus falls under the rubric of entertainment theology because much of it tends to be populist in nature, which is not to say that it is without substance but rather that it is without academic fencing. This is theology with a larger populist intention, the ultimate goal being the "saving" of Jesus, to quote a recent title.[138] Saving Jesus from what exactly? The stultifying, smothering confines of the church, and particularly the fundamentalists or conservatives, who, the consensus seems to say, have done Jesus a grave injustice by making him out to be what he obviously is not. In other words, Jesus has been made out to be just like them—uptight, overly religious in the pejorative sense, lacking a sense of humor, and disconnected from the way things really are. Quoting John L. Peterson, the secretary-general of the

Anglican Consultive Council in 1995, Bruce Bawer writes: "In certain parts of the world the word Christian has become an embarrassment because it has become aligned with movements which are contrary to the Loving Christ[139] that is at the heart of our message. I hold my head in shame to hear Jesus' name being affiliated with political movements that isolate, inhibit and breed hate and discontentment between human beings."[140] Other titles, such as Donald Spoto's *The Hidden Jesus*,[141] offer a similar result but use the mysterious "hidden" life of Jesus as his calling card. The idea that there are things about Jesus that have been missed, even by his contemporaries, is a major arena of discussion and engagement in the ongoing cultural conversation about Jesus. As one might expect, such conversation takes place largely outside the domain and confines of the church.

But, back to Madonna. Madonna is cool. She remains one of the most recognizable and admired celebrity icons today, and Madonna's endorsement makes Kabbalah cool. On one level, it really is that simple. How this plays out and whether public interest in Kabbalah will continue depends largely on reaction to its teaching after the initial excitement about its ideas and philosophies wears off. My instinct is that it will lose its present high profile and be absorbed into the larger pool of ideas, philosophies, and tools that are being employed to fashion the new religious imaginary. For now it remains under the rubric of the new gothic and is part of the neomedievalism at work in the postsecular age.

One final note about medievalism. The media culture, in spite of the hegemony of multinational media corporations, is going through a medieval experience itself. Because of disappointment with mainstream media—news media in particular—and continued developments in communications technology, media culture is developing new sites to gather, disseminate, and discuss ideas. I emphasize *discussion* because in the present climate participation and interaction are key, and many of the traditional forms of media are either unable or unwilling to provide avenues of interaction— they prefer to remain authoritarian mediators of information. Alternative arenas have thus emerged, particularly the Internet and blogs.[142] This "medievalism" is captured by Orville Schell of the Berkeley School of Journalism: "The Roman Empire that was mass media is breaking up, and we are entering an almost-feudal period where there will be many centers of power and influence."[143] Mass media and mass communication have gone the way of all the other totalizing ideologies of modernity, experiencing their own democratizing tendencies. In the postsecular, media represent a democratized site, a pluralized conglomeration of feudal sites of the cultural imaginary. The feudal nature of the media is a result of the reaction against the dominant ideologies of the major media conglomerates and the assertion of a concurrent people's media, which allow for a democratized, pluralized view of the present condition.

We turn attention now to a final rubric, one that would seem to be a singular element of the gothic. I choose to deal with it as a separate entity because it reflects a predominantly large portion of the reactions to and manifestations of the more traditional and particularly monotheistic faiths, namely, postsecular fundamentalism and the emergence of resistant communities.

Strong-Arming the World: The Rise of Resistant Communities

> The present-day fundamentalist movements are the true children of our time: unwanted children, perhaps, bastards of computerization and unemployment or of the population explosion and increasing literacy, and their cries and complaints in these closing years of the century spurs us to seek out their parentage and to retrace their unacknowledged genealogy. Like the workers' movements of yesteryear, today's religious movements have a singular capacity to reveal the ills of society, for which they have their own diagnosis.
>
> Gilles Kepel, *Radical Islam*

> Postmodernism celebrates evanescent flows, a state of no boundaries, the transgressive. If this sounds familiar, it is because these values are shared by the most ardent architects of both consumerism and capitalist globalization.
>
> John Zerzan, *Greasing the Rails to a Cyborg Future*

> Your religion consists of a few vague notions and empty expressions. The only place that will get you is hell.
>
> Street Preacher, Santa Monica, July 2004

The street preacher quoted above[144] is a published author and cohost of a weekly television program on a major Christian television network. For three months in the summer of 2004, I watched as he and a few coworkers attempted to engage the citizens of Santa Monica, along with numerous tourists, panhandlers, homeless, and packs of young people, with the "truth about Jesus." Their modus operandi was the same. They placed a dummy, covered with a white cloth and wearing Nike sports shoes, on the ground[145] in front of a small raised platform where the speaker stood. Next to this was an easel that held a few fairly large laminated posters, including a list of the Ten Commandments, a version of John 3:16, and a picture of the ascent of man from ape to human. A few feet away a microphone was set up. Each week I watched the same thing unfold again and again. One of the group would step up onto the platform and begin to preach. The content was essentially the same every time, as was the delivery. It was an angry declaration of God's impending judgment on a godless culture that was filled with lust, greed, and of course, sin. The entire time I watched them, they never drew more than twenty people, and that crowd would dissipate very quickly once the scenario progressed to the next level of damnation and judgment. After two or three people had preached, they would yell to passersby and invite them to ask any question they liked about God. This was their crowd-gathering device. Eventually some brave soul would step up to the microphone and their public humiliation would begin. It is not necessary to unfold the entire progression. Suffice it to say that unless the questioners agreed to affirm that Jesus was the only way to salvation and that they were a "born-again, Bible-believing Christian," they were harangued. They were told that their questions were pointless, as they were too fallen to be able to have an opinion of any value. It was disturbing to watch this week in and week out, and I never saw a positive result.[146]

In a discussion with one of the coworkers, I asked him what he thought they were accomplishing by this process. "We're telling people the good news." When I asked him to define "good news," he did so in negative terms, although he failed to understand this. He replied that the "good news" was that people were sinners and they were going to go to hell if they didn't repent of their sins. When I asked why he felt that the good news could only be couched in negative terms, he said that was the way "Jesus did it." When I asked him to show me in the Bible where Jesus took this approach, he resisted. When I asked him about their emphasis on using the Ten Commandments and wondered why those command-ments and not Jesus's commandment to love one another were used, he said that the Ten Commandments and keeping the Law were what it meant to be a real Christian. On noting the apparent lack of success of their approach, he replied that this was because people were godless and were blinded to the truth by Satan. We talked a little about the current rise of interest in spirituality and what he made of it. He said it was all worthless. Only Christianity was a real religion; the rest were New Age bunk and demonically inspired traps. In this he echoed the declarations from the platform.

I rehearse all of this to note that within the horizons of the new religious exploration and the emergence of a people's religion there lies a somewhat surprising turn to postmodern fundamentalism. I say postmodern fundamentalism because this is fundamentalism, or fundamentalisms, to be more accurate, that is firmly rooted in the postmodern turn. This fundamentalism may be viewed as a reaching back to premodern times in an attempt to insert some kind of religious orthodoxy, but rather than viewing it as an outburst of premodern irrationality, it is better seen as the iteration of an *alternative* rationality.[147] If modern fundamentalism raged against the "godless human being"[148] and the secular society that produced it, then postmodern fundamentalism directs its focus at both perceived notions of continuing secularity and the "empty religiosity" of the times. It presents itself as an alternative to the postmodern rationale, but it is, in fact, a product of that rationale. Postmodern fundamentalism is postmodern in part, in that it is publicly assertive, neotribal, and the result both indirectly and directly of globalization. Each claim warrants discussion.

First, by publicly assertive I mean that postmodern fundamentalism is firmly situated in the marketplace of ideas. It is but one of the many "voices from the margins" that postmodern philosophy has allowed to return. It is truly a "voice from below." But it is heard not merely in the railings of a street preacher here and there, for it is engaged in the public conversation, whether it be Jerry Falwell on *Crossfire* or Osama Bin Laden via Al-Jazeera. It is also directly engaged, if not obsessed, with the "other."

Part of the postmodern dynamic was the dismantling of the totalizing ideologies of modernity, as in Lyotard's "end of ideologies" or Derrida's deconstruction of totalization of all its forms. This was partly accomplished by the celebration of difference and the other.[149] This validation of the other, whether it be in the realm of cultural identity or philosophical idea, is the introduction of a new plurality—a level playing field where no singular hegemony exists and no idea or culture reigns. Here again is a central tenet of the postmodern.

Postmodern fundamentalism does not focus as much on its own world as it does the world of the other. It addresses others as if they were subject to its own set of values. This is the politics of difference rather than the celebration of difference; it reacts to the rise and perceived threat of the other, but at least the other is recognized. This is by no means a unified reaction. Islamic fundamentalism rises against the perceived threat of global capitalism, driven, in their view, by the imperialist and expansionist desires of the West. Christian fundamentalism focuses more on the other as a new religious move afoot in postsecular culture, which is perceived as anti-Christian, ungodly, and not the "truth." In this, then, it becomes a "set of strategies by which beleaguered believers attempt to preserve their distinctive identity, as a people or group, in response to a real or imagined attack from those who apparently threaten to draw them into a 'syncretistic, areligious, or irreligious' cultural milieu."[150] The social changes that have occurred have created great tension and anxiety within certain groups, more often than not within those groups associated with monotheistic faith.

This postmodern fundamentalism is linked not only to the issue of faith, for there are other fundamentalisms afoot as well. And, much like the gothic rubric, it is haunted by the uncertainty of a "community of desire."[151] In a commodified culture where consumer choice reigns and where desire without "proper object" (a view widely held by those of traditional faith persuasion) attends the cultural imaginary, fundamentalism functions as the politics of fear. Not simply in its outward manifestations but also in its inward processing of the present state of affairs, it lives in the apocalyptic twilight, seeing nothing but disaster on the horizon. As Bauman points out, "if typical modern fears were related to the threat of totalitarianism . . . postmodern fears arise from uncertainty as to the soundness and reliability of advice offered through the politics of desire. . . . Diffuse fears crystallize in the form of a suspicion that the agencies promoting desire are . . . oblivious or negligent of the damaging effects of their proposals."[152]

Fundamentalism in the postmodern also exists in the interregnum, the in-between time of the present moment, when the future has yet to come into full view. It is a reaction to the present circumstance and the sense that the hold of certain groups on the cultural imaginary is either lost or waning. Salman Rushdie defines the present relationship between Islam and the West as one that characterizes this interregnum (defined by Antonio Gramasci), in which "the old refuses to die, so that the new cannot be born, and all manner of morbid symptoms arise."[153]

Second, postmodern fundamentalism is neotribal. It is not tribal in the sense of particular ethnic identity, but it is neotribal in that it is the construction of tribal identity by individual association. Bauman expands on the idea of neotribalism as suggested by Michael Maffesoli and posits that the neotribes are formed as "concepts rather than integrated social bodies, by the multitude of individual acts of self-identification."[154]

The number of foreign fighters in Iraq, fighting with the Iraqi insurgents against the United States–led Coalition forces, is but one example of neotribalism. On some levels, this neotribalism echoes the gothic in that it presents the collapse of particular tribal identity in order to effect newer configurations. Or to put it another way, former and ongoing differences or particularities might be suspended in order to allow for an arrayed and united front against the "enemy" of all tribes in the neotribes purview. Appadurai speaks of "deterritorialization" and argues that "ethnoscapes," the global flow of peoples in various forms of transition both permanent and impermanent, contribute to the new global fundamentalism. "Deterritorialization, whether of Hindus, Sikhs, Palestinians, or Ukrainians, is now at the core of a variety of global fundamentalisms, including Islamic and Hindu fundamentalism."[155] The positive side of deterritorialization is that new markets are created for goods and services that link those deterritorialized with their homeland. But there is also exploitation from a number of sources that results in the linking of cultural reproduction to fundamentalism.

"Religious neotribalists have lost their connection to place but still function as 'community.' . . . Religion in its post-institutional phase seems to have become more cultural resource than a fixed identifiable entity."[156] This neotribalism is a means of creating a reductionist construct in which those who feel embattled by the uncertainty of postmodern life can retreat into a narrow "certainty" linked to particular responses to the current state of affairs. Manuel Castells, in a nod to the individuality that fuels neotribalism, terms it a "resistant identity," that it is, in fact, one more example of the fluid nature of the self in postmodernity. Postmodern fundamentalism is a choice, an identity construct, made in a consumer culture in which religion has been commodified. "The commodification and marketing of religious ideas as a set of lifestyle choices is highly advanced and thus, highly deterritorialized."[157]

Third, as already intimated, the emergence of postmodern fundamentalism is intrinsically linked with the globalizing tendencies of the postmodern era. "Human society is globalizing to the extent that human relationships and institutions can be converted from experience to information, to the extent it is arranged in space around the consumption of simulacra rather than the production of material objects, to the extent that value-commitments are badges of identity, to the extent that politics is the pursuit of lifestyle."[158] The indirect means by which globalization contributes to the rise of fundamentalism is related to the fact that the present state of affairs means that we all get to experience one another in previously unforeseen ways. The interconnectedness of the postmodern allows us to share in global triumph and despair and to experience the discontents of both modernity and postmodernity on a world scale. John Donne may have written that "no man is an island," but in the postmodern world, "no *island* is an island." In other times, religions may have been protected from these discontents, but now "religious systems are obliged to relativize themselves to global postmodernizing trends."[159] This relativizing can result in an embrace of the postmodern patterning, which Waters terms an *abstract humanistic ecumenism*. But it can also take the form of a "rejective search" for original traditions.[160]

Waters views this through a decidedly modernist lens. What he views as abstract ecumenism, a sort of theoretical unity based on universal ideas about the inherent similarity of religion, is a long way from the present condition as it emerges in the postsecular. I view the present situation not as a move toward some abstract ecumenism but as the shift toward *rhizomic sacralization*.[161] Poynor offers the following description of a rhizome: "Where trees have roots, linking them to a single point of origin, plants such as grasses and bamboos have an underground network of stems, a rhizome, which can sprout new plants at any point."[162]

Rhizomes also exist between things, forming a layer of contact between different elements. They are horizontal networks rather than root systems, which lead to a single point of origin. Rather than leading to a single point of origin, postmodernizing patterns lead to a complex web of interrelated ideas about the nature of the religious. This recalls our earlier discussion about the movie *Waterworld* and the idea of "surface as depth"—the fetishization process. Here is the "new depth." It is horizontal rather than vertical and derives breadth and depth from a wide range of influences gleaned from the interconnected surface of the rhizomic grid. Rather than digging down to a collective bedrock, a web of interconnected ideas forms a cover over the contours of postmodernity. This is a reflection of the leveling of the philosophical playing field in the postmodern situation wherein any number of diverse ideas are granted equal importance and are not categorized in a hierarchical manner. Ideas and philosophical constructs are exchanged across disciplines and fields with little regard for the boundaries set by modernity.

What Waters views as ecumenism[163] hints at universalism. The idea of religion as a tree, with each religion representing a particular branch in which all connect back to the trunk, is not the result of the postmodern embrace either. Rather than "ecumenism," I term it "sacralization," that is, the rejection of a single point of origin or particular religious hegemony in favor of a new contextualization of the religious. Here a plurality of interconnected ideas weave a complex web of potentialities from which new permutations can emerge. Rather than a theoretical unity based on ultimate similarity (abstract ecumenism), there is instead *actual* unity based on dissimilarity, or on the celebration of difference. This allows for the inclusion of those with no clearly defined concept of God in the traditional understanding to fall within the category of the "religious" in the postmodern context. At present, the shape of this rhizome follows the contours I have identified so far. What has emerged is a complex combination of permutations from within generally defined categories. This is the bricolage of the postmodern. The term "bricolage" was introduced by C. Levi-Strauss in his work *The Savage Mind*. He defines it as something that may be put together from available materials. It is an open-source enterprise that is both rational and improvised, the perfect postsecular mix.

To return to Waters for a moment, the direct relation of fundamentalism to globalization is linked to four interlocking developments: (1) Western cultural preference in the emerging global culture requires local particularism to be legitimated on Western terms, which means that the Universal Declaration of Human Rights is something that must be faced by all nations as the issue of the rights of women in things such as female genital circumcision is increasingly confronted; (2) the changing state of the nation-state society due to globalization, which results in a denial of superior allegiances to a church or particular gods; (3) the secularization and abstraction of law as the basis for social order; and (4) the establishment of the fact that the world is pluralistic and choice-driven and that there is not a single and superior culture.[164] I will not dwell on these points, as discussion over the demise of the nation-state, the challenge of human rights on the global scene, and the rising presence of international law (which countries such as the US agree to in principle, as long as it does not apply to them in the same manner) requires more space than can be allotted here.

Within the emergence of certain religious impulses in the postsecular, there are connections that can be made between these impulses and shifting globalization issues. For instance, international law challenges such things as *Sharia*, or Islamic law, which no longer fits into the global legal and ethical framework because of its rather brutal sense of religious justice. This development means that religions and religious cultures must wrestle with issues that emerge from outside their former horizons, forcing them to react to a larger social situation daily growing exponentially out of their control. Fundamentalism exists in a pluralized world. It functions within the horizon of a world that not only is conscious of but also legitimizes plurality (this is the horizontal aspect of the rhizome perspective). Fundamentalism also exists in its own pluralized state, where there is actually an amalgam of various fundamentalisms. "The Imam already lives next door to the Orthodox priest, the Quaker shares a taxi with the Christian evangelical, the Rabbi sits on a civic board with the Sikh. Words slip and slide."[165]

Bruce Lawrence offers three categories of fundamentalists: literalist, terrorist, and political activist.[166] Karen Armstrong notes that the roots of fundamentalism lie in the desire of certain groups of Christians to distance themselves from what is considered to be a liberal position by going back to the basics of Christian faith and reemphasizing the "fundamentals" of Christian faith, which is identified with a literal interpretation of Scripture and the acceptance of certain core doctrines.

Today, fundamentalism is an even more pejorative term. What has been lost in the cultural disdain is the originally intended nuance of meaning and manifestation. "It seems to suggest that fundamentalism is monolithic in all its manifestations. This is not the case. Each 'fundamentalism' is a law unto itself and has its own dynamic."[167] The early-twentieth-century version of fundamentalism reacted against secularism and science-based rationalism; today's version reacts to the postsecular situation. The paradox of fundamentalism is that it depends on difference for survival.[168] Fundamentalism needs an enemy, something to react against, for its survival. The early incarnation of fundamentalism was convinced the modern world was intent on destroying religion; postmodern fundamentalism is convinced either that the West is out to actively destroy its presence (particularly in the rise of Islamic fundamentalism) or that the West is out to actively destroy Christianity by drowning the world in a sea of generic spirituality that has room for everything but Christianity.[169] Neither perspective is true. "Fundamentalism's strident denunciation of its opponents is a sign of its weakness, its dogmatic authoritarianism is a pathological mutation of faith."[170]

To briefly broaden the conversation, there are signs of fundamentalist tendencies in many other areas of popular culture, such as the Dogme 95 approach to filmmaking developed by Lars Von Trier that has at its heart a reactionary response to the direction film is taking philosophically, commercially, and creatively. Dogme 95 is a purity movement seeking to put the brakes on what is occurring. Fundamentalist tendencies are also seen in the increasing polarization of television news and its purported right-wing

New Edges

bias or left-wing prejudice, depending on which side of the fundamentalist mouth is speaking. There are fundamentalist vegans, radically emphatic about their beliefs concerning raw foods and aggressively committed to the public assertion of their beliefs and opinions. PETA, the animal rights society, is equally aggressive in its proclamations, going so far as to picket cooking shows that boil lobsters. All this to say that at present there are fundamentalisms everywhere.

But let's return to religion. My friends witnessing on the street in Santa Monica are a good example of literalist fundamentalism. They take the Bible literally, so literally that they cannot even allow, almost not even conceive of, a position other than their own. They echo the approach of Jorge, the superstitious literalist of Eco's novel who was the nemesis of William of Baskerville. Jorge's singular reading of the text, taking everything at face value, precludes him from seeing the possibility of other horizons in his own faith.

The above-mentioned street preachers also represent one of the chief obstacles to traditional faiths in the twenty-first century. "A good part of the problem with religion is religious people,"[171] writes John Caputo, capturing what is a common reaction to the aggressively religious in our time. Author and avowed atheist Sam Harris released a book late in 2006 titled *Letter to a Christian Nation*, which was a response to often vitriolic and threatening communications he had received from large numbers of Christians about his previous book, *The End of Faith*, which explores the links between religious faith and violence. "Faced with a new Babylon, or a new Sodom, the fundamentalists clench their fists around the Word of God, which seems to them the one constant in a world gone mad. . . . The crazier the quilt of the world, the more tenaciously they clutch the letter and the more tightly they draw the net of a literalist religion,"[172] so says Caputo, and I couldn't agree more. Fundamentalism in our time is one of the mainstream theological issues I mentioned much earlier; it is here to stay and we must face the implications of it head on.

To explore the dynamic of postmodern fundamentalism in the context of the rise of entertainment theology, I direct our attention to one of the most contested religious books in recent years: Salman Rushdie's *The Satanic Verses*. This book is a work of fiction, but it is also a work of theology.

"To be born again," sang Gibreel Farishta tumbling from the heavens, "first you have to die. Ho ji! Ho ji! To land upon the bosomy earth, first one needs to fly. Tat-taa! Taka-thun! How to ever smile again, if first you won't cry? How to win the darling's love, mister, without a sigh? Baba, if you want to get born again . . ." Just before dawn one winter's morning, New Year's Day or thereabouts, two real, full-grown, living men fell from a great height, twenty-nine thousand and two feet, towards the English Channel, without benefit of parachute or wings, out of a clear sky.[173]

These opening lines of Rushdie's controversial novel also opened a new chapter in the brief history of postmodernity, as a new and reactionary form of fundamentalism rushed into the public psyche.

Bradford, a predominantly working-class town in northern England, whose glory days had passed with the end of the Industrial Age and thus is now characterized by a large immigrant population from mostly former colonial countries with Muslim citizens, was the herald of our entry into a brave new world of global religious fundamentalism. On January 4, 1989, a public, and very organized, book burning was held in the middle of Bradford. The object of the burning was Rushdie's book. There had been other protests, but somehow this event gained both national and international attention,[174] introducing a new and hostile element into the cultural imaginary: the rise of postmodern fundamentalism.

Rushdie's book galvanized the Islamic community because it was ultimately a theological clash; it was the sound of entertainment theology and the new religious colliding head on with a traditional faith that had not yet come to terms with the changing shape of the world. Waters notes that the emergence of the postmodern had direct effect on countries that were used to a more enclosed sense of national identity.[175] But just as the shape of global flows and politics was changing, so was Islam. The Islamic Revolution in Iran, which gave rise to a new Islamic state under the Sharia (Islamic law), occurred in 1979 under the guidance of Ayatollah Khomeini. Relations between the Middle East and the West have long been fraught with tension, but the rise of a theocracy in the latter decades of the twentieth century was confusing to many in the West.

This revolution captured the attention of Britain in particular. Other protest events had occurred, but they had failed to make a dent in the public conversation. Two specific components helped galvanize this particular protest. The first was the level of vitriol directed against a particular person. "Rushdie Must Die," the slogan on a number of placards at the book burning, seemed to catapult the issue onto a new trajectory, introducing a new and violent clash between private and public opinion.[176] This clash between the public and private nature of faith extends beyond this situation. Bawer notes that a similar issue is at work in the dynamics of Christian fundamentalism, in that the fundamentalists, whom Bawer defines as legalist or literalist interpreters of Jesus,[177] take their faith public and apply it to those for whom it is not even a religious reality. By contrast, the more silent, nonlegalistic arm of the church is still used to keeping matters of faith private. The postsecular context is a confusing one in that, while religion is a matter of public resource and discourse, its appropriation and creation are a highly individualized and private matter. The idea of outside imposition of values is anathema to the present context.[178] The second component was that this event introduced a new term into the British public's vernacular: Islamic Fundamentalism.

Reaction to the book began to spread throughout the world. On February 13, 1989, a number of Muslim protesters were shot at by police in Pakistan while they were angrily demonstrating against the book, and this was after similar protests and reactions in other Muslim nations. The next day was a landmark one in the history of religion in the West. From Iran, four months before his death, the Ayatollah Khomeini issued a proclamation:

> The author of the *Satanic Verses*, a text written, edited, and published against Islam, against the Prophet of Islam, and against the Qur'an, along with all editors and publishers aware of its contents, are condemned to capital punishment. I call on all valiant Muslims wherever they may be in the world to execute this sentence without delay, so that no one henceforth will dare insult the sacred beliefs of Muslims.[179]

This proclamation put the world on a new path and initiated the rise of a new kind of reactionary religion. Reactionary, that is, to its own new context, namely, the world. We see in this proclamation elements of Bauman's neotribalism—"Muslims wherever they may be in the world"—and Castells's view of "resistant identity." In her masterful work *The Battle for God*, Karen Armstrong notes that Khomeini's proclamation concerning *The Satanic Verses* came shortly after he, aware of Islam's changing relationship with the world, had initiated his own version of democracy, one in which the religious faith of the people could blend with the pressure to modernize and enter into wider relations with the rest of the world.

What exactly was Rushdie's blasphemous crime? It should be noted that it *was* indeed blasphemous, though from a certain Islamic perspective that was reductionistic in its own way. The title of the book refers to a hotly contested and familiar passage in the Qur'an, the sacred book of Islam that contains the words of the Prophet. In the midst of a revelation to the Prophet Muhammad that affirmed the absolute Oneness of God, the devil is said to have taken the form of the Archangel Gabriel, the one providing the revelation, to extol the virtues of certain goddesses in the pre-Islamic pantheon. The Prophet later amended this, but it remains a sore point within Islam. In suggesting in his novel that the Qur'an had been tainted by satanic influence and by presenting Muhammad as a "lecher, a tyrant and a charlatan,"[180] Rushdie simply crossed the line for some Muslims. That this was a much-debated issue within Islam was irrelevant; this was blasphemous to the Ayatollah, and Rushdie must pay the price.

At its heart, the Rushdie affair has allusions to the novel *The Name of the Rose*. Eco's narrative depicts the clash between Jorge the textual literalist, who is the fundamentalist of this story and who keeps a tight grip on anything that might threaten his superstitious beliefs, and William of Baskerville, a man of faith in changing and modern times who wishes to liberate his faith from its one-dimensional interpretation. In calling Qur'anic revelation into question, Rushdie walks the same path as Baskerville. He wishes to open up, not destroy, the possibility of differing views of the text, but the other parties resist. That Rushdie's novel opens with the words "to be born again" points to the ultimate purpose of the tale and the subtle contexts of the situation. Rushdie is a native of the East—India—but a citizen of the West. He is a Muslim by birth but not by practice. Still, he wants to open up the faith of his heritage and he employs a Western, and familiarly Christian, religious slogan to announce his intent. Nourrredine Saadi writes: "In his response to the zealots, Rushdie lucidly sets the stakes: 'Dr. Aadam Aziz, the patriarch of my novel *Midnight's Children*, loses his faith and is left with "a hole in him, a vacancy in a vital inner chamber." I also have this same hole left by God within me. Incapable of accepting the indisputable absolutes of religion, I have tried to fill the hole with literature.'"[181] For Rushdie, the employ of his imagination is to fill a hole left by his inability to accept the absolutes of religion that allow for no dialogue, no dispute, and no discussion. Literature becomes sacred for Rushdie, and yet, ironically, he uses what he regards as sacred to undermine what is viewed as sacred by the other side. It is the clash of the postmodern imagination and the self-preservation of the resistors. This is the complex dichotomy and reality in which postmodern fundamentalism exists.

The Rushdie affair is a battle. A battle between a man who has a "hole left by God," who uses writing to fill it, and a group for whom the protection of their community and the sacred text that gives rise to it is paramount. The dominant topic of *The Satanic Verses*, for which he received a death sentence, is the revitalization of the faith of his ethnic identity, Islam. But it is Islam in a new context, acknowledging its pluralistic potentiality. In a stunningly insightful essay, Zhor Ben Chamsi, a Moroccan writer and Muslim, writes that it is in fact the fundamentalists, the issuers of the fatwa,[182] who are the real blasphemers in the affair. He notes the unique events and circumstances of the affair: the fact that a "judge, a man" takes the place of God and orders every Muslim to commit murder and that this is done within a religion that considers faith a personal issue. But it is his comments on Rushdie that speak to the present situation and the role of the imaginary as something of vital importance to traditional faiths:

> Rushdie, for the first time, made use of certain elements from a Koranic text and from Muslim tradition; he did this for purposes related to the writing of fiction. He treated the sacred word as it happened to affect both the real and imaginary worlds of a modern Muslim living in London. Given the reigning orthodoxy, however, it would appear that the word of God could never germinate in this way; or ever be fecundated by the imaginary; or ever be made to appear as a myth from which to continue indefinitely building on.[183]

Here a Muslim argues for embracing the postmodern. He employs imagination, the tool of postmodern social production (Appadurai), as a means of revitalizing Islam. He challenges what he terms the "reigning orthodoxy," and believing it is not necessarily legitimate orthodoxy, he critiques its inability to be able to see that "any good could come of this venture,"[184] opting instead for the use of violence as a viable means of self-protection!

Another Muslim writer points out that the Qur'an itself affirms that the real book of truth lies within God alone and that the Qur'an is but a "readable copy of the timeless original" that "adopts a plurality of laws, languages, peoples, and readings."[185] Like most faiths, Islam is not a monolithic faith, but Muslim fundamentalism seeks to make it so, as do other forms of fundamentalism be they Christian or Buddhist. Benslama notes that Muslims long ago stopped studying and reflecting on their origins and opted instead for rehearsing that which has actually created a divide between the human and the transcendent. In this, to be a "Muslim today is to dance along the edge of an abyss."[186]

Rushdie is a marvelous writer who makes full use of language and imagination, creating worlds of complex beauty. *Satanic Verses* is filled with magical realism, a dominant tool of the postmodern imaginary. Dreams, visions, angels, and prophets are all interwoven in the story of two men falling to earth, Gibreel and Saladin. Their falling to earth is indicative of the novel's intent to address both the instability and the volatility of the postmodern world. That they fall from an exploding plane called *Bostan*, "garden" in Arabic,[187] only adds to the singular intention of his writing, for his is a quest for the meaning of existence in light of our banishment from the garden. The book challenges religious, national, and cultural orthodoxies, rejecting "fixed identities,"[188] the bane of the postmodern imagination. It is a novel whose purpose is to challenge settled habits and lazy authority. What takes place in the novel is a retelling, a recapitulation, of the story of the birth of Islam. These two men (or are they angels falling to earth?) who fall from an exploding airplane land in a world in which their miraculous escape from certain death sends them on a journey to the heart of faith, life, and God. Throughout the story they explore questions of ultimate meaning within the context of Islam, their "long standing rejecting of the eternal now beginning to look pretty foolish." In the particular encounter that comprises the book's title and the challenging event in the life of the Prophet, there is an insightful section that alludes to both the textual challenge dormant in the birth story of Islam and the *con*textual challenge of postmodern times:

> "I? Who am I?" Gibreel was startled into absurdity. The other nodded. . . .
> "These are problematic times, sir, for a moral man. When a man is unsure
> of his essence, how may he know if he be good or bad?" . . . "Tending as
> I do towards the pantheistic view . . . my own sympathy arises out of your
> willingness to portray deities of every conceivable water. You, sire, are a
> rainbow coalition of the celestial, a walking United Nations of gods! You
> are, in short, the future." . . . "I incline, sir," Maslama was saying, "towards
> the opinion that whatever name one calls It by is no more than a code; a
> cypher, Mr. Farishta, behind which the true names lies concealed."[189]

In this short passage the dilemma, the challenge, and the opportunity are laid bare. Encompassed here are all the anxieties and uncertainties of the present situation; questions of identity; the tenuous nature of the times; the search for essence and moral guidance; deities like water, an ocean not a stream; and the ultimate postmodern device—the literal as sign and signifier—as iconic means to unlock the nature of truth and reality in the present situation. The dilemma is to allow the suspect, contested elements to become the site of recontextualization in the new imaginary. The challenge is to allow the story to be owned by another time, to be open to the imaginary. And the opportunity is to be a part of the process of change rather than to be the one who seeks to hold back the story and keep it out of the new imaginary. Here can be heard echoes of the issues raised by a book such as *The Da Vinci Code*, which has elicited a parallel onslaught of defensive responses. Critiques of both novels sought to repudiate and dismiss all of the claims as either flights of fancy or mere myth. But in the postmodern imaginary, myth is seldom "mere myth."

Rushdie's book is fiction as entertainment, fiction as theology; it is essentially entertainment theology. Its potential threat to an existing reality was all too obviously noticed by the Islamic fundamentalists. Herein lies the new "creative tension site"[190] of the postsecular age. At the end of *The Satanic Verses*, the author looks to the future, as we also must now do. Rushdie closes his book with a certain resolve. The resolve is to a future in which faith has been written into existence. In writing the fiction, Rushdie has uncovered the momentum to move on, to move forward. The fairy tale, the myth, of monolithic hegemony has been replaced with a new vision that lies in the future, not the past.

Rushdie's is a singular quest for meaning, a quest that includes the meaning of identity, culture, civilization, and religion. We began with two men, two actors of sorts, one an angel (Gibreel Farishta), the other (Saladin Chamcha) a devil, and as a literary device, both were the same person.[191] Between them they occupy the dichotomy of the postmodern world, in which old allegiances are collapsed and new relations must be formed. Under Rushdie's pen the "preaching of origin must be distinguished from what it becomes in the hands of men in search of power."[192] And so at the end of the story, Gibreel, eaten by cancer, the incurable evil of the world, commits suicide and liberates himself from that world. And then the vision unfolds:

He stood at the window of his childhood and looked out at the Arabian Sea. The moon was almost full; moonlight, stretching from the rocks of Scandal Point out to the far horizon, created the illusion of a silver pathway, like a parting in the water's shining hair, like a road to miraculous lands. He shook his head; could no longer believe in fairy-tales. Childhood was over, and the view from this window was no more than an old and sentimental echo. To the devil with it! Let the bulldozers come. If the old refused to die, the new could not be born.

"Come along," Zeenat Vakil's voice said at his shoulder. It seemed that in spite of all his wrong-doing, weakness, guilt—in spite of his humanity—he was getting another chance. There was no accounting for one's good fortune, that was plain. There it simply was, taking his elbow in its hand. "My place," Zeeny offered. "Let's get the hell out of here."

"I'm coming," he answered her, and turned away from the view.[193]

Fundamentalism is not outside the postsecular context; it is part of the dynamic, part of the internal conflict that attends the times. It is a postmodern response to choice overload. As Ward rightly notes, this is not a clash of civilizations. Rather, it is the interregnum, the in-between time, the pull of civilizations old and new, modern and postmodern, as we witness the birth of the new.[194] The present state of fundamentalism bears witness to the changing times in its very plurality of expression. The various fundamentalisms, Caputo notes, have not just reacted against the high-tech world they find themselves in, they have also embraced it. "Fundamentalism has transplanted the advanced communications systems into its own body and, in order to tolerate the transplant, has suppressed its natural auto-immune systems."[195] This may account for the increased violence, both verbal and physical, that seems to characterize so much of fundamentalism today.

What we have seen, then, is the emergence of a new environment in which the religious now functions. It is the product of the reenchantment, the resacralization, of society. This resacralization is itself the product of a number of interrelated issues: the implosion of modernity via the postmodern; the world's continuing globalization resulting in an emerging global culture, connected by media technology and global flows of information, entertainment, and peoples; and the resultant role of the imagination as a major force for the production of social meaning.

Religion, in this context, is characterized by three particular elements: pluralism, economics, and fetishization. *Pluralism*, the very consciousness of the postmodern, offers the potentialities of many modes of existence (the new imaginary) within the new cultural flows, and in the realm of the religious it results in the democratization of spirit—the emergence of a people's religion. Again it must be said that the use of the term "people's religion" is not meant to evoke images of a new global form of religion to which all adherents now subscribe. Rather, it is meant to suggest that religion has entered a new evolutionary phase in which the power and influence of religious formation has shifted from the exclusive mediation of institutions and professional clergy, as with more traditional faith expressions, to the hands of individuals for whom the task of fashioning a connection with the divine is an intensely personal and creative venture. The notion of a people's religion is an acknowledgment that the democratization process common to postmodern culture has affected the realm of the religious as well.

Economics also characterizes religion in that the resacralization of culture is not the return to God as a matter of private faith (modernity's mode), or the adoption of premodern concepts, but the return of religion as public resource—a matter of consumer choice. In the consumer phase of global capitalism, religion is a matter of choice, related more to the construction of self-identity than to an allegiance to a particular and pre-established set of beliefs.

The process of *fetishization* shifts religion in the postsecular into a horizontal rhizomic configuration allowing for the emergence of new and seemingly unrelated realizations of the religious life. This is the means by which information and values are exchanged and embraced in the postsecular culture. On the surface of the new global flows, our own rootedness is increasingly related to the connections we make around the globe than to more traditional modes of rootedness: place, ethnic identity, and the such.

What emerges from this new context is a new incarnation of the religious: "spirituality," derived from any number of diverse sources available from the rhizomic grid. Central to this are democratized forms of information exchange. Advanced computer technologies, for example, are facilitating a participatory religious construct in which the self is the key determinant of how the religious is manifested in particular lives. Included in this is theology derived from the global mediascapes, or entertainment theology. Media in this construct, both personal and corporate, produce "image-centered and narrative-based accounts of strips of reality."[196] These provide the means for those who experience these elements to fashion them into new imaginaries of life in general and, for the sake of this study, of religion in particular. This complex web of interrelated global exchanges results in new contours of the religious, definable only in generalist terms.

This book presents four of these key contours as they appear on the Western cultural landscape at the present moment. To summarize those four contours, they are the Westernization of Asian thought, or the marriage of Western democratic capitalism with Eastern wisdom; rational mysticism, or the marriage of religion and science in new ways; postmodern gothic and neomedievalism, which is the attempt to return to premodern methods of engagement with the divine; and postmodern fundamentalism, or the attempt to return to a form of foundationalism in a world lacking foundation.

It could be argued that these four dynamics fall into two larger contours of expressions, one that looks forward, as with the East/West dynamic and the Rational Mystics, and one that looks back, retrograde. However, given the high degree of creativity and individual engagement afforded by the new global rhizome, the division is not that neat. Influences, narratives, and fragments are drawn together from an endless variety of global information flows to fit the mood of the current times. This is religion in a designer economy.

My goal up to this point has been not so much to critique these rubrics but to offer a description of what is out there. It has been an attempt to catch the mood, the inclinations, the directional impetus of religion as it manifests in the postsecular. This allows us by way of conclusion, then, to consider the role Christian faith might play in this new situation. The final section of this book, therefore, offers some reflection on how Christian faith might engage this democratization of spirit in meaningful ways.

Part 3

New Orthodoxies

Playing the Future

The Spirit blows wherever it pleases. You hear its sound, but you cannot tell where it comes from or where it is going.

John 3:8

But the spirit breathes where it wants, and the Romantic dream of a new religion remains, albeit partially, our dream.

Gianni Vattimo, After Christianity

My stepdaughter's paternal grandfather tap danced with Shirley Temple, starred in two television shows that are in continual syndication, and was the first actor to play the Tin Man in a movie called *The Wizard of Oz*. He was in a few of the early scenes but was then replaced because he almost died from the lead in the silver paint used to make him look like a man made of tin. Needless to say, this film has been the subject of numerous viewings in our household, as it is for many people, but with an extrapersonal connection. The film was based on a book titled *The Wonderful Wizard of Oz*, published in 1900 as a new century turned. The story, written by L. Frank Baum, is the tale of Dorothy, a young girl from Kansas who is caught up in a tornado and then finds herself set down in an unfamiliar but magical place called Oz. The film version expanded certain elements of the story, particularly the beginning and ending concerning Dorothy's home.

When the film opens, everything is in black and white. It reverberates with allusions to Americana, Norman Rockwell without color. But things aren't really black and white, they are gray, pallid. Gray is the color that sets the stage for the film. The opening scenes of the film are also very angular. If one looks carefully, there are lines and circles and triangles everywhere. Nothing complicated, just basic geometric shapes. Out of this dullness, this bleak and bare, uncomplicated Kansas landscape, comes the tornado that changes everything. It picks up the house Dorothy and her beloved dog Toto are hiding in. Dorothy gets knocked out as the tornado hits the house, and as it swirls through the air, we glimpse Hollywood's early attempt at special effects, objects and people and animals flying through the air. And then the storm ends.

Dorothy gets up from the bed where she has been lying and walks toward the front door of the house. When the door opens, something new meets her eyes: glorious Technicolor. The dull grayness of Kansas has been replaced with the vibrant colors of Oz. We forget the immense power of color in a world used to black and white. But in the early days of cinema, *The Wizard of Oz* employed strong colors—yellow, red, and emerald green—to great effect, contrasting the two worlds that Dorothy inhabits in the story. Stepping out into this strangely exotic world, she utters words that have become so familiar they have become part of the Western vernacular: "Toto, I have a feeling we're not in Kansas anymore."[1]

Salman Rushdie writes about this scene:

> Dorothy, stepping into color, framed by exotic foliage with a cluster of dwarfy cottages behind her and looking like a blue-smocked Snow White, no princess but a good demotic American gal, is clearly struck by the absence of her familiar homey gray. . . . She has done more than step out of gray into Technicolor. She has been unhoused, and her homelessness is underlined by the fact that, after all the door-play of the transitional sequence, she will not enter any interior until she reaches the Emerald City. From tornado to Oz, Dorothy never has a roof over her head.[2]

If we take this as metaphor, then here is a cinematic version of our present reality. "We are not in Kansas anymore, either." If Kansas is modernity, all black and white (but really gray), given its commitment to rationalism, to scientific method, to mathematics, to geometric shapes and simple understandings, and to its "maddening emptiness"—the ultimate price of the modern—then we are no longer in that place.[3] A tornado has whipped us away to a new world, one in which imagination reigns. We have truly entered Oz—the reenchanted world of the postsecular, bold, brash, and brightly colored.

The landscape, with its winding paths (yellow brick roads) and visual language (all circles and spheres), is not compatible with the angular, straight-edged world of Kansas as it is represented in the film. And consider its cast of characters, the surreal company of pilgrims: Tin Man, the man of science and myth; Cowardly Lion, the fundamentalist; Scarecrow and the Wicked Witch, the gothic; and, of course, the little Munchkins,

New Orthodoxies

who inhabit the landscape of Oz. Here is the employ of "special effect" to create the new context.

I do not wish to make the whole film an analogy of the postsecular, but I do wish to offer it as an allusion of being in a new place. Oz, which is decidedly unlike Kansas, is a useful device by which to experience the contrast. As Rushdie states, "If the overabundant new knowledge of the modern age is, let's say, a tornado, then Oz is the extraordinary, Technicolor world in which it has landed us, the world from which—life not being a movie—there is no way home. In the immortal words of Dorothy Gale, 'I have a feeling we are not in Kansas anymore,' to which one can only add; thank goodness, baby, amen."[4] There is no way home, if home means back to what once was. In the real world, stasis is not a possibility; nothing stays the same. But there is a new home, and it is being fashioned now, even as I write and you read.

We live in a time when spirit is ocean, not river, and it covers the re-sacralized postsecular, postmodern world of the emerging global culture. It is a time of creation and not form, a time of conflict even between form and spirit. And from the waters of spirit a multiverse of faiths emerge, characterized not by mutual objectives or necessarily shared desires but by *desire*. This desire is for more than modernity, for more than the old traditional ways of faith and practice, for new ways of living and being that resonate with the transcendent in a world full of diverse options for its manifestations. This dynamic emerges as a response to the complex world of interconnectedness. It responds to clusters of ideas and fragments that emerge on the surface via technologies.

It is a world in which Christianity, particularly for many in the West, is little more than a vapor trail, a fading path, once heavily walked on, now increasingly walked over. Thus, I don't think we can extend the present incarnations of Christian faith very far into the new situation. I say incarnations because, rather like Dorothy's Kansas, things are not really so black and white, so easily demarcated. The Christian faith is, like her home state in the movie, mostly shades of gray, the lines of division more conflicted and compromised than clearly demarcated.

Christianity is a plurality of broad ideas about Christ under the banner of the church. But if we think that is a monolithic, easily definable entity, one only has to consider the sheer number of denominations and theological nuances, differences, and divisions to realize the true reality of the situation. The current issues the church is wrestling with, such as the debate over gays or the leadership of women, demonstrate that it is clearly not a black-and-white world that the church lives in. I say this with no animosity, no ax to grind, no desire to undermine intention or effort. I welcome those who still find comfort in the way things are, even in the changing way things are. But I have my eye turned toward a different horizon. I want to focus on the new developments of religion in this emerging culture, where Christianity is an often rejected view, little more than a resource to be mined for other incarnations of faith. In this world, Christian faith creates little effect, makes little wake, beyond the adverse reaction to its universalist inclination and perceived posture of condescension.[5]

It is this missional horizon I wish to address.[6] I echo the belief and sentiment of Kester Brewin, who proposes that the church has reached a "local maximum" and thus in order to survive must change and find a "new way of being in an evolving world."[7] I write, then, for missiology, theology, and all of us who lay claim to God's love manifest in Christ.

I also write as someone who has tried to make his faith alive and who has come to the end of many things. Like Nick Cave, one of my favorite singer-songwriters, I don't believe in an "interventionist God."[8] Like Caputo, my view of God is somewhat postmetaphysical,[9] the name of an event that is bigger than all our attempts to capture it. Like Douglas Rushkoff, I believe that "nothing is sacred," and yet everything is sacred.[10] I could name and align myself with so many others who in differing ways and for reasons other than mine have come to the end of their own faith and to the beginnings of new things. I have come to the end of the need to be "right," to be certain that I hold the whole truth.

I caution that what follows is hardly a prescription, a systematic theology, or a decisive missiological plan. It is, rather, my own reflective response to the present mood. I am attempting to capture what theologian Catherine Keller and others describe as a "polyglossal matrix of conversation," a multidimensional, interdisciplinary approach to faith in the third millennium.[11] What I propose is born of a desire to "reclaim" the world and to accomplish this by bringing the entire world under the theological gaze. This attempt to "reclaim" is not to be read in any way as a desire to "Christianize" or to engage in colonization for institutional Christian faith. It is a desire to bring the world, all of it, back into the conversation and dialogue that Christian faith has with the world, to interact and involve all of life—politics, art, economics, sociology, and the like—in the work of thinking and acting religiously. This will be accomplished, as Milbank and others argue, "not simply [by] returning in nostalgia to the premodern, [but by] visit[ing] sites in which secularism has invested heavily—aesthetics, politics, sex, the body, personhood, visibility, space—and [by] resituat[ing] them from a Christian standpoint."[12]

This process begins with imagination. Imagination is the re-creation process that offers the hope of newness, of re-birth, if you will. Appadurai says that a prime function of imagination today (imagination that emerges from the consumption of global media flows) is to effect a number of responses, such as resistance, irony, and selectivity. But beyond these results, imagination functions even more importantly as *agency*,[13] or the very means by which we re-create ourselves in the postsecular. He also makes a distinction between imagination and fantasy, noting that fantasy carries with it the "inescapable connotation of thought divorced from projects and actions."[14] Fantasy has the tendency to dissipate; it is the stuff of escapism. Imagination is not about escape, and it becomes an important key for negotiating the present.

> The imagination, on the other hand, has a projective sense about it, the sense of being a prelude to some sort of expression, whether aesthetic or otherwise. . . . It is the imagination, in its collective forms, that creates the ideas of neighborhood and nationhood, of moral economies and unjust rule, of higher wages and foreign labor prospects. The imagination is today a staging ground for action, and not only for escape.[15]

One has only to consider the ways in which imagination has been recently used in cinema, particularly in the big summer blockbuster movies such as *Lord of the Rings* or *Batman* or even *Harry Potter*. These imaginary worlds are so fully realized, so complete, if you will, that they function as viable and valid locales rather than as mere settings for the unfolding of story. These movies often come with associated Web sites that expand these imaginary worlds even more, creating a sense that they hold some clue about how to fashion life in the future.[16]

It is with this understanding of imagination—as agency to project, as staging ground for action—that I offer my reflections on the role of church and Christian theology in the postsecular. I will focus primarily on three elements: a shift in identity, a typology for a missional theology, and a new encoding of message.

In true "Oz" fashion, these should be understood not as independent geometric lines of demarcation but as a cluster of interlocking shapes—a "yellow brick road"—that leads us to the "Emerald City," that complex and sparkling world of the postsecular. Just to be clear, this is not simply the exercise of postmodern deconstruction. Deconstruction was the early phase of the postmodern dynamic; we are not in those times anymore. The central dynamic of the present state of the postmodern trajectory is the search for a voice, a search for new ways of being that are not merely reactive or obsessed with the state of the past but rather are concerned with playing the future, with finding a new voice with which to speak about the divine.[17] I offer my reflections in this light and in this spirit. In this I realize that I walk a tightrope, but Ludwig Wittgenstein perhaps said it best when he said that an "honest religious thinker is like a tightrope walker." He almost looks as though he were walking on air. His support is the slenderest possible, and yet it really is possible to walk on it. What I offer is the slenderest of threads but a thread nonetheless.

After Christianity

It's the end of the world as we know it, and I feel fine.

R.E.M., "The End of the World"

Every act of imagination has a starting point, a "once upon a time." My act of imagination begins with the phrase, "Once upon a time there was Christianity, but this Christianity is no more." In saying this I acknowledge that such a thing *does* exist in the imaginary of a number of adherents for whom the idea continues to have resonance. I also say this as someone who participates regularly in Christian worship. But in the emerging global culture, in this new time of the democratization of spirit and the rise of an entertainment theology, Christianity as it has traditionally been understood is no more. To generalize, the Christianity I am referring to is the traditional religion of the followers of Jesus; a totalizing ideology; an organization with universal desires, creeds, and intentions. It is a religion whose ascendancy was long and rich, but which has been, or more correctly is being, eclipsed in these new times by something else, something other. It is an ecumenical form of the Christian faith, with many branches, all tracing themselves back to a singular perception of the dominance and ascendancy of Christian faith and belief above all others.

Any new imagination of the cause of Jesus Christ in our present context must be willing to work "after Christianity." To be honest, I do not think we have had such a Christianity for a long time,[1] but in the modern era we were at least willing to live with the *illusion* of its continued existence. One could argue that since the Reformation, we have not had Christianity. The split in the church gave rise to the secular state, which in the end did away with Christendom and its global pretensions. Christianity has existed in fragmented division ever since. And in the last decades of the twentieth century, those fragments often turned into particles.

But to focus on the issue at hand, what do I mean by "after Christianity"? I mean that Christianity, as we have known it, is a religion.

However, this is not the age of religion but of spirit and spirituality. A wedge has developed between "ideas regarding religion" and "spirituality," the two being interpreted as binary opposites rather than as partners in process.[2] If we choose to retain religion, then I point to the church's function in the new religious space as a resource, a wellspring for the myriad of spiritualities emerging. This is the function of religion in the postsecular world. Its ideas, values, and practices are there to be mined for new incarnations and expressions of spirituality. So it is in this context that I propose a radical break with Christianity and a turn to something else—*Christian spiritualities*.

Theologian John Drane observes that "it is ironic, to say the least, that the church is in serious decline at exactly the same time as our whole culture is experiencing a rising tide of spiritual concern—and that many of today's spiritual searchers dismiss the church, not because it is irrelevant or old-fashioned, but because in their minds it is 'unspiritual.'"[3] Drane goes on to argue for a gospel more mystical and numinous in focus. Karl Rahner had earlier taken this even further, saying that the Christian "of the future will be a mystic or he or she will not exist at all."[4] It would seem that a break with linearity and regimented systems as a determining element for theological reflection and faith practice is a basic requirement of the new situation. And this would seem to be exactly what is happening. This move is being reflected in the wider Christian culture in the rise of such things as the concept of Ancient-Future Worship,[5] the interest in monasticism, and the practice of spiritual disciplines.

But I am not sure that even this is enough. Such a move may well suffice in terms of reinvigorating the spiritual lives of existing Christians, but I don't think it will work missionally in the long term. This is because it remains an attempt to gather people under the existing, though perhaps modified, constructs of Christian faith and practice, namely, the concrete theological structures of the reigning orthodoxies of Christian faith. I say "reigning" because this perceived orthodoxy is largely viewed through the lens of scientific rationalism. It is the church in modernity that tends to dominate the Christian imaginary. This is why I advocate a shift *beyond Christianity* and a move toward Christian spiritualities.

To be more specific, I mean a form of Christian spirituality characterized by a move from dependence on modernist structures of organization to a new encounter with mystery. "The process of globalization and the crisis in organized Christianity lead us back to paleo-Christianity, that is, to the Christian faith," argues Boff. He goes on to declare that the distinction between Christianity (for which he sees no place in the global civilization) and the Christian faith is that faith "always implies a profound encounter with the Mystery that inhabits this world, that religions and scholars have deciphered as being God."[6] This shift away from the more organizational mode of Christianity to manifestations of Christian faith extends from buildings to theology—but particularly theology, which continually links people to organizational structures. "Religion is the Temple when God has left the building," says Bono from the Irish band U2. This statement is a postmodern version of Karl Barth's contention that religion is a form of idolatry. The perception that religion is linked to specific space, institutional space, can be a major hindrance to the ongoing effort of Christian mission in the postsecular world. Linking things to specific space[7] can play a part, but it cannot be the central dynamic. There is a growing sense of the sacredness of the earth, not merely the acknowledgment of certain humanly designated sacred spaces.[8]

I am not arguing for the end of the "church," but I am arguing for a different understanding of faith itself, and this will result in a different incarnation of church that is not dependent on the traditional ecclesial, organizational, and structural approaches. Over the years I have heard probably hundreds of sermons that include a statement along the lines of, "the church is not the building, it's the people." But people still speak of "going to church," and in spite of the best efforts of many to change this attitude, as long as the church building is the prime locus of Christian spiritual activity, we will have this issue to deal with.

The present situation is about much more than what "church looks like." The shift must be toward the presentation of Christian faith as a means of addressing the spiritual hunger and searching of the postsecular era. Mystery cannot be bottled; rather, it is something not fully understood, and as such it cannot be brought under the totalizing tendencies of universal ideologies. This is why, according to Max Weber, mystery was banished from the modern forest. In modernity, it was presumed that all could be explained, all brought under the domain and understanding of the rationalizing efforts of the modern, secular mind. The church remains one of the last bastions of "rational-material thought."[9]

This commitment to mystery will also demand that we give up the quest for relevance in a particular incarnation, something that at present seems to characterize the church, particularly in its forms of Western and Westernized Christianity, wherever they are found in the global flow of the postsecular. The general trend seems to be engaging in desperate attention-seeking practices as if to say, "look at us, we do count, we are cool." But as any arbiter of cool will tell you, "cool" cannot be claimed, only conferred.

Kester Brewin argues for the church to become "wombs of the divine,"[10] effecting rebirth of Christian faith and spirituality into the host culture. Another element of this shift, then, will be the move from a praxis-based spirituality. Mystery is an ongoing interaction with the unexplained, the hard to categorize. This is not to say that the affects of faith should be completely abandoned, but rather that we should focus on our search for God again.[11]

Slavoj Žižek proposes that we read Paul's declaration in his second letter to the Corinthians in a new and radical light. In his book *The Fragile Absolute*, he argues as a Marxist in defense of Christianity. Žižek believes that Paul's declaration in 2 Corinthians 5:16–17[12] asserts a radical break[13] with the past for the believer. As a Marxist, Žižek calls this the "revolutionary logic."[14] In my particular view of the evolutionary nature of spirituality in the postmodern context, I argue that the break with the past is the shift into the new world. The break is in part imposed from without in that it is no longer possible to live according to the old ways in the new world.

To return to the analogy of the movie *Waterworld*, it is simply impossible to live the life one once lived on dry land in a world made of water. This break is also internal, a response to the call of the new world, a call to reinvent, to rethink, to reimagine. To be more precise, this decisive break is not with the past, per se, but with the *modes* of the past. There is no "return to Kansas," no return to the supposed black-and-white practices of the early church that we so often hear preachers calling for in response to the complexity of the times—"if we could just go back, things would be all right." But there is no going back.

The radical possibility of Jesus continues to herald both a break in the old order and a new mode of existence. My proposal is that we make a radical break with the form of Christianity as we have known it, with the "religion of Christianity." This is not to dismiss or negate. It is simply to assert a new order of engagement. Jesus gave his disciples a "new commandment," which did not negate the old ones but established a new order and criteria for acting and being in the world. Following Nietzsche, Žižek argues that St. Paul formulated the basic tenets of Christian faith. "There is no Christ outside Saint Paul; in exactly the same way, there is no authentic Marx, that can be approached directly, bypassing Lenin."[15] Žižek notes that Paul was not a part of Christ's inner circle and argues that this externality is the only possible way of retrieving the true impulse of Jesus's message.

There are three pertinent observations from Žižek in this regard. First, from his external position, Paul is able to reinscribe the original teaching of Jesus into a different context. Second, it is only through such a "violent displacement" that the original theory can be put to work, fulfilling its potential. And third, there is no middle ground, no "third way," for Christianity. This has particular resonance for me. To call for an end to the present form of Christianity is truly not meant to be merely an inflammatory statement. It is rooted in a conviction that a big problem for the presence of the church in the world is that it is almost inextricably linked, in its present mode, with Western culture and does not have a truly global understanding of the state of humanity. The current crisis in the Anglican communion highlights some of these issues. The church in the "global south," in a period of strength and growth, is attempting to assert its dominance and authority within the communion. The Western church, in crisis and decline, is desperately seeking to find a middle way in order to keep the communion together. Both are products of modernity, at opposite ends of the spectrum, arguing over issues that are rooted in Enlightenment realities, which no longer reflect the approach to reality that much of the world is living in or beginning to move toward. It is little more than shuffling deck chairs on the Titanic. There is no room for a "universal church" in the present situation because a form of religion rooted in a different space and time cannot conceive of the present realities in such a way as to promote true equality, to be truly universal.

In the third millennium the task is to retrieve the unique moment when the "thought already transposes itself into a collective organization, but does not yet fix itself into an institution."[16] For Žižek, this moment of transposition is the two-way dialogue between Christian faith and Marxism. He places the work of both Lenin and St. Paul on similar ground. My intent is not to address Marxist dialectics or to explore the link between two ideologies but rather to acknowledge that Žižek's basic theory carries some significance for the present task. Žižek goes on to say: "[This moment of transposition] aims neither at nostalgically reenacting the 'good old revolutionary times,' nor at the opportunistic-pragmatic adjustment of the old program to 'new conditions,' but at repeating, in the present world-wide conditions, the (Leninist) gesture of initiating a (political) project."[17]

My call for a break with Christianity is not a call to go home (nostalgia), where there is nothing for us in this new context but a call back to the evolutionary moment of radical break with the past that was initiated by Paul and from which sprang the future of the gospel. Rushkoff terms this movement "recapitulation"—the repetition of the evolutionary stages of the development of a particular organism.[18] This is more than contextualization that usually seeks to reiterate a certain body of ideas in a new situation without consideration of whether those ideas are consistent with the cultural transformation. Recapitulation, however, is neither the abandonment of orthodoxy nor the rejection of a heritage with its classic expressions of faith. It is not even a denial of the accomplishments and expansions of the church in modernity. Rather, it is the seeking of a return of the gospel in new situations.

This is the "end of the world as we know it, and I feel fine," to quote the familiar pop song. I feel fine because I know the end of all things is but the beginning of new things with God: the recapitulation of the gospel of Jesus. I can celebrate and honor the past, and will be forever haunted by its ghosts (as is the present situation), but I am liberated from its tendencies and must live, as writer Liz Gilbert says, on that "shimmering line between your old thinking and your new understanding."[19]

The work of Dietrich Bonhoeffer, and his letters on religionless Christianity[20] in particular, were also instrumental in shaping some of my thinking here. Writing before the end of the Second World War, Bonhoeffer was living in a time quite different from the present and his assumptions about the potential shape of the future were deeply affected by the events that were taking place in his life. In a prison cell awaiting an uncertain future, he could foresee a "world come of age" in which there was no place for religion. A world come of age for Bonhoeffer was one in which there was no apparent need for God. This possibility caused him to reflect on what the future of Christianity might be in such an environment. Living in the first half of the twentieth century, Bonhoeffer did not live to see the things we see now. He thought that the secularists would triumph and that the banishment of God would be permanent, and his thoughts on a religionless faith were posited in the light of that eventuality.

I see things differently. My conclusions about the world's attitude toward religion and the future of Christianity are quite different. But Bonhoeffer raised many issues that resonate with the present situation. We live in a world where religion has not died but has been replaced with a democratized approach to belief that negates traditional faiths in much the same way Bonhoeffer envisioned: "We are moving towards a completely religionless time; people as they are now cannot be religious anymore. Even those who honestly describe themselves as 'religious' do not in the least act up to it, and so they presumably mean something quite different by 'religious.'"[21] Whether or not the present impulses regarding religion are what Bonhoeffer imagined, the fact remains that what most people mean by "religious" today has little in common with past understandings of the word. In the confines of his prison cell, Bonhoeffer wrestled with many issues about Christianity in a changing world. His call for a religionless Christianity was an attempt to come to terms with what Christianity would have to face in a world in which "presuppositions of metaphysics and inwardness" have been replaced. I, of course, contend that with the implosion of modernity we have entered a postsecular time in which much can be found in common with Bonhoeffer's wrestlings. He seemed to have a fairly negative view toward all of this, something that I do not share.

I think these are exciting times for the realm of faith and belief. We live in a world where metaphysics is challenged, where interconnectedness has replaced inwardness as a key religious impulse, and where religions that once held the imagination and cradled the faith of many are no longer seen as vital sources and resources for life and living. Bonhoeffer also wondered whether there was a future for the Western form of Christianity and asked some hard questions about the shape of Christian faith in the light of its demise:

> If our final judgment must be that the western form of Christianity, too, was only a preliminary stage to a complete absence of religion, what kind of situation emerges for us, for the church? How can Christ become the Lord of the religionless as well? Are there religionless Christians? If religion is only a garment of Christianity—and even this garment has looked very different at different times—then what is religionless Christianity?[22]

My contention is that religion is only a garment of Christianity, one which no longer fits well and therefore needs to be discarded in favor of something other to regain the vitality of the message of Jesus. It is once again, and perhaps as never before, a time for new wineskins.

I call for an expansion of the somewhat limiting perspective and an evolutionary move into the present situation. The Christian faith needs a new purpose, if you like, because the old one has almost run its course. Religion, in general, has traditionally had at least two social functions. One deals with what Christianity calls our "fallen nature." The golden rule found in most faiths is an aid against and a challenge to the tendency in all of us to selfish and destructive living. Religion reminds us and often operates as a means of control, personally as well as corporately. The other end of religion's spectrum, or at least of Western versions of religion, is that of inspiration; it intends to lift the soul, inspire the heart, challenge the status quo, and elevate the human being to new levels of relationship with

God and fellow humans. Douglas Rushkoff says that religion's role is "to provide the tools for human evolution."[23] I couldn't agree more, and if I am writing about anything in the pages of this book, that sentiment is at the heart of it all. Christian faith needs to evolve into something else.[24]

My advocacy of a break with Christianity and a concomitant shift into spiritual Christianities is attended by the three elements I mentioned earlier: identity shifting, theological typology, and a re-encoding of the message.

Identity Shifting

Lot's wife looked back, and she became a pillar of salt.

Genesis 19:26

In an earlier section on the emergence of postmodern fundamentalism, we discussed Manuel Castells's theory of fundamentalism as an example of "resistant identity," as a response to the manifold uncertainty of the present age. He also identified two other modes of identity. "Legitimating" identities are imposed from the "top down" by nation-states or other entities (this form of identity is perhaps less significant for the current social imaginary because of the shifting social landscape, which generates suspicion toward identities legitimized by institutions and more rigid understandings of social organization).[25] Castells's third category is the one that resonates most with my intention: "project identity."

"Project identity," for Castells, is a forward-looking identity, fashioned in and by the tendencies of the present.[26] Because this identity construct is a product of the new socializing forces at work in the postmodern world and is fluid, we need not imagine that it lacks either ethical seriousness or association with legitimate identity. In other words, this is not the adoption of a "form of the self" taken on in some flippant manner or in a desperate attempt to connect with the culture. Rather, it is an identity shaped by a new social imaginary, not as a herald of the past but as a *participant in the present*. As Castells states:

> In this case the building of identity is a project of a different life but expanding towards the transformation of society as the prolongation of this project of identity . . . as in . . . a post-patriarchal society liberating men, women and children through the realization of women's identity. Or . . . the final reconciliation of all human beings as believers, brothers and sisters under the guidance of God's Law.[27]

New Orthodoxies

Project identity is forward looking. This forward looking is not merely a posture. It is "proactive" rather than "reactive," like the other two modes Castells identifies: legitimate and resistant. It is a sense of being, or to be more specific, the sense of being in this moment, the postsecular age. Unlike resistant and legitimate identities, which seek to connect with the past in the present, project identity is at home in the present. This is not to say that project identity cannot be influenced or aided either by the past or by legitimizing activities, but whatever legitimizing activities occur, they will occur as a means to moor the person in the present time. Herein lies the significance of the postmodern gothic and of ancient-future theological perspectives. To embrace project identity is to understand oneself as living fully in the realities of the present moment, "cognizant of different identities but without espousing individualism or fundamentalism, favoring transformation without utopian absolutes."[28]

This proactive identity is also characterized by its search to resituate the holy in the here and now, connecting it with the present condition. Here there is once again resonance with Bonhoeffer's reflections on religionless Christianity, which seem to be an attempt to consider how Christianity might resituate itself into what he perceived as the emerging context, namely, that of a "world come of age."[29] In other words, "The sacred establishes itself with respect to the profane."[30]

In 1 Samuel 21:1–6 we encounter a moment of life-transforming crisis in the life of David. The future king is on the run from Saul's charge of treason. Arriving harassed and hungry in the city of Nob, he seeks food from Ahimelech, the priest. The only food available is consecrated bread, reserved for those engaged in the service of God. The priest, desiring to maintain piety, questions David as to the nature of his mission and whether or not his mission and his men qualify for consecrated, "holy" bread. There is a certain amount of ambiguity to the "holiness" of David's mission, but David seems to ignore those ambiguities and simply declares that his mission qualifies by appealing to a proviso in the laws regarding consecrated bread that broadens the horizons of qualification (1 Sam. 21:5). Walter Brueggemann says that the story revolves around the juxtaposition of two Hebrew words: *hol* and *qodes* ("profane" and "holy"), with David rejecting the conventional ideas upheld by the priest of what is holy:

> Thus he breaks the notion of holy away from the shrine and moves it out into the normal affairs of men. . . . Either way David is not bound by the normal notion of what is holy. . . . If "holy" still functions as a meaning-

ful term, it now refers to the well-being of his party on the way to royal power. Against the narrower notions of holy which had been held, this is a revolutionary affirmation made good by his readiness to act upon it. He risks a new idea of what holy is.[31]

Brueggemann's description is interesting in that he goes on to decisively link this recapitulation with the ministry of Jesus. In Mark 2:23–28 Jesus encounters the Pharisees in a grain field through which he and his disciples have been walking on the Sabbath. His disciples have been eating the heads of grain (the essential ingredient of bread), and the Pharisees question Jesus as to the legitimacy of their actions, an action that if done on the Sabbath was deemed unlawful by these upholders of the law, these arbiters of what is holy and what is profane. In response, Jesus recites an event in the history of Israel: "Have you never read what David did when he and his companions were hungry and in need? . . . He entered the house of God and ate the consecrated bread" (vv. 25–26). Of this event Brueggemann says, "The way in which Jesus makes reference to this story in Mark 2:23–28 confirms the point our discussion makes. Jesus utilizes the text to overturn conventional notions of what is sacred. David is his bold predecessor in the same effort."[32]

This is not to say that this idea grants license to do and live as one pleases, simply by shifting the line between holy and profane so that it encompasses more and more. It is important that in both of the above scriptural situations, the notion of holiness is *redefined in juxtaposition to existing ideas of the holy*. In both cases, consecrated bread is broken in the ordinary world of the human and not in the confines of conventional religious space. This, it seems to me, is the order of the day. To redraw the lines between the holy and the profane is to take the consecrated bread and break it in the broader culture. But it remains consecrated bread. Rowan Williams points to this when he states:

> To explore the continuities of Christian patterns of holiness is to explore the effect of Jesus, living, dying and rising; and it is inevitable that the tradition about Jesus is re-read and re-worked so that it will make sense of these lived patterns as they evolve. We constantly return to imagine the life of Jesus in a way that will help us to understand how it sets up a continuous pattern of human living before God.[33]

Nick Cave is an insightful singer-songwriter who practices a form of advanced entertainment theology in the apocalyptic punk music he has generated for over twenty years with his band the Bad Seeds. What makes

New Orthodoxies

his work so remarkable is that his particular musical genres and influences—punk, Goth rock, and art-house burlesque—are hardly environments in which one would expect to find theology being done. More surprising is that it is particularly Christian theologizing.

In a song released in 2000, titled "God Is in the House," Cave tells the story of an anonymous town in America. It is a place of white-picket fences, neat lawns, and order. The town is lit so that there is no "place for crime to hide," and at the center of the town is a church, painted white, where citizens go "in the safety of the night, as quiet as a mouse for word is getting out that God is in the house." As the verses of the song unfold, what lies behind these neat and orderly lives is revealed as a self-constituted sense of holiness that results in nothing but bitterness and judgment for those deemed profane by the community, which is essentially everyone but the churchgoers. They are a bastion of suburban, middle-class values, progressive enough to have a woman for a mayor, but not like the big city where "packs of queers roam the streets and crime is everywhere." The refrain, "God is in the house," is an allusion to their sense of holiness. The town has no time for psychotherapy or twelve-step groups, which cater to those for whom there should be no mercy.

This is a somewhat harsh and stereotypical characterization of the religious impulse in suburbia, but it is close enough to require some acknowledgment of the veracity of the claims. In a shift of focus, from the posture of the town that seeks to keep God locked up in "their house," Cave echoes a plaintive refrain, "God is in the house, God is in the house, I wish he would come out, God is in the house." To redraw the line of holiness is to take holiness out of its safe, conventional house and let it interact and engage with the world as it is and not as we think it should be.

The movie *Chocolat*, released in 2000, made a similar point. A woman and her daughter move into a small French community and open a chocolate store. The store opens with Sunday hours, which causes a clash with the rigid morality of the church-centered community. The community is pious, but it is also riddled with judgmentalism and callousness. They are as "gray as Kansas," and it is precisely their religion that has made them this way. Vianne (Julliette Binoche), the chocolatier, becomes a vehicle for change in the community, her simple devotion to chocolate becoming a lightning rod for renewal.

A final element of project identity is its demand and creation of struggle. This is a notion Gramsci speaks of as the "struggle for a new culture," which is a struggle that is focused on the discovery of a "new moral life" but which acknowledges that this cannot be "intimately connected to a new intuition of life until it becomes a new way of feeling and seeing reality."[34]

It is impossible to speak of moving into the realm of rhizomic sacralization—this time of democratized spirit and entertainment theology—and not recognize the considerable struggle this portends for anyone who would be serious about the missional dynamic of the church. Before leaving this idea and moving on to the next consideration, it is also worth noting that in the new social process, social network, and not social structure, is the key. Rather than rootedness, there is the complex, diverse relationship with the shifting global flows of the postmodern situation. "Believers are one with each other because they are joined to Christ. The temptation is to reverse these priorities so that by being joined to church one is joined to Christ."[35]

God-Talk in the Postsecular: Missional Theology for a Radically Different World

> In thought of tomorrow there is a power to upheave all thy creed, all the creeds, all the literature of nations.
>
> Ralph Waldo Emerson, *Essays and Poems*

> We were wise indeed, could we discern truly the signs of our own time; and by that knowledge of its wants and advantages, wisely adjust our own position to it. Instead of gazing idly into the obscure distance, look calmly around us, for a little, on the perplexed scene where we stand. Perhaps, on a more serious inspection, something of its perplexity will disappear, some of its distinctive characters and deeper tendencies more clearly reveal themselves; whereby our own relations to it, our true aims and endeavors in it, may also become clearer.
>
> Thomas Carlyle, *Signs of the Times*

The perplexity and complexity of the current station is beyond doubt. How far theology goes toward clarifying either is subject to discussion and debate. I hesitate to speak of postmodern or postsecular theology because it seems to imply a totalizing system or construct into which all things can be quantified, subjected to scrutiny, and reconfigured. This is far from the case and far from my intention.

I should perhaps clarify what I mean by theology, because it means different things to different people. My view of theology is that it is quite simply "god-talk," Phyllis Tickle's brilliant term for how we engage in the theological enterprise. This may be much too simplistic for some, but for me, theology is no longer a specialized field to be left to those deemed qualified. It is a wide-open and ever-growing field of passionate desire for that which cannot be completely named.

What I do have to say about the "doing of theology" in the present context, and why it is a different venture from other theological exercises, is that I believe, with Graham Ward and others, there is a relationship between our thinking and our cultural context.[36] Theology is both producer and product in the postsecular realm, and this interests me. Doing theology in the present situation means recapitulating the radical break, referenced in the opening of this section, with the emergence of the postmodern, and its facilitation of the return of God. I cannot say, nor would I want to, that there is a "postmodern theology," but there are surely postmodern theologies. The loss of a certain foundational framework in the latter years of the twentieth century gave rise to whole new theologies that no longer neatly traveled the liberal-conservative theological continuum.[37] The rise of new theologies has grown exponentially since then.

Christian theology is a pluralism of theologies and has never been in anyway monolithic. Theology in the present situation will be no different. What it cannot be is monochromatic. What it *must* be is missional and faithful. It must be missional in the sense that it must "go" to the culture and engage it, and it must be faithful in that it must seek to explore the *effect* of Jesus—living, dying, and rising—in the present situation.[38] Whatever else it will be remains to be seen. It is to create a new imaginary, a new mood, and a new dream as much as a construct. This is no easy task, for it is fraught with challenges. In fact, one could even say that it is an act of madness. As Kliever points out, "Words inevitably lose their meaning when that setting changes unless they are redefined to fit the new situation. . . . Even in new settings, efforts at redefinition become extremely difficult because stereotyped images of past meaning and use linger."[39]

To speak of theology is to speak of words, words about God, the word *of* God. But words about God are no exception to this process of meaning loss or change mentioned by Kliever in the above quote. To redefine theology, to redefine images and words about God, is to alter the social context in which speaking of God occurs.[40] "Words are what we use to write God into existence, they are the blanket we throw upon the invisible to make it visible," says Nick Cave.[41] Bonhoeffer asks how we might speak about God in a religionless world, how we might speak in what he calls a "secular way,"[42] as people who belong to the world. The theology of which I write must first undergo a relocation and be situated in the world. It must be for the world, practiced in the marketplace imaginary—a network of the new cultural—rather than in the synagogue.[43] "Il s'agit de saisir ce qui ne passe dans ce qui passe" (what matters is to grasp what does not pass away in what passes away).[44]

What I offer is a posture, or a new attitude, toward the process of doing theology, and then I outline three central dynamics that hold the potential to aid in the release of the words of God into the new situation.

Attitudes

> Literature remains alive only if we set ourselves immeasurable goals, far beyond all hope of achievement. Only if poets and writers set themselves tasks that no one else dares imagine will literature continue to have a function.
>
> Italo Calvino, *Six Memos for the Next Millennium*

I open with this quote from Italian writer Italo Calvino for a number of reasons, not the least of which is my desire to emphasize the poetic element of the theological endeavor of which I write. This endeavor must necessarily be poetic, because it must perform prophetic function: to herald the poetry, the love song, of God into the new situation. "The poet/prophet is a voice that shatters the shattered reality (or perhaps in this case, the unsettled reality) and evokes new possibility in the listening assembly. . . . Poetic speech . . . is a construal of a world beyond the one taken for granted."[45] But *what* to say is a bigger question.

Second, it is Calvino to whom I will now turn to develop some sense and shape of the manner of speech, of theology, that we might offer the world. Italo Calvino died suddenly in 1985, just as he was to depart for Harvard where he was to deliver the Charles Eliot Norton Lectures 1985–86. In his preparation for the lectures, Calvino looked ahead to a world he did not know then that he would not see and reflected on the nature of writing, of creating stories, of his own method and intentions. He had the idea for a series of eight lectures and had finished five at the time of his death. One lecture was left unfinished, and the remaining two are unknown except for a single working title. After his death, his wife gathered the five lectures and one unfinished idea and released them in a book titled *Six Memos for the Next Millennium*.[46] I will use these five finished ideas, and one idea "in title," as a sounding board for thinking about a posture and an attitude toward the theological process.

Calvino was brave and adventurous, and it is in that spirit that I invite us to consider how his approach to writing could translate into the way we approach theology today. He was a writer who wrote for his audience, not for himself. He provides us insight into the shape of a practical theology. His most famous novel *If on a Winter's Night a Traveler* opens with this line: "You are about to begin reading Italo Calvino's most famous novel, if on a winter's night a traveler."[47] He begins by literally inserting the reader into the text. This is writing for the reader, and the task before us is to theologize for the public. Calvino also distinguished between writers and thinkers who made one think, "Yes, that's the way it is," and others who made one say, "I never supposed it could be like that." The latter voices a new world, a new possibility.[48] I cannot overemphasize how important I believe it is to have a new approach to theology, how vital thoughtful words about God are for the church at this juncture. At first, I was tempted to recommend a theology of silence, because I fear we have spoken too much. I thought that there has been too much prose, too much opinion, too much anger and frustration, too much pabulum in the guise of truth to warrant another call to, as Brueggemann calls it, "daring speech for proclamation."[49] But silence is not a long-term answer, though it would be better to be silent than to keep repeating the same tired propositions that have become the benchmark of a Christianity no longer in tune with the surrounding culture and consequently without prophetic voice. What is called for, what needs to be discerned and voiced, is a new style, a whole new approach. So I offer these thoughts with timidity.[50] The six elements of writing that Calvino suggests are lightness, quickness, exactitude, visibility, multiplicity, and consistency.

Calvino is reflecting on forty years as a writer as he prepares to deliver these lectures, and he is trying to identify what his working method is. He determines that it is the removal of weight. Not substance, but weight. "I will devote my first lecture to the opposition of lightness and weight, and will uphold the value of lightness."[51] As Calvino develops it, lightness is what gives a story wings to fly, allows it to rise into the air. Lightness in theology is linked to the removal of its own weight, its baggage, if you will. On one of their most recent releases, the Irish band U2 gave an obscure title to their album: *All That You Can't Leave Behind*.[52] The clue to the meaning of this statement was found in the imagery on the album cover, which featured members of the band posed in various ways around an airport, and in the songs on the recording itself. A further clue was in the suitcase logo that accompanied their world tour. The enigmatic statement "all that you can't leave behind" is the response to the question, "What is in your suitcase?" On the edge of a new millennium, and of a new era for a band that had fought through a creative and interpersonal malaise, the album was a celebration of all the important things one must carry when one journeys somewhere new. Theology in the postsecular must ask the same question and consider what it is that will give us wings to fly. Lightness must mark the new context. In a time of journey, in the shift to a new environment, lightness of words carries its own weight.

Quickness is the second of Calvino's memos. "The secret of the story lies in its economy."[53] The quickness, or economy, of which he speaks is not rapidity, a telling of the story hurriedly so that listeners can hear it all before they move on. There is much talk in the culture about the short attention span of everyone, but I am not sure this is true. Concerning this, Rushkoff says, "The child of the remote control may indeed have a 'shorter' attention span as defined by the behavioral psychologists of our pre-chaotic culture's academic institutions. But this same child also has a much broader attention range. The skill to be valued in the twenty-first century is not the length of attention span, but the ability to multitask—to do many things at once."[54] Quickness is not rushing to tell the story, but being alert to the times in which the story is to be told (i.e., being aware of social, historical, and cultural contexts). We seldom consider breadth as a viable means of growth in a "depth" culture. But we have already discussed the rhizomic nature of the present age, one in which information, ideas, and stories float across a multiverse of interconnected global flows. Quickness in this situation is words that make one think, that can make one stop and listen. "A writer's work has to take account of many rhythms,"[55] writes Calvino, as does a theologian's. Rather than constantly bemoaning and critiquing the rhythms of these times, we should start to feel them and then see what can be done with theology. Great writing and great theology begin as a response to the rhythm of the times and end speaking to eternity.

Exactitude, Calvino's third memo, sounds more like a term to apply to theology than the first two. Calvino understands this to be a well-defined, well-developed plan; an evocation of clear, incisive, and memorable images; a language as precise as possible in its choice of words and subtleties of expression. Perhaps we could understand it as fewer words with more meaning. Exactitude means to rehearse the story before its telling; it is to consider the hearer. Earlier I recounted my encounters with the street preachers in Santa Monica. There was no consideration of audience, just assumption—they are all "sinners in need of a Savior." There was no sense of the rhythm, the feel of the space they were in, which was a shopping promenade where people go to eat and drink and enjoy the stuff of life. Here was the sort of place and the kind of people the Pharisees disparagingly accused Jesus of associating with. To rehearse the story before its telling is not to learn and be able to repeat it by rote, as the succession of ardent street evangelists did. It is, in fact, just the opposite. It is to consider the way in which words might capture the imagination of the listener; it is the careful telling of the story in such a way that the audience is hanging on every word. People were so amazed at the things Jesus had to say that they forgot about their other obligations. The world melted away and they were captivated: "Who has ever heard such teaching? He speaks with such authority!"

Calvino's lecture on the fourth of his memos, visibility, begins with a quote from Dante: "There is a line in Dante (*Purgatorio* XVII.25) that reads: 'Poi piovve dentro a l'alta fantasia' (then rained down into the high fantasy . . .). I will start out this evening with an assertion: fantasy is a place where it rains."[56]

What Calvino considers with this idea of visibility is the role that imagination plays in his writing, how it precedes or is "simultaneous" with verbal imagination. It seems strange to say that in doing theology we must remain open to God, to the potential for the encounter that transforms, but it shouldn't. All too often we begin our theologizing with a point to prove. Calvino notes that Dante's *Commedia* was the product of a series of visions, "Moveti lume che nel ciel s'informa" (You are moved by a light that is formed in heaven).[57] Given Dante's geometric universe with its layers and hierarchies of realms, it is no wonder that he considers that which comes from God to descend from above. In our resacralized world, that light may appear more often horizontally. For us, the challenge is to be open to the possibility of unexpected light—light that brings us visions of things we never expected—that shapes our world. Calvino notes that at the beginning of his manual *Spiritual Exercises*, Ignatius of Loyola "prescribes the visual composition of the place."[58] To engage with the new religious sensibility, we must not simply move into spaces like tourists, but we must also live there, because it is in these realms that light comes and spirit speaks, across the surface of the reenchanted world.

I said earlier that theology in the postmodern, in the postsecular, world is a multidisciplinary venture. It is about the intersecting and networking of ideas and theories that produce new permutations. This seems to be what Calvino was alluding to when he tackled the idea of multiplicity, the fifth memo. He began his exploration of multiplicity by echoing Gadda's view that the contemporary novel must be seen as "an encyclopedia, as a method of knowledge, and above all as a network of connections between the events, the people, and the things of the world."[59]

In modernity we created one theological connection point for the entire world: "You are a sinner who will die in your sins unless you repent. You must be born again." This sounds theologically correct, but is it really the case that this is the only connection with God through the Jesus story? I think not, though I think it is *a* connection to Christianity and has been the dominant mode of connection in the church post-Reformation. But it is not the sole means. And in postmodernity, such exclusion has little chance of connecting with the seekers and practitioners in the new religious economy. Multiplicity, a network of connections, is necessary, making room for both the sinners and the sinned against, the broken and the whole. Speaking more of the writer Gadda, Calvino says, "Whatever the starting point, the matter in hand spreads out and out, encompassing ever vaster horizons, and if it were permitted to go on further and further in every direction, it would end by embracing the entire universe."[60]

Writing, for Calvino, is the casting of a wide net, the inviting of all avenues of influence to feed into his imagination and find their way out through his stories. If with visibility the implication was to be open to the light, to the divine, then multiplicity is to allow our own lives and experiences into our theologizing. This may sound too subjective for some, but I do not know how to engage the world I live in if I don't insert my own life experience into my theology. This is not so self-consumed as it sounds. It might possibly be the reverse. Calvino speaks of the tendency to view the writer and the writing process as occurring in what he calls a "unicom"—a singular version of a vacuum, a place devoid of matter. What could be more self-centered than that? In response to this he offers a dual perspective, first acknowledging that we are:

> a combinatoria of experiences, informations, books we have read, things imagined. Each life is an encyclopedia . . . an inventory of objects, a series of styles, everything that can be constantly shuffled and reordered in every way conceivable. . . . But think what it would be to have a work conceived outside of the self, a work that could escape the limited perspective of the individual ego . . . to give speech to that which has no language.[61]

There is a certain finality to Calvino's lecture on multiplicity. He died before he could finish his other lectures. Going through his desk, not long after his death, his wife found a sheet of paper. On it, written in

New Orthodoxies

pencil, were the words: Six memos for the next millennium: 1—lightness; 2—quickness; 3—exactitude; 4—visibility; 5—multiplicity; 6—consistency. There were lectures on five of the words and just the one word to signal the direction of his last point. What Calvino would have to say about *consistency* remains between him and God. For our task, I would say that consistency is related to aesthetics. Consistency in style and approach is what defines the identity of a person. Consistency in the context of the new theological and missional horizon is the creation of a new aesthetic of the Christian life.

Armed with these thoughts, at least as a shaping reflection for the practice of theology, I would like to say a little about certain aspects of theology that I believe should be included in the practice and development of missional theologies. Again, the goal of these reflections is twofold: to begin to offer shape to a missional theological response to the postsecular moment and to address the dynamics and contours of the experience of the religious in this context.

Theological Containers

We have to struggle to replace a functionalist, bureaucrat, God with an artist God—that is to say a God who loves both beauty and risk. The goodness of God may be hard to argue from the creation—the flamboyance, the abundance, the sheer ebullience of God however is not.

Sara Maitland, *A Big Enough God*

The spiritual landscape, rather than the religious tradition, has become the arena for theological exploration.

Diarmuid O'Murchu, *Quantum Theology*

The Christian claim, then, is bound always to be something evolving and acquiring definition in the conversations of history.

Rowan D. Williams, *On Christian Theology*

There seem to be many kinds of postmodern theologies: postliberal, post-metaphysical, deconstructive, reconstructive, feminist, radical, and many others. I am not sure where mine fits in all of this. I imagine that mine includes elements of all of them, because there are so many people I have read and been influenced by. Friedrich Schleiermacher was not afraid to call his theology mystical; I am not afraid to term mine *artistic*. The approaches share something in common I think. There is a mystery to the intensely communicative power of the arts that has a symbolic function that often bypasses the reason. "Each generation has to create its own imaginative conception of God, just as each poet has to experience truth upon his own pulse."[1] So I lean on the artistic as a theological tool in hope that the employment of the arts will aid in the process of imagining God for our time. I am also a fan of mystery and am aware that there is something of the domain of mystery that does not show its face too often in the present situation. What I offer here are some coordinates by which I have been practicing theology recently, coordinates that I believe form a certain pod of actions I undertake when I think theologically. They are:

participatory, prophetic, and practical. They are performances of theology in specific settings, designed to stimulate the missional endeavor of the church into new settings and contribute to the emergence of Christian spiritualities.

Participatory Theology

Participatory theology is theology as cultural analysis and engagement. This is the outward function of theology. A theology of participation seeks to fulfill the aim of Milbank, that theology should seek to reclaim the whole world. Not in the sense of trying to bring everything back under the roof of the church, attempting to take over the conversation, but in the sense of acknowledging that in the present situation theology is being done outside the church. A participatory theology seeks to visit those sites where theology is at work and to join the conversation. This is theological dialogue in and with the present situation; it is theology done in a missional posture. Its impetus might be linked to Jesus's oft-used response to those who came to him with questions: "What do *you* say?" But this is not simply engagement with the culture's theological conversation, for there are larger dynamics at work. Participatory theology acknowledges that no field of study stands alone or apart. The present situation is one in which old categories have been dissolved and boundaries separating fields of study are being erased. In light of this, Mieke Bal observes:

> If "culture" is the object of study in the disciplines of art history, literary studies, classics and such social disciplines as anthropology, then the endeavor, again, must be an understanding of the present as integrative and dynamic. This conviction entails a need for interdisciplinary work as an indispensable framework for any study within separate disciplines. . . . Moreover, no field within this large arena can afford to limit itself to traditional self-understanding.[2]

The postsecular age represents the collapse of the old order and a new permeability; thus, the return to God is signaled in art, literature, and movies. A participatory theology, then, visits those places where elements of the religious emerge in the present situation and engages in dialogue and reflection within that framework.

This process is about exploring spirituality in the postsecular as a *lived experience*. There is a more radical side to this approach. It focuses on *this* side, the human side, of the religious equation. It is theology in conversation and partnership, seeking not so much to influence as to understand. It is also the case that such an approach leads to the shaping of theology itself, shaped in this context sometimes by non-Christian sources. Going perhaps further than I would, Mieke Bal, who views the theological task as primarily cultural analysis, proffers an "atheological theology" that includes the possibility of being able to break open the confining limitations imposed by authoritarian religion and open up possibilities for different forms of relationship that are insensitive to old, ill-conceived taboos. I have no desire to be insensitive to the old, and I am not sure she fully reads the situation for what it is. But sadly, the authoritarian religions have little to say in the present situation. They are usually not present in the conversation because dialogue is usually taking place out of the reach of their limited forays into the cultural imagination. But that said, there is the potential for considering new theological approaches by bringing the whole of life as it is being expressed back into the theological conversation. I also view this as a theology that affirms and continues to affirm difference. By this I mean that it will be a theological impulse informed by awareness of plurality and divergent opinions on all issues. Rather than seeking to be a "final voice" on the matter, it will recognize itself as but one voice in the ongoing cultural conversation about God.

Prophetic Theology

A prophetic theology relates to the awakening of the theological imaginary and explores the potential for the capacity of witness in a number of cultural situations. If participatory theology has at its heart a certain posture of engagement and absorption of the present situation, then prophetic theology is the rehearsing of the gospel in the idiom, language, and rhetoric of the postsecular. It is the discovery of a new voice. It could be argued that this represents a more classic view of theological method, for it seems to point to the historic engagement of the church with other idioms: the recovery of Greek philosophical thought and the subsequent use of its language and theories in the work of Aquinas or the use of Marxist rhetoric in Liberation Theology. An idea behind this is that not only can there be positive conversation with the present circumstance, but beyond the potential of positive engagement is the opportunity that the idioms of the other setting can, in fact, allow for the discovery of other elements of the gospel story.

New Orthodoxies

Take for instance Matthew 5:5, which says, "Blessed are the meek, for they will inherit the earth." Now the French Louis Second version translates the same verse this way: "Hereux les débonnaires, cars ils hériteront la terre!" "Les débonnaire" is in French the "easy-going." In my mind this is not too far from "meek," but it is also not the same. But consider now the appropriation of the word "debonair" into the English language where the definition now becomes: "suave, urbane." Suddenly what I assumed I knew has changed drastically, because my understanding of the text has been influenced by another mode of engagement: "blessed are the meek because they dance like Fred Astaire." It doesn't mean that things have changed, but what has changed is my ability to communicate the story in other contexts and circumstances with a new emphasis and dynamic. So if I engage the democratization of spirit in the postsecular and learn the new language of the spirit-talk, can it inform my theological constructs and allow me to express them in new ways? I am convinced it can.

This mode requires confidence in the fact that there is something to be held on to and which can be held on to. I find that there is often a lack of confidence among some of the most vocally ardent advocates of more fundamentalist positions when it comes to issues like this. Any changing of categories or language or dynamic is seen as a move away from the perceived solid center. If the present situation speaks of God as the sacred or the divine, can my theology handle the shift? And more than that, can I still articulate the story while remaining faithful to the tradition? I referenced a Muslim writer, named Zhor Ben Chamsi, who wrote in support of Salman Rushdie's right to create his art. What he said bears repeating and expanding slightly here. In an essay called "Being Open to the Imaginary," Chamsi had this to say about his own faith's approach to situations in which its stories are rehearsed in new ways:

> He [Rushdie] treated the sacred word as it happened to affect both the real and imaginary worlds of a modern Muslim living in London. Given the reigning orthodoxy it would appear that the word of God could never germinate in this way; or ever be fecundated by the imaginary; or ever be made to appear as a myth from which to continue indefinitely building on. Yet this is exactly what is said in the Koran apropos Mary. Mary was fecundated by the word or breath of God after her cousin Joseph had been presented to her by the angel.[3]

A prophetic theology considers that the Word of God could germinate this way or that and opens itself up to any number of potential expressions.

Practical Theology

> Time, perhaps, to propose a new thesis of the post-frontier; to assert that the emergence, in the age of mass migration, mass displacement, globalized finance and industries, of this new, permeable, post-frontier is the distinguishing feature of our times, and . . . explains our development as nothing else can. For all their permeability, the borders snaking across our world have never been of greater importance. This is the dance of history in our age: slow, slow, quick, quick, slow, back and forth and from side to side, we step across these fixed and shifting lines.
>
> Salman Rushdie, *Step Across This Line*

> Christianity is thinkable only if it is alive. And there is no life without new risks in our actual situation . . . only new departures manifest and will continue to manifest Christianity as still *alive*. . . . It is impossible to be Christian without a common risk, without the creation of a new divergence in relation to our past and to our present, without being alive.
>
> Michel de Certeau, *To Step Forward*

The final ingredient of my theological grid, practical theology, probably needs little said about it. It is hardly a new term to the conversation. I include it here because there is no missional response to the incarnation of religion in the postsecular without risk, and for me practical theology is all about risk. Practical theology, in my mind, is daring to believe that life and not theory is where the theological enterprise begins. If we don't take the step, Christianity remains not a living faith but a dead resource; its bones all but picked clean of any sign of life. The only potential for the future of Christian faith lies in the doing, the going, the practice. A practical theology is not the taking of theology and applying it to a certain situation, but rather it is a beginning, as Michel de Certeau argues. In his seminal work *Transforming Mission*, David Bosch closes his account of the state of mission with this statement: "Looked at from this perspective, mission is, quite simply, the participation of Christians in the liberating mission of Jesus."[4] This is a good definition of mission, but I think it might be a little more complicated than that. I think mission might be the *journey* of Christians into all the world to *discover* the liberating mission of Jesus in transforming encounter with others, and discovery is almost always the result of adventure, creativity, and risk. These theological performances aspire to such a risk.

There remains one final topic of exploration. On the heels of adopting a project identity, forging a new attitude toward the new theological moment, and exploring how theology might be performed in the postsecular situation, I must direct our attention to a final point: a new encoding of message. For many, the claims of Christianity no longer ring true. The stories seem lifeless or at least disconnected from this life. The language seems weighted down with concepts and ideas that no longer resonate. To encode the message in new ways is more than contextualization, it is a reframing or a reimagining of the story and the discovery of a new language for proclamation.

Making Signs
Encoding the Message

When the world shook and the sun was wiped out of heaven, it was not at the crucifixion, but at the very cry from the cross: the cry which confesses that God was forsaken of God. And now let the revolutionists choose a creed from all the creeds and a god from all the gods of the world . . . they will not find another god who has himself been in revolt. . . . They will find . . . only one religion in which God seemed for an instant to be an atheist.

G. K. Chesterton, *Orthodoxy*

The problem with Christians is they've put a padlock on paradise and lost Jesus in a bunch of bad songs.

Glenn Frey, musician

Hans Holbein the Younger was a painter at the court of Henry VIII. The German-born artist created many memorable works that can be found in museums across Europe. One of his most famous pieces is called *The Ambassadors*. It has been the focus of much attention over the centuries because of its beauty, its complex design, and its enigmatic meaning. *The Ambassadors*, painted in 1533, is an example of a technique called *anamorphosis*. Anamorphic art features an image that is intentionally compressed and stretched so that it cannot be seen for what it is in conventional viewings. Holbein's painting of two French ambassadors to the court is a meditation on man's scientific achievements and the growing religious divisions in the light of the Protestant Reformation. Surprisingly, it also features a large anamorphic skull in the bottom of the painting. The reason for the insertion of this image into the painting has been the source of much debate, with theories that range from its being a meditation on mortality to a loose reference to Holbein's name (Holbein can be loosely translated as "hollow bone," from its German roots). The skull can only be seen when the painting is viewed in an unconventional way, but when viewed from the new angle, things come into perspective.

Like Holbein, Spanish surrealist painter Salvador Dali traded his whole career in mind-bending images that forced the viewer to stretch themselves in order to comprehend what they were seeing. Fifty thousand people went to view Salvador Dali's work *Christ of St. John of the Cross* when it was first shown in Glasgow, Scotland, in 1954. The painting was a revelation, a reinterpretation of one of the most familiar and oft-replicated icons of Christian art: Christ on the cross. What made Dali's work so monumental and generated such interest was the challenge and the paradoxes it presented to the viewer. Drawing inspiration from a sketch of the crucified Christ done by St. John of the Cross, Dali took the familiar image and changed it. He made it contemporary by setting the painting in a local landscape familiar to him and then set about presenting the image. This painting offers a new perspective, both in the manner in which his painting presents the image and in the purpose for the painting. The painting can be a little disorienting, for the viewer simultaneously looks down on and up at the figure of Christ on the cross. Dali paints Christ as hanging over the world, yet we seem to be looking down on him. Christ himself in the painting is a revelation. Of this work, Dali says, "My aesthetic ambition was completely opposite of all the Christs painted by most of the modern painters, who have all interpreted him in the expressionistic and contortionistic sense, thus obtaining emotion through ugliness. My principal preoccupation was that my Christ would be as beautiful as the God that he is."[1]

In contrast to centuries of portrayals of Christ in art, in which the focus is on the suffering on the cross, Dali attempts to make a statement by appealing to beauty. A marked shift particularly from more medieval representations, such as those reflected in Mel Gibson's movie *The Passion of the Christ*. Dali's painting was influenced by a number of other issues in his life. Produced at a time when he was deeply troubled by the potential for nuclear destruction, was experimenting with hallucinogenic drugs, and was exploring Christian mysticism, his paintings of that period tried to capture the intersections of all those differing ideas. The painting presents the circle of Jesus's head as the nexus of a triangular configuration that traces its shape along the extended arms of Jesus and forms a triangle as the painted space between the extended arms and the Savior's head. This, for Dali, was symbolic of the nucleus of the atom. It was within the scope of his own situation that Dali wished to present Christ. His Christ is only partially visible, and what is seen is not the usual bruised and battered body of Christ. He writes, "I want to paint a Christ that is a painting with more beauty and joy than has ever been painted before. I want to paint a Christ that is the absolute opposite of Grunewald's materialistic and savagely anti-mystical one."[2]

In this statement we discover Dali's intention and his foil. His particular foil is a painting by Matthius Grunewald. *The Crucifixion*, painted between 1510 and 1516, was part of an altarpiece commissioned by an Antonine monastery.[3] Christ in Grunewald's painting is ugly, characterized by an emaciated body and long tendril-like fingers curling around the nails in his palms. The light over Christ's body creates a pallid tone in his flesh and is made even more harsh by the virtually black background of the painting. His grotesque state of immense suffering is further underscored by the figures witnessing this event: his mother, who is fainting into the arms of John, the beloved disciple; a penitent Mary Magdalene weeping at his feet again; a lamb, its right front limb wrapped around a cross as blood pours from its heart into a communion cup; and the figure of John the Baptist pointing at the cross, as if there is not enough to draw our attention to the Christ image. Floating in the black background are John's words spoken when he was questioned about Jesus: "He must increase, but I must decrease." In the painting, even though he is in the foreground, John is dwarfed by the figure on the cross. This is a masterful piece of medieval religious symbolism: Christ is the man of sorrows, the lamb slain for our transgressions. John baptized with water, but Jesus washed our sins away in his blood. As Dali comments:

> It is horror with a purpose—to teach us one understanding of the theology of the Crucifixion. He suffers so much, because he loves us so much. The pain Christ endures has to be great enough to redeem the sins of the whole world, past, present, future. The conclusion is simple: the more we sin, the more he must suffer to save us. And the speed with which we grasp the enormity of that equation is the measure of Grunewald's achievement.[4]

It is against this that Dali contrasts his work. For him there is no redemption in resorting to shock tactics or through ugliness or even through the sublime, which is the gothic means of shocking us into response. Dali seeks instead to present the mystical beauty of Christ as an antidote to his world's fascination with nuclear destruction. He accomplishes this by finding a new way of presenting the image of Jesus. To encode the message of Jesus in the postsecular is to perform a similar task. It is to approach the story from other directions, to bring out other elements.

This not to say that there is simply one way of doing this. In fact, I would argue that we must avoid attempting to totalize our encodings and realize that there is never just one way to tell a story, convey a truth, or transmit an idea.

Another recent representation of Christ is a statue commissioned by the National Gallery in London, which invited the creators of a number of works to display them outside the entrance to the museum on a plinth in Trafalgar Square, that imposing homage to Britain's global dominance through empire. Situated in the middle of London, Trafalgar Square features a central column that literally raises Nelson, Britain's great military hero, to the heavens and is protected on each of its corners by four huge statues of lions, symbolic of Britain's quiet but imposing regal strength. It was in this context that Mark Wallinger presented his rather less imposing statue titled *Ecco Homo* ("Behold the man!"), which depicts the event of Pilate washing his hands, thereby symbolically absolving himself from all involvement and responsibility in the volatile "Jesus" affair. A three-dimensional statue was made of resin mixed with white marble, which creates a ghostlike white. The statue was made out of a mold of a clean-shaven art student who wore a cap over his head and kept his eyes firmly closed. The result was a very human statue that echoes and reverberates with allusion to the historic Christ figure and yet reveals other aspects, in particular, his humanity. Because of the rubber cap worn by the student, there is no long, flowing mane of hair, no piercing eyes, no marks of torture. The body is smooth, its appearance both contemporary and timeless. Instead of a crown of thorns, there is a crown fashioned from barbed wire. In Trafalgar Square, this rather slight figure of Jesus stood, arms clasped quietly behind his back, before all the iconic celebrations of human, and particularly British, power and aspiration. Of his statue Wallinger said, "Whether or not we regard Jesus as a deity, he was at the very least a political leader of an oppressed people. The sculpture alludes to the recent historical past and its sad record of religious and racial intolerance."[5]

This is Christ for this age but also a Christ for all ages. Images of Jesus are historical and contextual, as are recitations of the gospel. Things are added and subtracted; there are differences in focus and emphasis. My opening quote from Chesterton is of help here. Chesterton wrote at a time when atheism was a significant and growing alternative to faith. The rise of scientific-rationalism, including new theories such as Darwin's evolutionary model, were undermining the already embattled Christian faith that Chesterton held. The gift Chesterton offers is the power of a new perspective. Rather than address issues of sin, salvation, and redemption, he appeals directly to the "atheistic" potential in the Jesus story, the singular moment in the Passion where a conversation about atheism and God is a viable one. This is what I mean when I say that we must once again encode the message of Jesus.

In the present situation it seems that some are willing to change, rearrange, and rethink form, but there is little attention paid to change of content in the presentation of the Christian message in the postsecular. My sense is that it is the message, the very content, that which we present as being representative of Christian faith that is the one thing that needs to be revisited and re-encoded. The dynamic at the center of the democratization of spirit occurring in our time is creativity, the creative imagining and fashioning of various elements into a livable expression of a person's connection with the sacred. It is too easy to dismiss this as folly. But in some sense, as long as Christianity remains a vapor trail of modern and premodern concepts about how the relation between the human and the divine is achieved, Christian thinking will not contribute much to the matters at hand. The shift in times demands a new reiteration of the message, one that is a pertinent and timely iteration of the timeless Christ story for our cultural context. The message needs to speak to our time, not times past. Chesterton made room for atheists at the foot of the cross, not by denying other realities of the story, but by isolating the very point of connection by which the potential for engagement might be effected.

We may need to make less room for atheists at the foot of the cross than Chesterton's time needed to. In the postsecular, the issue is not so much reaching those who don't believe as it is communicating with those who believe in *something else*, something other, and seeking to provide them with links to the sacred as it is expressed through the gospel. There is no singular message to encode; there is instead multiple codings of the story as it intersects with our lives in the present situation.[6] My modest proposal is that we join the people's religion, that in effect we democratize Christianity and allow for the emergence of Christian spiritualities, connected not by singular identity and meaning but by the living, dying, and rising Jesus as he is rehearsed in our lives.

A Final Thought

What I have tried to do in these pages is capture something of the mood and landscape of the present time. I want to accept what is going on in the realms of the spiritual as valid and invite the reader to embrace the dominant expression of religion in our time, namely, spirituality, which in the postsecular manifests itself as "a people's religion." Democratized spirituality is the result of the democratization of spirit along with pretty much everything else through the new globalized cultural imaginary. I have also attempted to employ something of the contour and dynamics of "entertainment theology" in my populist approach to the situation. In arguing for a move to Christian spiritualities, and a move *away* from old-fashioned Christianity, it is my desire that our imaginations be attuned to the realities of the present situation and that our missional impetus be challenged by the times.

I am in effect arguing that Christian faith needs to move into the current religious moment and manifest itself not as a religion of the past but as a religion of the present *and* the future. It must derive its missional impetus from the present time and see the democratization around us as a gift and an opportunity. Christianity must also realize that the diffusion of the message is not contingent on some centralized authority but on the wind of the true Spirit that still moves across the waters of these turbulent and chaotic times.

Notes

Introduction

1. Leonardo Boff, *Global Civilization: Challenges to Society and Christianity* (London: Equinox, 2005), 11.

2. Diarmuid O'Murchu, *Quantum Theology* (New York: Crossroad, 1997), 21.

3. Douglas Rushkoff, *Playing the Future* (New York: Riverhead Books, 1996), 5.

4. Leonard Sweet, *Quantum Spirituality* (Dayton, OH: Whaleprint, 1991), 21.

5. I use the word "stable" quite loosely, for change is always with us. However, I do believe that the changes we are experiencing today are more than cosmetic and herald seismic changes in the ways we understand ourselves as human beings.

6. Sandra Schneiders, "Religion and Spirituality: Strangers, Rivals, or Partners?" The Santa Clara Lectures, Santa Clara University, Santa Clara, CA, February 6, 2000, 1.

7. David Hay and Kate Hunt, "Is Britain's Soul Waking Up?" *Tablet*, London, June 27, 2000, 846.

8. I use the term "spirit" to highlight the fact that this is not Holy Spirit, or Great Spirit, or any other of the permutations by which the presence of God has been characterized in other times by both the church and other faiths, but rather a new understanding of spirit not bound necessarily by any religious affiliation or association.

9. For an expansion of this thought see Graham Ward, *True Religion* (Oxford: Blackwell, 2003), chap. 1.

10. Quoted in Graham Cray, ed., *Mission-Shaped Church: Church Planting and Fresh Expressions of Church in a Changing Context* (London: Church House Publishing, 2004), 11.

11. The use of Scripture may not be enough to convince some that the show is therefore "spiritual" or faith focused. However, the point is that there is no problem with invoking the spiritual to serve the purposes of the story and lend greater meaning to the events unfolding before the audience.

12. Bruce Mau, ed., *Massive Change* (New York: Phaidon, 2004), 16.

13. Colleen McDannell, *Material Christianity: Religion and Popular Culture in America* (New Haven, CT: Yale University Press, 1995), 1.

14. See note 9 above.

15. Ward, *True Religion*, 125.

16. Cray, ed., *Mission-Shaped Church*, 41.

Part 1 New Horizons

1. David Lyon, *Jesus in Disneyland: Religion in Postmodern Times* (Cambridge: Polity, 2000), 41.

2. I use the term "reenchantment" to signify the return of interest in religion and spirituality in contemporary postmodern society. It reflects a shift away from what Max Weber called "die Entzauberung der Welt"—the disenchantment of the world.

3. Please note that I use the terms postmodern and postsecular interchangeably. For me, to speak of the postmodern is to speak of the postsecular. I trust the reader will not find this too confusing. The use of postmodern terminologies is like walking a minefield of minutiae, and this probably adds yet one more layer of terminology. But in true postmodern fashion, I take license with my use of terms and words!

Magical, Mystical Polish

1. William E. Connolly, *Why I Am Not a Secularist* (Minneapolis: University of Minnesota Press, 1999), 19.

2. Bryan R. Wilson, *Religion in Secular Society: A Sociological Comment* (London: Watts, 1966), 14.

3. Lonnie D. Kliever, *The Shattered Spectrum: A Survey of Contemporary Theology* (Atlanta: John Knox, 1981), 8.

4. By "mediated" I refer to the theory of sociologist Arjun Apadurai, who posits that we now live in five scapes: ethnoscape, technoscape, financescape, mediascape, and ideoscape (Arjun Appadurai, *Modernity at Large: Cultural Dimension of Globalization* [Minneapolis: University of Minnesota Press, 1996], 33).

5. Robert C. Tucker, ed., *The Marx-Engels Reader* (New York: Norton, 1978), 145.

6. Alan Aldridge, *Religion in the Contemporary World: A Sociological Introduction* (Cambridge: Polity, 2000), 60.

7. Abstract from the Introduction to "Contribution to the Critique of Hegel's Philosophy of Right," *Marx/Engels Internet Archive*, www.marxists.org.

8. Aldridge, *Religion in the Contemporary World*, 61.

9. Ibid., 63.

10. Richard Cimino and Don Lattin, *Shopping for Faith: American Religion in the New Millennium* (San Francisco: Jossey-Bass, 1998), 11.

11. Ibid., 15.

12. We should not dismiss this as extreme individualism run rampant, however. Contemporary society is characterized by a deep belief in the connectedness of all things, and particularities of personal belief are not necessarily viewed as hindrances to communal expression of belief. These particularities simply represent individual interpretations of the collective conscience that many people accept as a reality.

13. Max Weber, *The Protestant Work Ethic and the Spirit of Capitalism* (London: Allen and Unwin, 1930), 182, quoted in Aldridge, *Religion in the Contemporary World*, 66.

14. Aldridge, *Religion in the Contemporary World*, 68.

15. Ibid.

16. Jacques Derrida, "Faith and Knowledge," in *Religion*, ed. Jacques Derrida and Gianni Vattimo, trans. Samuel Weber (Cambridge: Polity, 1998), 1–78.

17. Ward, *True Religion*, 129.

18. Ibid.

19. It would seem that C. S. Lewis and J. R. R. Tolkien were precursors of this shift.

20. Angela Rippon, one of the BBC's most well-known television news presenters, offered *Harry Potter and the Sorcerer's Stone* as her choice for the best book in Britain in a survey conducted by the BBC during April 2003, called "The Big Read." It was a national survey designed to discover Britain's all-time favorite book.

21. There is also a wealth of religio-spiritual themes in contemporary pop music, underscoring the ongoing reenchantment of society. Many of the artists, while quick to distance themselves from organized religion, are in fact engaging with forms of traditional religions. These include Bono (Christianity), the Beastie Boys (Buddhism), and Madonna (Kabbalah, a mystical expression of Judaism).

22. James Redfield, *The Celestine Prophecy: An Adventure* (New York: Warner Books, 1993).

23. Paolo Coehlo, *The Alchemist: A Fable about Following Your Dream* (New York: HarperCollins, 1993).

24. Rick Warren, *The Purpose-Driven Life: What on Earth Am I Here For?* (Grand Rapids: Zondervan, 2002).

25. Tim F. LaHaye and Jerry B. Jenkins, *Left Behind: A Novel of the Earth's Last Days* (Wheaton: Tyndale House, 1995).

26. The last two works mentioned fall into a slightly different category in that they specifically address traditional Christian views. They show, however, the continuing audience for such works. Both books meet the criteria for contemporary books on spirituality. *The Purpose-Driven Life* is a Christianized self-help book, and the *Left Behind* series is Christian eschatology told in story form. Inspirational fiction is a common category on bookstore shelves these days, a development that emerged in the mid-1990s.

27. Ross Robertson, "Searching for a Postmodern Religion on the Set of the *Celestine Prophecy*," *What Is Enlightenment?* November 2004–February 2005, 65.

The Implosion of Modernity and the Rise of the Postsecular

1. Peter Steinfels, "Swapping 'Religion' for 'Postsecularism,'" *New York Times*, August 3, 2002.

2. Ibid.

3. Graham Ward, ed., *The Postmodern God: A Theological Reader* (Malden, MA: Blackwell, 1997), xv.

4. Ibid.

5. Old ages die slowly, if at all. There seems to be a cumulative buildup of systems, ideas, philosophies, and worldviews that form an ever-wider pool of resources for the creation of the self in postsecular times.

6. This is reflected in a variety of ways. The recent invasion of Iraq is at some level fueled by the idea that Western democratic values concerning human rights and freedom need to be made available to everyone, everywhere, with no regard for differing views on the matter.

7. Ward, *Postmodern God*, xvii.

8. Manuel Castells, *The Information Age*, vol. 1, *The Rise of the Network Society* (Malden, MA: Blackwell, 1996), 433.

9. Ibid.

10. This is reflected in pop culture's love of space in the waning days of modernity, whether in the form of science fiction novels and comics or television shows such as *Lost in Space* and *The Jetsons*, or movies such as *Flash Gordon* or *Planet of the Apes*.

11. Anthony Giddens, *Modernity and Self-identity* (London: Polity, 1991), 17.

12. This was also the result of other early developments in modernity, such as the shift away from the liturgical calendar (space time) and the rise of the civic state.

13. David Harvey, *The Condition of Postmodernity* (London: Blackwell, 1990), 240.

14. Lyon, *Jesus in Disneyland*, 139.

15. For the following interpretation of *Romeo and Juliet*, I am deeply indebted to Ward, *True Religion*.

16. Anthony Holden, *William Shakespeare: His Life and Work* (London: Abacus, 1999), 140–47.

17. *Romeo and Juliet*, act 1, scene 1. Text references are to act, scene, and line.

18. Ward, *True Religion*, 6–9.

19. I recommend Holden, *William Shakespeare*; Frank Kermode, *The Age of Shakespeare* (New York: Modern Library, 2003); Dennis Taylor and David N. Beauregard, eds., *Shakespeare and the Culture of Christianity in Early Modern England* (New York: Fordham University Press, 2003). See also Ward, *True Religion*.

20. Desiderus Erasmus, *Prayer to the Lord Jesus for Peace in the Church*, trans. Charles J. McDonough, in *Collected Works of Erasmus: Spiritualia and Pastoralia*, ed. John W. O'Malley and Louis A. Perraud (Toronto: University of Toronto Press, 1999), 109.

21. Changes in the understanding of the nature of time and space invariably affect cosmology, and the relationship between cosmology and religion is made more firm as our understanding of the nature and composition of the universe and its functions shift.

22. Holden, *William Shakespeare*, 12.

23. Ibid.

24. Quoted in Steve Solimer, "Shakespeare's Time: Riddles in *Romeo and Juliet* Solved," *English Literary Renaissance* 35, no. 407 (November 2005).

25. A number of acts were passed, ostensibly to promote better Christian living. But given the Reformers' intense aversion to the adoration of saints and their attendant icons and ritualized practices, these changes can also be viewed as an attempt to consolidate the new Protestant religion by structuring the lives of the people within a new religious framework.

26. Eamon Duffy, *Marking the Hours: English People and Their Prayers, 1240–1570* (New Haven, CT: Yale University Press, 2006).

27. "I think, therefore I am" (Rene Descartes, *A Discourse on Method* 6.1637).

28. In spite of the continuing fascination with watches and a particular trend with watches as fashion accessories, I see fewer and fewer people wearing watches. More and more of us use our increasingly multifunctional cell phones and Blackberries as timekeepers, calendars, etc., thus eradicating the need for watches and other more traditional sources for telling time.

29. Margaret Wertheim, *The Pearly Gates of Cyberspace: A History of Space from Dante to the Internet* (New York: Norton & Company, 1999), 30–31.

30. Ibid., 33.

31. Franco Zeffirelli adopted a similar posture in another of his films, *Brother Sun, Sister Moon*, the story of St. Francis and Clare of Assisi. In both films he presents the medieval context as romanticized, idealized, "purer times." An innocence reigns, in contrast to the advancing complexities and compromises of his own times—the age of the sexual revolution, etc.

32. The following ideas are my own, but I must acknowledge my debt to Graham Ward, both in private conversation and through his book *True Religion*, for inspiration and affirmation.

33. See the opening scenes of the play, where the innuendo between "swords" and "pricks" frames the exploration of a deeper kind of love and erotic sensibility as the relationship between the two young lovers unfolds.

34. There are certain stories that permeate Western culture, with which most of us are familiar. Along with those stories are certain expectations: we "know how the story goes," and we are prepared to experience it in a certain way. This is what I term "prefocus."

35. Ward, *True Religion*, chap. 1.

36. Wertheim, *Pearly Gates of Cyberspace*, 36.

37. The development of sacred space as an aesthetic in and of itself was a dominant theme in post-Reformation architecture. The church as "sacred space," in contrast to secular space, was a key development in church aesthetics, as icons, statues, and other artistic devices employed to provide access to the divine were abandoned by the Reformers. The loss of visual imagery led to the creation of space itself as a means of communion with the divine.

38. This stands in stark contrast to Kant, an Enlightenment (and thus modernist) thinker, who believed that space and time were a priori concepts that we imposed on the world and by which we understood our world.

39. Ray Pahl, *After Success: Fin-de-Siecle Anxiety and Identity* (Cambridge: Polity Press, 1995), quoted in Lyons, *Jesus in Disneyland*, 89.

40. Manuel Castells, *The Power of Identity* (Malden, MA: Blackwell, 1997).

41. Lyon, *Jesus in Disneyland*, 91.

42. This issue of the self will be taken up more thoroughly when I explore the rise of postmodernity and the challenges it creates for contemporary Christian theology in particular.

43. Appadurai, *Modernity at Large*, 53, emphasis mine.

44. Ibid., 54.

45. Lyon, *Jesus in Disneyland*, 91–92.

46. Ibid., 18.

47. This sacralization of the self is in all likelihood not demonstrated by a shift toward more traditional religious affiliation or expression but rather will manifest in new spiritual permutations. I recommend George Rawlyk, *Is Jesus Your Personal Savior? In Search of Canadian Evangelicalism in the 1990s* (Montreal: McGill-Queen's University Press, 1996).

48. James B. Nelson, *Body Theology* (Louisville: Westminster John Knox, 1992).

49. Gerard Loughlin, *Alien Sex: The Body and Desire in Cinema and Theology* (Oxford: Blackwell, 2004).

50. Joan Smith, *Moralities: Sex, Money, and Power in the 21st Century* (London: Allen Lane, 2001), 86.

51. Ibid., 87.

52. This performance is archived on a number of Web sites and is also available in *Madonna's Greatest Video Hits* released by Universal Music, 2000.

53. It is not the idea of another world that is problematic as much as it is the linearity of many theological formulations. Every time people attend the screening of a film they visit other worlds, other imaginaries, other ways of being human. The complexity and technological advancement of computer-driven special effects allow for the re-creation on the screen of incredibly complex and thorough "other worlds." Simply by going to the cinema, we already "inhabit" other worlds.

54. Elaine Graham, "Post/Human Conditions," *Theology and Sexuality: The Journal of the Centre for the Study of Christianity and Sexuality* 10, no. 2 (March 2004): 10.

55. Ibid., 13–16.

56. The social and cultural ramifications of these developments are immense and complex. A close friend of mine has a child who was carried to term and birthed by his mother-in-law. A fertilized egg was taken from his wife, who was unable to carry a baby in pregnancy, and placed in her mother, who then carried the embryo until birth. The mother of a child is usually the one who gives birth, but in this case the mother was merely a receptacle for someone else's eggs and sperms. Combined with other issues, such as surrogacy, adoption, and in vitro fertilization, modalities of parenting and family are being radically redefined.

57. We will return to this theme as it unfolds in one of the categorizations of postsecular religion.

58. Graham, "Post/Human Conditions," 13.

59. Ibid.

60. Ibid., 14.

61. This is a postmodern form of possession, not by the demonic but by the alien outsider, which seeks to inhabit the human form to perform its evil intention against humanity. This is a dominant theme in a world in which God's absence is keenly felt by a number of people.

62. Stellarc, performance artist, quoted in Graham, "Post/Human Conditions," 15.

63. Ibid., 15–16.

64. Ibid.

65. Mark Poster, "Introduction to the Forum on 'A Magna Carta for the Knowledge Age': Cyberspace and the American Dream," 188–89 in Graham, "Post/Human Conditions," 16.

66. http://TallSkinnyKiwi.com.

67. The coffee, however, has to be made by the cyberguest in his or her own "real world" situation!

68. This was a continual response by those I questioned for a research paper I wrote on tattooing and body modification for my Master's degree, Fuller Seminary, summer quarter, 1998. What I write about here is the tattooing and body piercing related to self-ritualization and marking life passages. This is in direct contrast to the growing number of people for whom body mutilation, cutting, and self-harm are illnesses.

69. Interestingly, the cover story of a recent issue of *Christian Century* was on Christians and tattooing. See Tim Keel, "Tattooed: Body Art Goes Mainstream," *Christian Century*, May 15, 2007, 18–20; see also Beth Felker Jones, "Marked for Life," *Christian Century*, May 15, 2007, 18–20.

70. See www.herstory/ws/web/articles/body_self-injury.html.

71. A slang term for those who practice self-wounding.

72. Slavoj Žižek, *On Belief* (New York: Routledge, 2001), 10.

73. O'Murchu, *Quantum Theology*, 190.

74. Ibid., 191.

75. See Weber, *Protestant Work Ethic*.

76. On the "network society," I recommend Manuel Castells, *The Information Age*, 3 vols. (Malden, MA: Blackwell, 1996–98).

77. Two members of my own religious group defined themselves in this way.

78. Frankie is a play on Francis and an allusion to St. Francis of Assisi, who is often credited with being the first person to verifiably receive stigmata, or the wounds of Christ.

79. Suspicion and distrust of authority manifest in many instances of conspiracy theories that permeate contemporary culture. It reflects a growing sense

that institutions naturally prevent ordinary citizens from having access to information that might affect social ordering. The explosion of information has been attended by a dynamic of conspiracy theories, and these are reflected in a number of sites throughout the postsecular world. Whether it is in the television show *The X-Files* or in films like *Conspiracy Theory*, this idea is both reflected and disseminated in and through pop culture.

80. This issue is raised in another film, *The Third Miracle*, which revolves around the story of an unwed mother put forward as a candidate for elevation to sainthood. The film explored the resistance of the church to such a person as being a viable candidate for sainthood, while hundreds of ordinary people were already interacting with the woman as though she were already elevated.

81. Sulak Sivaraksa, founder and director of the International Network of Engaged Buddhists, as quoted in Carter Phipps and Craig Hamilton, "If Heaven Were a Place on Earth: A Pilgrimage to the 2004 World Parliament of Religions," *What Is Enlightenment?* November 2004–February 2005, 11. Phipps and Hamilton also quote primatologist Jane Goodall as noting that the "religious traditions have been lagging behind what's actually going on in the world today" (ibid.).

Evolution Not Revolution

1. James Twitchell, *Lead Us into Temptation* (New York: Columbia University Press, 1999), 6.

2. Ken Wilber in *What Is Enlightenment?* November 2004–February 2005.

3. Pitirim A. Sorokin, *Social and Cultural Dynamics: A Study of Change in Major Systems of Art, Truth, Ethics, Law, and Social Relationships* (London: Transaction Publishers, 1985).

4. Ibid., 20–40. See also, Frederick W. Bave, *The Spiritual Society: What Lurks beyond Postmodernism* (Wheaton, IL: Crossway Books, 2001), esp. pp. 43–50.

5. These findings were eventually gathered together in his definitive work on the subject, *Social and Cultural Dynamics*, first published in 1937.

6. Ibid., 63–73.

7. Gianni Vattimo, *After Christianity*, trans. Luca D'Isanto (New York: Columbia University Press, 2002).

8. Joachim of Fiore, at www.pbs.org/wgbh/pages/frontline/shows/apocalypse/explanation/joachim.html.

9. Quoted in Vattimo, *After Christianity*, 29–30.
10. Ibid., 30.
11. Ibid.
12. Ibid.
13. Ibid.

14. Although hardly what would be termed a traditional, orthodox faith, but there again the traditional faiths are not exempt from the democratizing efforts of the people's religion either.

15. Vattimo, *After Christianity*, 6.

16. Mark I. Wallace finds a thorough and quite compelling argument for this position in *Fragments of the Spirit: Nature, Violence, and the Renewal of Creation* (Harrisburg, PA: Trinity Press, 2002).

17. Vattimo, *After Christianity*, 31.

18. Ibid.

19. This can be contrasted with some of the recorded comments made by victims of the December 26, 2004, tsunami that devastated areas surrounding the Indian Ocean. Many of those people, particularly those practicing traditional Hindu faith, wondered what they had done to make God so angry and punish them so severely. See *Los Angeles Times*, December 27–29, 2004, lead articles.

20. Vattimo, *After Christianity*, 33.

21. Mark I. Wallace, "Earth God: Cultivating the Spirit in an Ecocidal Culture," in *Blackwell Companion to Postmodern Theology*, ed. Graham Ward (Oxford: Blackwell, 2001), 210.

22. "Always on My Mind," written by Mark Wallinger and presented on the album *Dumbing Up* by World Party, Universal Records, 1998.

23. Leszek Kolakowski, *Religion: If There Is No God . . . On God, the Devil, Sin and Other Worries of the So-Called Philosophy of Religion* (London: Fontana, 1982), 194, 199, quoted in Zygmunt Bauman, "Postmodern Religion?" in *Religion, Modernity, and Postmodernity*, ed. Paul Heelas (Oxford: Blackwell, 1998), 58.

24. Mieke Bal, "Postmodern Theology as Cultural Analysis," in Ward, *Blackwell Companion to Postmodern Theology*, 5.

25. Vattimo, *After Christianity*, 15.

26. Steve Bruce, "Cathedrals to Cults: The Evolving Form of the Religious Life," in Heelas, *Religion, Modernity, and Postmodernity*, 30.

27. Ibid., 30.

28. Jean-Francois Lyotard, *The Postmodern Condition: A Report on Knowledge*, trans. Geoff Bennington and Brian Massumi (Minneapolis: University of Minnesota Press, 1979).

29. David Tracy, *On Naming the Present: Reflections on God, Hermeneutics, and Church* (Maryknoll, NY: Orbis Books, 1994), 16, quoted in Roger Haight, *Jesus, Symbol of God* (Maryknoll, NY: Orbis Books, 2000), 333.

30. Ward, *True Religion*, 75.

Emerging Global Culture and the Symbolic Universe of the Media Generation

1. This is yet another hotly contested arena in the twenty-first century. I realize that by invoking the term

"global culture" I invite a tidal wave of opinion, and I leave myself little room in this text to fully defend my position. That said, I could find no better term than global culture to use at present, so I will gladly accept the hits.

2. Appadurai, *Modernity at Large*, 14.

3. Ibid., 27.

4. Ibid. Religions of conversion are faiths that seek converts and actively proselytize. Islam, Christianity, and Buddhism are some examples of such religions.

5. Ibid., 31.

6. Ibid., 28.

7. Ibid.

8. Ibid.

9. Ibid., 29.

10. Ibid.

11. Wayne Ellwood, *The No-Nonsense Guide to Globalization* (London: Verso, 2001), 12.

12. John Tomlinson, "Globalized Culture: The Triumph of the West?" in *Culture and Global Change*, ed. Tracey Skelton and Tim Allen (London: Routledge, 1999), 29.

13. Appadurai, *Modernity at Large*, 29.

14. Ibid., 31.

15. Ibid.

16. Appadurai terms this "ethnoscapes"—the landscape of persons who constitute the shifting world in which we live. Tourists, immigrants, refugees, exiles, guest workers, and other moving groups and individuals constitute an essential feature of and appear to affect the politics of (and between) nations to a hitherto unprecedented degree (ibid., 33).

17. Rushkoff, *Playing the Future*, 5.

18. Ibid.

19. Marshall McLuhan and Quentin Fiore, *The Medium Is the Massage* (New York: Random, 1967), 260.

20. Rushkoff, *Playing the Future*, 7.

21. Appadurai, *Modernity at Large*, 5.

22. Ibid., 33.

23. By mythography, I mean the rendering of myths in the arts.

24. Appadurai, *Modernity at Large*, 36.

25. Ibid., 7.

26. Ibid.

27. Ibid., 8.

28. Ibid.

29. Wallace, *Fragments of the Spirit*, 30.

30. Mau, *Massive Change*, 118.

31. Dr. Seuss, *The Lorax* (New York: Random House, 1971).

32. Rushkoff, *Playing the Future*.

33. Barna Research Group Ltd., "How America's Faith has Changed since 9/11," November 26, 2001, www.barna.org. Twenty-five percent replied that they made choices based on their emotions, fourteen per-cent based on childhood lessons, and thirteen percent based on the Bible.

34. Quoted in Elizabeth Diebold, "Shifting Moral Ground: The Dilemma of Ethics in an Out-of-Control World," *What Is Enlightenment?* February/April 2004, 58.

35. Phyllis Tickle, "Preface," in Frederic and Mary Ann Brussat, "Spiritual Literacy: Reading the Sacred in Everyday Life," in *God-Talk in America*, ed. Phyllis Tickle (New York: Crossroad, 1997).

36. The continued success of books seems to challenge ideas about the "end of the word" posited by some. Instead of the written word becoming obsolete, there is merely an adjustment of priorities and a new cumulative literacy emerging.

37. Consider for instance the sheer number of Christian publications under the heading of "The Gospel according to . . ." This attempt to use pop culture as a site for the dissemination of Christian faith and ideology includes these titles:

The Gospel according to the Simpsons, by Mark L. Pinsky (Louisville: Westminster John Knox, 2000).

The Gospel according to Harry Potter, by Connie Neal (Louisville: Westminster John Knox, 2002).

The Gospel according to Tony Soprano, by Chris Seay (Lake Mary, FL: Relevant Books, 2002).

The Gospel according to Peanuts, by Robert L. Short (Louisville: Westminster John Knox, 2000).

The Gospel according to Tolkien, by Ralph C. Wood (Louisville: Westminster John Knox, 2003).

The Gospel according to Disney, by Mark L. Pinsky (Louisville: Westminster John Knox, 2004).

The Gospel according to Dr. Seuss, by James W. Kemp (Valley Forge, PA: Judson, 2004).

38. F. David Peat, *From Certainty to Uncertainty: The Story of Science and Ideas in the Twentieth Century* (Washington, DC: Joseph Henry, 2005).

Part 2 New Edges

1. Lyon, *Jesus in Disneyland*, 91.

Surface as Depth

1. The film was beset with problems almost from the beginning. Arguments with his long-time producer and director Kevin Reynolds left Kevin Costner in charge of a disheartened crew. Shooting in Hawaii, where the movie was being filmed, was interrupted by a series of unexpected storms that destroyed the water-based movie set. Expensive reshoots because of problems with Kevin Costner's hair, which apparently looked too thin and balding in the largely water-based environment of the film, created only more animosity between cast, crew, and film studio.

2. Gerard Kelly, *Get a Grip on the Future without Losing Your Hold on the Past* (London: Monarch Books, 1999), 51.

3. Ibid., 51–54.

4. Ibid., 52.

5. Ibid.

6. Ibid.

7. Appadurai, *Modernity at Large*, 30.

8. Craig Detweiler and Barry Taylor, *A Matrix of Meanings: Finding God in Pop Culture* (Grand Rapids: Baker Academic, 2003), 222.

9. Kelly, *Get a Grip*, 53.

10. A mariner is "one who navigates."

11. Kelly, *Get a Grip*, 53.

12. Mark Magnier, "Good Things in Small Packages," *Los Angeles Times*, May 23, 2003.

13. These charms are now available in the West and are sold in kiosks and specialty cell-phone stores throughout the US and Europe.

14. Žižek, *On Belief*, 14.

15. Ward, *True Religion*, 133.

16. Ibid.

17. Laura Cerwinske, *In a Spiritual Style: The Home as Sanctuary* (London: Thames and Hudson, 1998).

18. Ward, *True Religion*, 133.

19. Ibid.

20. Ibid., 132–33.

21. Ibid.

22. McLuhan and Fiore, *Medium Is the Massage*, 29.

23. Timo Kopomaa, "Speaking Mobile: The City in Your Pocket," in YTK's electronic publications, April 4, 2004, www.hut.fi/Ysikot/YTK/julkaisu/mobile.html.

24. Ibid.

25. As I write, there are signs that some Christians who have been hovering "above the waters of the new age" are almost ready to dive in and rethink the missional project within postsecularity. I cannot point to any particular group but would point to the so-called emergent churches as a potential site for the transformation of Christian faith for the new millennium.

Shopping for God

1. Zygmunt Bauman, *Intimations of Postmodernity* (London: Routledge, 1992), 49.

2. Lyon, *Jesus in Disneyland*, 30.

3. Bauman, *Intimations of Postmodernity*, 223.

4. Ibid., 278.

5. Ibid.

6. Ibid., 50.

7. Ibid.

8. Ward, *True Religion*, 133.

9. See Eccles. 9:7–10; 2:24–26.

10. Ward, *True Religion*, 133.

11. Bauman, *Intimations of Postmodernity*, 51.

12. Cimino and Lattin, *Shopping for Faith*, 56.

13. Ibid., 11.

14. Twitchell, *Lead Us into Temptation*, 12.

15. Bauman, *Intimations of Postmodernity*, 59.

16. Twitchell, *Lead Us into Temptation*, 57.

17. Ibid.

18. Ibid., 61.

19. Mike Featherstone, *Consumer Culture and Postmodernism* (London: Sage, 1991), quoted in Lyon, *Jesus in Disneyland*, 78–79.

20. Lyon, *Jesus in Disneyland*, 78.

21. Ibid.

22. Ibid.

23. Ibid.

24. Ibid.

25. Ibid., 79.

26. Ibid., 92.

27. Ibid.

28. John Grant, *New Marketing Manifesto* (London: Orion Business, 1999), quoted in David Boyle, *Authenticity: Brands, Fakes, Spin, and the Lust for Real Life* (London: Flamingo, 2003), 26.

29. Ward, *True Religion*, 133.

30. Lyon, *Jesus in Disneyland*, 81.

31. Featherstone, *Consumer Culture*, 126.

32. Lyon, *Jesus in Disneyland*, 82–83.

33. Ibid.

34. Ibid.

35. The basis for and use of mystery-based practices in Christianity goes back to the early days of the church. For instance, Cyril, bishop of Jerusalem from ca. 349, incorporated features of the mystery religions of his day into the lectures he delivered to catechumens. See esp. his "Catechetical Lectures" (*Nicene and Post-Nicene Fathers*, series 2, 14 vols. [1885–96; repr. Grand Rapids: Eerdmans, 1983–87], 7:1–157).

36. Ward, *True Religion*, 123.

37. Ibid.

Entertainment Theology

1. Ward, *True Religion*, 125.

2. Ibid.

3. John Drane has written often about the role of secularity in modern religion. I recommend particularly *The McDonaldization of the Church: Spirituality, Creativity, and the Future of the Church* (London: Darton, Longman and Todd, 2000).

4. Slavoj Žižek, *The Plague of Fantasies* (London: Verso, 1997), 7.

5. I do not mean fantasy in the escapist sense of the word, as we will explore through Appadurai's work. Rather than escaping through imagination and fantasy, postmodern culture employs it as a tool for reordering society.

6. Žižek, *Plague of Fantasies*, 7.

7. Ibid.

8. Tickle, *God-Talk in America*.

9. Ward, *True Religion*, 133.

10. On this, see the excellent study by Jean Baudrillard, *Simulacra and Simulation*, trans. Sheila Faria Glaser (Ann Arbor: University of Michigan Press, 1994).

11. Tom Beaudoin, *Virtual Faith: The Irreverent Spiritual Quest of Generation X* (San Francisco: Jossey-Bass, 1998), 13.

12. Ward, *Blackwell Companion to Postmodern Theology*, xv.

13. Ward, *True Religion*, 133.

14. Of course it depends on one's particular scientific approach to the collation of data—the linear, factual elements of a Newtonian-based scientific view or the chaos-theory version of the Einsteinian era. I go with the latter!

Postsecular Soul Space

1. Ward, *True Religion*, 133.

2. John D. Caputo, *On Religion* (New York: Routledge, 2001), 9.

3. Žižek, *On Belief*, 10.

4. Ibid.

5. Ibid., 11.

6. Jonas Ridderstråle and Kjell Nordström, *Funky Business: Talent Makes Capital Dance* (London: Financial Times Publications, 2000), 63.

7. Ibid., 64.

8. Žižek, *On Belief*, 11.

9. The best of Buddhism and other Eastern traditions present themselves not so much as bodies of eternal truth, as Christianity might, but as a system of tools and guidelines for developing more spacious views of reality.

10. Karen Armstrong, *Buddha* (New York: Viking, 2001), 201.

11. Wallace, *Fragments of the Spirit*, 23.

12. Lyotard, *Postmodern Condition*, introduction.

13. Wallace, *Fragments of the Spirit*, 23.

14. Ibid.

15. Lyon, *Jesus in Disneyland*, 93.

16. Ward, *True Religion*, 133.

17. "Our Advaita and Buddhism" issue, *What Is Enlightenment?* 14, Fall/Winter 1998, introduction.

18. Philip Sudo, *Zen Guitar* (New York: Simon and Schuster, 1997), from the back cover.

19. Orville Schell, *Virtual Tibet: Searching for Shangri-La from the Himalayas to Hollywood* (New York: Metropolitan Books, 2000), 18.

20. Ibid., 37.

21. Ward, *True Religion*, 133.

22. Noah Levine, *Dharma Punx: A Memoir* (New York: HarperSanFrancisco, 2003).

23. I recommend Greil Marcus, *Lipstick Traces* (Cambridge, MA: Harvard University Press, 1989), as a seminal work on punk music and the movement it sparked.

24. Rick Poynor, *No More Rules: Graphic Design and Postmodernism* (New Haven, CT: Yale University Press, 2003), 38. Poynor posits that graphic design employed in the service of punk music reflected the early engagement of pop culture and graphic design in particular with postmodernism. This was reflected in the deconstructive nature of both forms of pop culture: they both sought to dismantle the "old order."

25. Marcus, *Lipstick Traces*, 6.

26. Brad Warner, *Hardcore Zen: Punk Rock, Monster Movies and the Truth about Reality* (Boston: Wisdom, 2003), 14.

27. Žižek, *On Belief*, 66.

28. I mean Western in the sense of the cowboy western, not simply the culture known as Western.

29. *Spirited Away* was a Japanese film produced and distributed by the Walt Disney Company.

30. Sofia Coppola quoted on Ritz Filmball: Movies to Talk About (http://www.ritzfilmball.com).

31. Walter Truett Anderson, *The Next Enlightenment: Integrating East and West in a New Vision of Human Evolution* (New York: St. Martin's Press, 2003), 15, to which I am indebted for many of the ideas posited here. This book was instrumental in helping me coalesce ideas and feelings about changes in the world of religion. I am also indebted to the New Age magazine *What Is Enlightenment?* and also the many writings of Ken Wilber. *Wired* magazine, a technology journal, is also a source of much inspiration. See, for instance, the article by Gregg Easterbrook, "The New Convergence: Religion and Science," *Wired*, December 2002.

32. Kenneth Gergen, *Realities and Relationships: Soundings in Social Construction* (Cambridge, MA: Harvard University Press, 1994), 209.

33. See F. David Peat, *From Certainty to Uncertainty: The Story of Science and Ideas in the Twentieth Century* (Washington, DC: John Henry Press, 2002).

34. The one exception to this rule in virtually all media representations is the African-American faith community, which is probably the worthy subject of another dissertation. Generally the African-American church is experienced by the broader culture as something to be affirmed and enjoyed. Perhaps it is the perception of its highly emotional representation of faith that contrasts with the more staid offerings of most white churches (i.e., black church = fun; white church = boring). Gospel music is still extremely supported as a musical genre by believers and nonbelievers alike, its emotional center hard to resist. In one edition of the weekly television show *Lost*, the

Notes to Pages 104–22

single African-American woman in the cast was shown leading another cast member in prayer. This remains acceptable in the larger culture whereas other presentations of Christian faith in particular are viewed with suspicion.

35. This rejection of spiritual guides extends even to the realm of the New Age movement, long known for its fascination with gurus. The destabilization of the New Age movement is part of the new religious dynamic. A recent edition of *What Is Enlightenment?* magazine discussed whether we needed gurus anymore (see Elizabeth Debold, "The Future of the Student Teacher Relationship: Definitely Not Just a Book Review of Maria Caplan's *Do You Need a Guru?" What Is Enlightenment?* Spring–Summer 2003).

36. Ward, *True Religion*, 2.

37. Cybil (age 25), personal communication, January 6, 2005.

38. John Drane, *What the New Age Is Still Saying to the Church* (London: Darton, Longman and Todd, 1991), 25.

39. Ibid.

40. Ibid.

41. Ibid.

42. Marilyn Ferguson, *The Aquarian Conspiracy: Personal and Social Transformation in Our Times* (Los Angeles: J. P. Tarcher, 1980), 26.

43. Ibid., 29.

44. Inner Traditions, One Park St., Rochester, VT 05767.

45. Wallace, *Fragments of the Spirit*, 60.

46. Žižek, *On Belief*, 36.

47. Anderson, *Next Enlightenment*, 6.

48. Ibid.

49. Ibid., 18.

50. Ibid., 17–18.

51. Please note that my intent is not to critique these emergings as much as it is to acknowledge their existence and argue that they should legitimately be included in our understanding of the nature of the religious experience and expression in the postsecular. Beyond that, my desire is to explore how the church might respond in and to such times of emerging movements.

52. Friedrich Nietzsche, *Ecce Homo: How to Become What You Are*, quoted in Anderson, *Next Enlightenment*.

53. Devin Friedman, "David O. Russell's Existential Crisis," *GQ*, October 2004, 214.

54. Bruce Sterling, "Every Other Movie Is the Blue Pill," in *Exploring the Matrix*, ed. Bruce Sterling (New York: St. Martin's Press, 2003), 23–24.

55. "Wake Up Neo," *What Is Enlightenment?* August–October 2004, 29.

56. Ken Wilber, *A Theory of Everything: An Integral Vision for Business, Politics, Science, and Spirituality* (Boston: Shambhala, 2001).

57. Ibid., 12.

58. Paul H. Ray and Sherry Ruth Anderson, *The Cultural Creatives: How 50 Million People Are Changing the World* (New York: Harmony Books, 2000).

59. Ibid., 14.

60. Ibid., 14–42.

61. Ibid.

62. Monological holism is a theory, influenced by things such as systems theory, that refers to a hierarchy of interrelated systems featuring multiple ideas working in sync with one another. This is in contrast to "flat holism," which is a single theory idea. Wilber is a believer in the idea of "nested hierarchy," or "holarchy," which was developed by Arthur Koestler.

63. Wilber, *Theory of Everything*, 31.

64. Ibid.

65. Ibid., 132. By "divine mysticism," Wilber seems to mean nondogmatic spiritual experience, that is, an integration of the whole person into a new state. This new state is envisioned as a nondual union (i.e., the collapse of binary oppositions such as soul/body and divine/human) that reworks or rewords the idea of oneness that pervades much contemporary spiritual conversation.

66. Anderson, *Next Enlightenment*.

67. Easterbrook, "New Convergence," 176.

68. Dan Brown, *The Da Vinci Code* (New York: Doubleday, 2003).

69. See Umberto Eco, *Travels in Hyperreality*, trans. William Weaver (New York: Harvest Books, 1983).

70. Andrew Blake, *The Irresistible Rise of Harry Potter* (London: Verso, 2002), 8. The word "retrolution" emerged from the world of commercial advertising in 1994, when it was used in conjunction with the release of a new model of the Jaguar XJ series automobile. The new car was at once a mix of new and old. The publicity material called the design philosophy "retrolutionary." The new was packaged for those who apparently did not much like the new (ibid., 16).

71. Ibid., 17.

72. Eco, *Travels in Hyperreality*, 65.

73. *The American Heritage Dictionary of the English Language*, 3rd ed. (New York: Houghton Mifflin, 1992), s.v. "symbol."

74. Fred Botting, *Gothic* (London: Routledge, 1996), 39.

75. Such use of the gothic could also be a tool to help unfold meaning in other areas of contemporary life, to "read" Quentin Tarantino movies, for instance. His use of gothic levels of fright, destruction, violence, and complex worlds are filled with so much information it cannot be absorbed rationally. However, if we employ this understanding of gothic, then we can see that a basic premise inherent in Tarantino's

film-making—a "message," if you will—is that if we learn to stay cool in times of chaos then we will get through them. I recommend particularly the *Kill Bill* films along with *Pulp Fiction* as exemplary expressions of this postmodern gothic sentiment.

76. Botting, *Gothic*, 3.

77. Appadurai, *Modernity at Large*, 31.

78. Botting, *Gothic*.

79. Ibid., 3.

80. The Christmas "number one" hit is a national obsession in Britain. This British eccentricity was used to good effect in the movie *Love Actually*, a story about the battle for the number one slot between a washed-up old singer who is down on his luck and a glamorous, overhyped, and overproduced boy band. What made "Mad World's" place at the top of the charts so interesting was that it was such a melancholy song, with no overt signs of Christmas cheer or any other of the usual characteristics of a Christmas number one. Rather than being a glossy, well-produced pop production, it was in fact a home-studio recording of limited quality. But this did nothing to inhibit its success.

81. Ward, *True Religion*, 130.

82. Ibid.

83. See also *Fight Club, Panic Room*, and *The Game*.

84. Fincher has made a career out of these elements. Most of his movies trade in low light, rain, dark and decaying environments, etc.

85. Botting, *Gothic*, 3–4.

86. Ibid., 4.

87. See Detweiler and Taylor, *Matrix of Meanings*, for a more thorough exploration of rock music dynamics.

88. Botting, *Gothic*, 38.

89. Ibid.

90. Ibid., 39.

91. Ward, *True Religion*, 130–33.

92. Tom Waits and Kathleen Brenneman, "The Day after Tomorrow," *Real Gone*, Anti, 2004.

93. Camilla Paglia, *Sexual Personae: Art and Decadence from Nefertiti to Emily Dickinson* (Harmondsworth: Penguin Books, 1992), 346, as quoted in Loughlin, *Alien Sex*, 49.

94. McLuhan and Fiore, *Medium Is the Massage*, 146.

95. Jana Riess, *What Would Buffy Do?* (San Francisco: Jossey-Bass, 2004).

96. Ibid., xiii.

97. Ibid.

98. Botting, *Gothic*, 5.

99. Changing attitudes toward sexuality are everywhere on the postmodern horizon, but within the realm of the gothic there is a tradition of "transgression" toward socially acceptable norms, particularly with regard to sexuality, the Marquis de Sade being but one notorious gothic figure who characterizes this element of the gothic.

100. Angela McRobbie, *Postmodernism and Popular Culture* (London: Routledge, 1994), 55.

101. Botting, *Gothic*, 7.

102. Tony Myers, *Slavoj Žižek* (New York: Routledge, 2003), 52.

103. Chuck Palahniuk, *Fight Club* (New York: Henry Holt, 1996).

104. Blake, *Rise of Harry Potter*, 46.

105. Alain Minc, *Le Nouveau Moyen Age* (Paris: Gallimard, 1994).

106. Botting, *Gothic*, 171–72.

107. Umberto Eco, *The Name of the Rose*, trans. William Weaver (London: Pan Books, 1980), 500.

108. Botting, *Gothic*, 22.

109. Robert Webber, *Ancient-Future Faith: Rethinking Evangelicalism for the Postmodern World* (Grand Rapids: Baker Books, 1999).

110. www.tallskinnykiwi.com.

111. Peter Finch, "Towards a New Monasticism," www.vineyard.ca.

112. Ibid.

113. www.spiritdublin.com.

114. Wicca was formerly known as witchcraft but now has little to do with it. Wicca is a modern practice with mythical medieval roots. It is largely a goddess-based and earth-centered self-realization and self-responsibility movement, revering the divine in all things. If it has a creed at all it is the statement: "Harm no one and do what you will." What the "goddess" is exactly is proffered by Starhawk, one of Wicca's most well-known proponents: We must remember that our basis is in people's real, direct experience of that deep interconnectedness to all things. There is a journal devoted to Neo-Pagan studies: *Pomegranate: International Journal of Pagan Studies*, ed. Chas Clifton, Colorado State University, Pueblo, and published by Equinox Publications Limited, London.

115. It is very much in debate what kind of event Burning Man is, even among its key leaders. At best it is a transitional and experimental community gathered in mutual desire to declare their longing for alternative forms of communal life and social ordering. I recommend Brian Doherty, *This Is Burning Man: The Rise of a New American Underground* (New York: Little, Brown and Company, 2004). In other words, it seems to be the postmodern gothic.

116. *Sefer Ha Zohar* (*The Book of Splendour*). Written around 1280 in Spain, it was translated into modern Hebrew by Yehuda HaLevi Ashlag in 1953 and then into English in 2003 by the Kabbalah Center of Los Angeles. See also Kim Zetter, *Simple Kabbalah* (York Beach, NY: Conari, 2000). Who actually wrote the original Zohar is a matter of dispute, some attributing it to Simon bar Yochai, a hermit

who lived in Palestine, others to Moses de Leon, a Spanish Jew. Given its mystical nature, this only adds to the mystery.

117. Maura R. O'Connor, "Twenty-first Century Kabbalah," *What Is Enlightenment?* November 2004–February 2005, 90–92.

118. Zetter, *Simple Kabbalah*, 1.

119. Ibid.

120. Rabbi Philip Berg, quoted in O'Connor, "Twenty-first Century Kabbalah," 95.

121. Ibid.

122. I addressed these issues more expansively in Detweiler and Taylor, *Matrix of Meanings*, 29–59.

123. McLuhan and Fiore, *Medium Is the Massage*, 81.

124. Ziauddin Sardar, *The A to Z of Postmodern Life: Essays on Global Culture in the Noughties* (London: Vision, 2002), 34–35.

125. See Detweiler and Taylor, *Matrix of Meanings*, 89–124.

126. Sardar, *A to Z of Postmodern Life*, 35.

127. Twitchell, *Lead Us into Temptation*, 80.

128. Sardar, *A to Z of Postmodern Life*, 37.

129. I explore this further in chap. 4 of Detweiler and Taylor, *Matrix of Meanings*.

130. McLuhan and Fiore, *Medium Is the Massage*, 45.

131. Sardar, *A to Z of Postmodern Life*, 37.

132. Twitchell, *Lead Us into Temptation*, 52.

133. It is not always the case that celebrities know nothing of a particular topic. What is more important to note is the fact that their opinions are actively sought on virtually every issue.

134. Dick Pountain and David Robins, *Cool Rules: Anatomy of an Attitude* (London: Reaktion Books, 2000), 13.

135. Ibid., 18.

136. "Cool youth now votes for the Democrats not because it likes them, but because it detests the moralizing Christian right more" (ibid., 173).

137. The detaching of Jesus from the church also extends to taking away the "Christ" aspect. Here we are speaking of Jesus the national icon, not necessarily the Jesus Christ of historic Christian faith, although in the pluralized world of today this will not always be the case. There has been a rash of work and research done on this phenomenon, and again as my project is focused more on the new religious dynamic and its additions to the cultural religious imaginary I refer the reader to two salient works that address this topic in greater depth than I am able to offer here: Stephen Prothero, *American Jesus: How the Son of God Became a National Icon* (New York: Farrar, Straus and Giroux, 2003); Richard Wightman Fox, *Jesus in America: Personal Savior, Cultural Hero, National Obsession* (San Francisco: HarperSan-Francisco, 2004).

138. Carter Heyward, *Saving Jesus from Those Who Are Right: Rethinking What It Means to Be Christian* (Minneapolis: Fortress, 1999).

139. Jesus's cool factor is linked to the cultural perception that he is nonjudgmental and inclusive, whereas the church seems to amplify judgmentalism and exclusion.

140. Bruce Bawer, *Stealing Jesus: How Fundamentalism Betrays Christianity* (New York: Crown, 1997), 13.

141. Donald Spoto, *The Hidden Jesus: A New Life* (New York: St. Martin's Press, 1989).

142. Blogs or weblogs are personal Web sites that are updated frequently like a diary, are usually interactive, and are user friendly. There are currently about 70 million blogsites worldwide, but the US has an average of 110 million people per day interacting and reading blogs—www.blog.com.

143. Quoted in Tim Rutten, "Regarding Media," *Los Angeles Times*, January 8, 2005, calendar section, 1.

144. I refrain from using the man's name as it is not necessary to the points being made. He also resisted being interviewed when I told him what I was doing.

145. An allusion to the thirty-nine members of the Heaven's Gate cult who committed mass suicide dressed in identical Nike shoes and covered in white cloths, in Rancho Sante Fe, CA, in March 1997. The suicide was a symbolic statement of the opinion this group held about contemporary religion in general.

146. That is not to say there were not positive results, but I saw no public proclamations of faith in response to this, and as I usually waited around for a couple of hours, there were never any people who returned.

147. Bauman, *Liquid Modernity*, 74.

148. Karl Barth's notion, referenced in Ward, *True Religion*, 134.

149. Anselm Kyongsuk Min, *The Solidarity of Others in a Divided World: A Postmodern Theology after Postmodernism* (New York: T&T Clark, 2004), 30.

150. Ibid.

151. Bauman, *Intimations of Postmodernity*, 199.

152. Ibid.

153. Salman Rushdie, *Step Across This Line: Collected Nonfiction 1992–2002* (New York: Modern Library, 2002), 286.

154. Bauman, *Intimations of Postmodernity*, 136.

155. Appadurai, *Modernity at Large*, 38.

156. Lyon, *Jesus in Disneyland*, 105.

157. Malcolm Waters, *Globalization* (New York: Routledge, 1995), 156.

158. Ibid.

159. Robertson, as quoted in Waters, *Globalization*, 130.

160. Ibid.

161. This concept was introduced into postmodern discourse through the writings of Gilles Deleuze and Felix Guattari: "A Rhizome has no beginning and no end" (*A Thousand Plateaus: Capitalism and Schizophrenia* [London: Athlone, 1988], chap. 1).

162. Poynor, *No More Rules*, 108.

163. Ecumenism also carries the utopian fantasy of modern universalism. Žižek argues that when looking at religion, we are tempted to say that there is a universal concept or genus of religion and that within that universality are particular varieties such as Buddhism, Christianity, etc. Not so, says Žižek: "Christianity is not simply different from Judaism and Islam; within its horizon, the very difference that separates it from the other two 'religions of the Book' appears in a way which is unacceptable for the other two. In other words, when a Christian debates with a Muslim, they do not simply disagree—they disagree about their very disagreement: about what makes the difference between their religions" (in Myers, *Slavoj Žižek*, 114).

164. Waters, *Globalization*, 13.

165. Ward, *True Religion*, 153.

166. Bruce B. Lawrence, "From Fundamentalism to Fundamentalists: A Religious Ideology in Multiple Forms," in Heelas, *Religion, Modernity, and Postmodernity*, 89.

167. Karen Armstrong, *The Battle for God* (New York: Alfred A. Knopf, 2000), x.

168. Alistair McGrath, *The Future of Christianity* (Oxford: Blackwell, 2002), 75.

169. Christianity has imploded in much the same way modernity has. Its commitment to the values of modernity, particularly to the totalizing claims of western hegemony, is indicative of what is at work in the fabric of Christian faith at present. It is as much a problem from within as without. John Henry Newman noted that if the "church is to remain the same, it must change" (quoted in McGrath, *Future of Christianity*, 73). Christianity, to quote Captain Kirk of *Star Trek*, is "locked in a time warp." That time warp is modernity, and until it moves forward Christianity will largely be forced to resort to a dominant fundamentalist perception in the postsecular psyche. Our commitment to change has largely been cosmetic—it is time to pull up the roots and plant ourselves in the rhizome.

170. Giddens, summarized in Aldridge, *Religion in the Contemporary World*, 185.

171. Caputo, *On Religion*, 92.

172. Ibid., 102.

173. Salman Rushdie, *The Satanic Verses* (New York: Picador Books, 1988), 1.

174. Ward, *True Religion*, 140.

175. Waters, *Globalization*.

176. Ward, *True Religion*, 140.

177. Bawer, *Stealing Jesus*.

178. This even extends to the New Age religions that have a long association with gurus and mentors of all shapes and sizes. However, in the twenty-first century, this particular characteristic is losing popularity (see *What Is Enlightenment?* magazine, November2004–February2005 issue).

179. Quoted in Ayatollah Djalal Gandjeih, "For Rushdie," in *For Rushdie: Essays by Arab and Muslim Writers in Defense of Free Speech*, ed. Anouar Abdallah (New York: George Braziller, 1994), 149.

180. Armstrong, *Battle for God*, 331.

181. Nourrredine Saadi, "The Hole Left by God," quoted in Abdallah, *For Rushdie*, 256.

182. A fatwa is a judgment made by an Islamic scholar capable of issuing judgment based on Sharia, Islamic law.

183. Zhor Ben Chamsi, "Being Open to the Imaginary," in Abdallah, *For Rushdie*, 97.

184. Ibid.

185. Fethi Benslama, "Rushdie, or the Textual Question," in Abdallah, *For Rushdie*, 84.

186. Ibid., 86.

187. Ibid., 236.

188. Ibid., 260.

189. Rushdie, *Satanic Verses*, 199.

190. Lyon, *Jesus in Disneyland*, 39.

191. Samir Nair, "How to Read the *Satanic Verses?*" in Abdallah, *For Rushdie*, 237.

192. Ibid.

193. Rushdie, *Satanic Verses*, 561.

194. Ward, *True Religion*, 135.

195. Caputo, *On Religion*, 106.

196. Appadurai, *Modernity at Large*, 35.

Playing the Future

1. L. Frank Baum, *The Wizard of Oz*, quoted in Rushdie, *Step Across This Line*, 17.

2. Ibid.

3. Ibid., 12–15.

4. Ibid., 282.

5. These are, of course, stereotypes and generalizations about Christianity that inhabit the cultural imaginary, but it is often the case with stereotypes that they are built on a kernel of truth. Sometimes I think frustration is the driving force behind the church's attitude toward the culture. The church was once in the ascendancy, in authority and power, but this is no longer the case. And yet, it clings to the idea that the potential for this still holds.

6. Slavoj Žižek, *The Fragile Absolute, or, Why Is the Christian Legacy Worth Fighting For?* (London: Verso, 2000).

7. Kester Brewin, *The Complex Christ: Signs of Emergence in the Urban Church* (London: SPCK, 2004), 153.

8. Nick Cave, "Into Your Arms," Mute Records, 1997.

9. See John D. Caputo, *The Weakness of God: A Theology of the Event* (Bloomington: Indiana University Press, 2006).

10. Douglas Rushkoff, *Nothing Sacred: The Truth about Judaism* (New York: Three Rivers, 2003).

11. See Keller's paper, given at the Drew Colloquia in Transdisciplinary Theological Studies, at http://depts.drew.edu/tsfac/colloquium.

12. John Milbank, Catherine Pickstock, and Graham Ward, eds., *Radical Orthodoxy: A New Theology* (London: Routledge, 1999), 1.

13. Appadurai, *Modernity at Large*, 7.

14. Ibid.

15. Ibid.

16. There are also a number of Web sites, such as Edge.org, that invite key thinkers and strategists to offer ideas for new ways of being in the world, new ideas for congregating in community. The imagination has become an accepted resource for thinking and acting in the postsecular world.

17. This look to the future and the desire to discover a new voice are emerging in a number of fields within the postsecular horizon. For example, recent trends in graphic design point toward this dynamic as being central to the rise of a new generation of designers who no longer wish to labor under the boundaries, categories, and practices of the modern era. I recommend Poynor, *No More Rules*.

After Christianity

1. A five-line summary of the history of Christianity is not sufficient to capture the two-thousand-year history of the Christian faith, but again, I am trying to capture the mood of the present situation toward the very idea of a Christianity that has totalizing tendencies—a Constantinian Christianity.

2. I have referenced this dynamic and simply alert the reader again to the wealth of discussion, ad nauseam, that attests to this reality.

3. John Drane, *Cultural Change and Biblical Faith: The Future of the Church. Biblical and Missiological Essays for the New Century* (Cumbria: Paternoster, 2000), 76.

4. Karl Rahner, *Theological Investigations*, vol. 20, *Concern for the Church* (London: Darton, Longman and Todd, 1981), 149.

5. This has become a dominant rubric under which a number of ecclesial structures from mainline denominations to Pentecostal, charismatic, and evangelical expressions of faith seem to be discovering resonance and help.

6. Boff, *Global Civilization*, 40.

7. Space here refers to "physical space." We still seem to work on the idea that while God is at work in the world, the real engagement happens in designated sacred spaces at specific times, i.e., in church on Sunday. The cultural shift that is presently underway appreciates designated holy space but sees God as available and accessible outside those mediated spaces.

8. I am not, and would not, argue for the elimination of sacred space—such space offers beauty, an environment of worshipfulness, and an alternative to the other spaces we live in. What I mean here is the commonly accepted idea that "church" means tangible sacred space rather than people following a certain way of life and practice.

9. Drane, *McDonaldization of the Church*, 76.

10. Brewin, *Complex Christ*, 70.

11. Some may argue against searching for a God already found in the revelation of Christian teaching. This search is not to deny the reality of revelation but rather a seeking out of God in this particular postsecular situation.

12. "So from now on we regard no one from a worldly point of view. Though we once regarded Christ in this way, we do so no longer. Therefore, if anyone is in Christ, he is a new creation; the old has gone, the new has come!"

13. Michel de Certeau terms Christ the "inaugurating rupture," which resonates with the idea posited here (*The Practice of Everyday Life*, vol. 2, *Living and Cooking*, ed. Luce Giard, trans. Timothy J. Tomasik [Minneapolis: University of Minnesota Press, 1998]).

14. Žižek, *On Belief*, introduction.

15. Ibid., 2.

16. Ibid., 4.

17. Ibid.

18. Rushkoff, *Playing the Future*, 221–40.

19. Elizabeth Gilbert, *Eat, Pray, Love: One Woman's Search for Everything across Italy, India, and Indonesia* (New York: Viking, 2006), 203.

20. Dietrich Bonhoeffer, *Letters and Papers from Prison*, ed. Eberhard Bethge (New York: Macmillan, 1953), 275–78.

21. Ibid., 279.

22. Ibid., 280.

23. Douglas Rushkoff, *Nothing Sacred* (New York: Three Rivers, 2003), 216.

24. Richard Rorty has stated: "My sense of the holy is bound up with the hope that someday my remote descendants will live in a global civilization in which life is pretty much the only law" (Santiago Zabala, ed. *The Future of Religion: Richard Rorty and Gianni Vattimo* [New York: Columbia University Press, 2005], 40). I think this is the role religion is supposed to play. It is reflected in Jesus's statement in John 13:34—A new command I give you: love one another as I have loved you; by this all will know you are my disciples. When religion continues to fund,

support, and drive human violence, war, injustice, marginalization of the poor, and any value that benefits some at the expense of others, it is of no help to human evolution as far as I can see.

25. Castells, *Power of Identity*.

26. See Lyon, *Jesus in Disneyland*, 90.

27. Castells, *Power of Identity*, 10.

28. Castells, *Rise of the Network Society*, 4.

29. Bonhoeffer, *Letters and Papers*, 280.

30. Ward, *True Religion*, chap. 1.

31. Walter Brueggemann, *In Man We Trust: The Neglected Side of Biblical Faith* (Atlanta: John Knox, 1972), 35.

32. Ibid.

33. Rowan Williams, *On Christian Theology* (Oxford: Blackwell, 2000), 25.

34. Antonio Gramsci, *Selections from Cultural Writings* (London: Lawrence and Wishart, 1985), 98.

35. Graham Ward, *Cities of God* (London: Routledge, 2002), 186.

36. Ward, *Blackwell Companion to Postmodern Theology*, xii.

37. See Kliever's *Shattered Spectrum*.

38. Williams, *On Christian Theology*, 25.

39. Kliever, *Shattered Spectrum*, 31.

40. Ibid.

41. Nick Cave, "The Flesh Made Word," from *The Secret Life of the Love Song and the Flesh Made Word: Two Lectures by Nick Cave*. Kmob Records. London, 1999, compact disc.

42. Bonhoeffer, *Letters and Papers*, 280–81.

43. See Detweiler and Taylor, *Matrix of Meanings*.

44. Victor Hugo.

45. Walter Brueggemann, *Finally Comes the Poet: Daring Speech for Proclamation* (Minneapolis: Fortress, 1989), 4.

46. Italo Calvino, *Six Memos for the Next Millennium: The Charles Eliot Norton Lectures 1985–86*, trans. Patrick Creagh (Cambridge, MA: Harvard University Press, 1988).

47. Italo Calvino, *If On a Winter's Night a Traveler* (New York: Harcourt, 1981).

48. See Brueggemann, *Finally Comes the Poet*.

49. The subtitle to ibid.

50. I am indebted to Calvino for the basic ideas and categories, but the reflections on their implication for theology and mission are my own. For that I ask his forgiveness.

51. Calvino, *Six Memos*, 3.

52. U2, *All That You Can't Leave Behind*, Island Records, 2001.

53. Calvino, *Six Memos*, 3.

54. Rushkoff, *Playing the Future*, 50.

55. Calvino, *Six Memos*, 3.

56. Ibid., 81.

57. Ibid., 82.

58. Ibid., 84.

59. Ibid., 105.

60. Ibid., 107.

61. Ibid., 124.

Theological Containers

1. Karen Armstrong, *A History of God* (London: Heinemann, 1993), 403.

2. Mieke Bal, "Postmodern Theology as Cultural Analysis," in Ward, *Blackwell Companion to Postmodern Theology*, 7.

3. Chamsi, "Being Open to the Imaginary," in Abdallah, *For Rushdie*, 97.

4. David J. Bosch, *Transforming Mission: Paradigm Shifts in Theology of Mission* (Maryknoll, NY: Orbis Books, 1991), 519.

Making Signs

1. Dali, as quoted in Neil MacGregor and Erika Langmuir, *Seeing Salvation* (New Haven, CT: Yale University Press, 2001), 198.

2. Ibid.

3. Ibid., 129.

4. Ibid., 136–37.

5. Ibid., 115.

6. I realize this raises a host of other theological questions, hence my offer of a certain performance of the practice of theology for times like these.

Bibliography

Aldridge, Alan. *Religion in the Contemporary World: A Sociological Introduction*. Cambridge: Polity, 2000.

Althaus-Reid, Marcella. *Indecent Theology: Theological Perversions in Sex, Gender, and Politics*. London: Routledge, 2000.

Altman, Dennis. *Global Sex*. Chicago: University of Chicago Press, 2001.

Anderson, Perry. *The Origins of Postmodernity*. London: Verso, 1998.

Anderson, Walter Truett. *The Fontana Postmodernism Reader*. Edited by Walter Truett Anderson. London: Fontana, 1995.

———. *The Next Enlightenment: Integrating East and West in a New Vision of Human Evolution*. New York: St. Martin's Press, 2003.

Appadurai, Arjun. *Modernity at Large: Cultural Dimension of Globalization*. Minneapolis: University of Minnesota Press, 1996.

Appignanesi, Richard, et al., eds. *Introducing Postmodernism*. New York: Totem Books, 1998.

Armstrong, Karen. *The Battle for God*. New York: Alfred A. Knopf, 2000.

———. *Buddha*. New York: Viking, 2001.

———. *A History of God*. London: Heinemann, 1993.

Arnold, Rebecca. *Fashion, Desire, and Anxiety: Image and Morality in the 20th Century*. London: Tauris, 2001.

Bal, Mieke. "Postmodern Theology as Cultural Analysis." In *The Blackwell Companion to Postmodern Theology*, New Edition, edited by Graham Ward, 3–23. Oxford: Blackwell, 2004.

Barber, Benjamin R. *Jihad vs. McWorld: Terrorism's Challenge to Democracy*. New York: Ballantine Books, 1995.

Bauman, Zygmunt. *Intimations of Postmodernity*. London: Routledge, 1992.

———. *Liquid Love: On the Frailty of Human Bonds*. Cambridge: Polity, 2003.

———. *Liquid Modernity*. Cambridge: Polity, 2000.

———. "Postmodern Religion?" In *Religion, Modernity, and Postmodernity*, edited by Paul Heelas, 55–78. Oxford: Blackwell, 1998.

Bave, Frederic W. *The Spiritual Society: What Lurks beyond Postmodernism*. Wheaton, IL: Crossway Books, 2001.

Bawer, Bruce. *Stealing Jesus: How Fundamentalism Betrays Christianity*. New York: Crown, 1997.

Beaudoin, Tom. *Virtual Faith: The Irreverent Spiritual Quest of Generation X*. San Francisco: Jossey-Bass, 1998.

Beaudrillard, Jean. *Cool Memories II, 1987–1990*. Translated by Chris Turner. Durham, NC: Duke University Press, 1996.

Ben Chamsi, Zhor. "Being Open to the Imaginary." In *For Rushdie: Essays by Arab and Muslim Writers in Defense of Free Speech*, edited by Anouar Abdallah, 97–99. New York: George Braziller, 1994.

Bennett, Andy. *Consuming Faith: Integrating Who We Are with What We Buy*. Lanham, MD: Sheed and Ward, 2003.

———. *Popular Music and Youth Culture: Music, Identity, and Place*. London: Macmillan, 2000.

Bernard, H. Russell. *Research Methods in Anthropology: Qualitative and Quantitative Approaches*. Walnut Creek, CA: AltaMira, 1995.

Best, Steven, and Douglas Kellner. *Postmodern Theology: Critical Interrogations*. New York: Guilford, 1991.

———. *The Postmodern Turn*. New York: Guilford, 1997.

Blake, Andrew. *The Irresistible Rise of Harry Potter*. London: Verso, 2002.

Boff, Leonardo. *Global Civilization: Challenges to Society and Christianity*. London: Equinox, 2005.

Bonhoeffer, Dietrich. *Letters and Papers from Prison*. Edited by Eberhard Bethge. New York: Macmillan, 1953.

Borg, Marcus, and Ross Mackenzie, eds. *God at 2000*. Harrisburg, PA: Morehouse, 2000.

Borg, Marcus, and N. T. Wright. *The Meaning of Jesus: Two Visions*. New York: HarperSanFrancisco, 1999.

Bosch, David J. *Transforming Mission: Paradigm Shifts in Theology of Mission*. Maryknoll, NY: Orbis Books, 1991.

Botting, Fred. *Gothic*. London: Routledge, 1996.

Bouma-Prediger, Steven. *For the Beauty of the Earth: A Christian Vision for Creation Care*. Grand Rapids: Baker Academic, 2001.

Boyle, David. *Authenticity: Brands, Fakes, Spin, and the Lust for Real Life*. London: Flamingo, 2003.

Bracewell, Michael. *When Surface Was Depth: Death by Cappuccino and Other Reflections on Music and Culture in the 1990s*. Cambridge, MA: De Capo, 2002.

Brewin, Kester. *The Complex Christ: Signs of Emergence in the Urban Church.* London: SPCK, 2004.

Bromell, Nick. *Tomorrow Never Knows: Rock and Psychedelics in the 1960s.* Chicago: University of Chicago Press, 2000.

Brown, Dan. *The Da Vinci Code.* New York: Doubleday, 2003.

Brown, Deborah A., ed. *Christianity in the 21st Century.* New York: Crossroad, 2000.

Brown, Mick. *The Spiritual Tourist: A Personal Odyssey through the Outer Reaches of Belief.* New York: Bloomsbury, 1998.

Browning, Don S. *A Fundamental Practical Theology: Descriptive and Strategic Proposals.* Minneapolis: Fortress, 1996.

Bruce, Steve. "Cathedrals to Cults: The Evolving Form of the Religious Life." In *Religion, Modernity, and Postmodernity*, edited by Paul Heelas, 19–35. Oxford: Blackwell, 1998.

Brueggemann, Walter. *Finally Comes the Poet: Daring Speech for Proclamation.* Minneapolis: Fortress, 1989.

———. *In Man We Trust: The Neglected Side of Biblical Faith.* Atlanta: John Knox, 1972.

Brussat, Frederic, and Mary Ann Brussat. "Spiritual Literacy: Reading the Sacred in Everyday Life." Introduction in *God-Talk in America*, edited by Phyllis Tickle. New York: Crossroad, 1997.

Burnham, Frederic B. *Postmodern Theology: Christian Faith in a Pluralist World.* New York: HarperSanFrancisco, 1989.

Calvino, Italo. *If On a Winter's Night a Traveler.* New York: Harcourt, 1981.

———. *Six Memos for the Next Millennium: The Charles Eliot Norton Lectures 1985–86.* Translated by Patrick Creagh. Cambridge, MA: Harvard University Press, 1988.

Caputo, John D. *On Religion.* New York: Routledge, 2001.

———. *The Weakness of God: A Theology of the Event.* Bloomington: Indiana University Press, 2006.

Caputo, John, and Michael J. Scanlon, eds. *God, the Gift, and Postmodernism.* Bloomington: Indiana University Press, 1999.

Castells, Manuel. *The Information Age.* 3 vols. Malden, MA: Blackwell, 1996–98.

———. *The Informational City.* Oxford: Blackwell, 1989.

———. *The Power of Identity.* Vol. 2 of *The Information Age.* Malden, MA: Blackwell, 1997.

———. *The Rise of the Network Society.* Vol. 1 of *The Information Age.* Malden, MA: Blackwell, 1996.

Cerwinske, Laura. *In a Spiritual Style: The Home as Sanctuary.* London: Thames and Hudson, 1998.

Chopra, Deepak. *How to Know God: The Soul's Journey into the Mystery of Mysteries*. New York: Harmony Books, 2000.

Cimino, Richard, and Don Lattin. *Shopping for Faith: American Religion in the New Millennium*. San Francisco: Jossey-Bass, 1998.

Cobley, Paul, and Litza Jansz. *Introducing Semiotics*. Edited by Richard Appignanesi. New York: Totem Books, 1997.

Coelho, Paulo. *The Alchemist*. Translated by Alan R. Clarke. New York: Harper Perennial, 1988.

Collins, Jeff, and Bill Mayblin. *Introducing Derrida*. Edited by Richard Appignanesi. New York: Totem Books, 1996.

Connolly, William E. *Why I Am Not a Secularist*. Minneapolis: University of Minnesota Press, 1999.

Coupland, Douglas. *Hey Nostradamus!* New York: Bloomsbury, 2003.

Cowen, Tyler. *In Praise of Commercial Culture*. Cambridge, MA: Harvard University Press, 1998.

Crane, Julia G., and Michael V. Angrosino. *Field Projects in Anthropology: A Student Handbook*. Prospect Heights, IL: Waveland, 1984.

Cray, G., ed. *Mission-Shaped Church: Church Planting and Fresh Expressions of Church in a Changing Context*. London: Church House Publishing, 2004.

Cupitt, Don. *After God: The Future of Religion*. New York: Basic Books, 1997.

———. *The Revelation of Being*. London: SCM, 1998.

Curran, James, and Myung-Jin Park, eds. *De-Westernizing Media Studies*. London: Routledge, 2000.

Dark, David. *Everyday Apocalypse: The Sacred Revealed in* Radiohead, The Simpsons *and Other Pop Culture Icons*. Grand Rapids: Brazos, 2002.

Debord, Guy. *The Society of the Spectacle*. Translated by Donald Nicholson-Smith. New York: Zone Books, 1967.

de Certeau, Michel, Luce Giard, and Pierre Mayol. *The Practice of Everyday Life*. Vol. 2, *Living and Cooking*. Edited by Luce Giard. Translated by Timothy J. Tomasik. Minneapolis: University of Minnesota Press, 1998.

Deleuze, Gilles, and Felix Guattari. *A Thousand Plateaus: Capitalism and Schizophrenia*. London: Athlone, 1988.

Detweiler, Craig, and Barry Taylor. *A Matrix of Meanings: Finding God in Pop Culture*. Grand Rapids: Baker Academic, 2003.

Docker, John. *Postmodernism and Popular Culture: A Cultural History*. Cambridge: Cambridge University Press, 1994.

Dockery, David S., ed. *The Challenge of Postmodernism: An Evangelical Engagement*. Grand Rapids: Baker Academic, 1995.

Doherty, Brian. *This Is Burning Man: The Rise of a New American Underground*. New York: Little, Brown and Company, 2004.

Downes, Brenda, and Steve Miller. *Media Studies*. London: Hoddler Headline, 1998.

Drane, John. *Cultural Change and Biblical Faith: The Future of the Church. Biblical and Missiological Essays for the New Century.* Cumbria: Paternoster, 2000.

———. *The McDonaldization of the Church: Spirituality, Creativity, and the Future of the Church.* London: Darton, Longman and Todd, 2000.

———. *What the New Age Is Still Saying to the Church.* London: Darton, Longman and Todd, 1991.

Drane, John, Ross Clifford, and Philip Johnson. *Beyond Prediction: The Tarot and Your Spirituality.* Oxford: Lion, 2001.

Duff, David, ed. *Modern Genre Theory.* Harlow: Longman, 2000.

Easterbrook, Gregg. "The New Convergence: Religion and Science." *Wired,* December 2002.

Eck, Diana L. *A New Religious America: How a "Christian Country" Has Become the World's Most Religiously Diverse Nation.* New York: HarperSanFrancisco, 2001.

Eco, Umberto. *The Name of the Rose.* Translated by William Weaver. London: Pan Books, 1980.

———. *Travels in Hyperreality.* Translated by William Weaver. New York: Harvest Books, 1983.

Ehrlich, Dimitri, ed. *Inside the Music: Conversations with Contemporary Musicians about Spirituality, Creativity, and Consciousness.* Boston: Shambhala, 1997.

Elliott, Neil. *Liberating Paul: The Justice of God and the Politics of the Apostle.* Maryknoll, NY: Orbis Books, 1994.

Ellwood, Wayne. *The No-Nonsense Guide to Globalization.* London: Verso, 2001.

Featherstone, Mike. *Consumer Culture and Postmodernism.* London: Sage, 1991.

Ferguson, Marilyn. *The Aquarian Conspiracy: Personal and Social Transformation in Our Times.* Los Angeles: J. P. Tarcher, 1980.

Fetterman, David M. *Ethnography: Step by Step.* Thousand Oaks, CA: Sage, 1998.

Forbes, Bruce David, and Jeffrey H. Mahan, eds. *Religion and Popular Culture in America.* Berkeley: University of California Press, 2000.

Fox, Matthew. *Sins of the Spirit, Blessings of the Flesh: Lessons for Transforming Evil in Soul and Society.* New York: Harmony Books, 1999.

Fox, Richard Wightman. *Jesus in America: Personal Savior, Cultural Hero, National Obsession.* San Francisco: HarperSanFrancisco, 2004.

Frend, W. H. C. *The Rise of Christianity.* Philadelphia: Fortress, 1984.

Friedman, Devin. "David O. Russell's Existential Crisis." *GQ,* October 2004.

Gallagher, Winifred. *Working on God.* New York: Random, 1999.

Gandieih, Djaial. "For Rushdie." In *For Rushdie: Essays by Arab and Muslim Writers in Defense of Free Speech*, edited by Anouar Abdallah, 149. New York: George Braziller, 1994.

Gans, Herbert J. *Popular Culture and High Culture: An Analysis and Evaluation of Taste.* New York: Basic Books, 1999.

Giddens, Anthony. *Modernity and Self-Identity.* London: Polity, 1991.

Gilbert, Elizabeth. *Eat, Pray, Love: One Woman's Search for Everything across Italy, India, and Indonesia.* New York: Viking, 2006.

Godawa, Brian. *Hollywood Worldviews: Watching Films with Wisdom and Discernment.* Downers Grove, IL: InterVarsity, 2002.

Goldstein, Niles Elliot. *Spiritual Manifestos: Visions for Renewing Religious Life in America from Young Spiritual Leaders of Many Faiths.* Woodstock, VT: Skylight Paths, 1999.

Gooch, Brad. *Godtalk: Travels in Spiritual America.* New York: Alfred A. Knopf, 2002.

Gorringe, T. J. *The Education of Desire: Towards a Theology of the Senses.* Harrisburg, PA: Trinity Press, 2001.

Gould, Stephen Jay, Umberto Eco, Jean-Claude Carriere, and Jean Delumeau. *Conversations about the End of Time.* Edited by Catherine David, Frederic Lenoir, and Jean-Philippe de Tonnac. Translated by Ian Maclean and Roger Pearson. New York: Fromm, 1998.

Graham, Elaine. "Post/Human Conditions." *Theology and Sexuality: The Journal of the Centre for the Study of Christianity and Sexuality* 10, no. 2 (March 2004): 10–32.

Gramsci, Antonio. *Selections from Cultural Writings.* London: Lawrence and Wishart, 1985.

Grenz, Stanley J. *Renewing the Center: Evangelical Theology in a Post-Theological Era.* Grand Rapids: Baker Academic, 2000.

Griffin, David Ray. *God and Religion in the Postmodern World: Essays in Postmodern Theology.* Albany: State University of New York Press, 1989.

Grossberg, Lawrence, Cary Nelson, and Paula Treichler, eds. *Cultural Studies.* London: Routledge, 1992.

Gudorf, Christine E. *Body, Sex, and Pleasure: Reconstructing Christian Sexual Ethics.* Cleveland: Pilgrim, 1994.

Guehenno, Jean-Marie. *The End of the Nation-State.* Translated by Victoria Elliott. Minneapolis: University of Minnesota Press, 1995.

Haber, Karen, ed. *Exploring the Matrix: Visions of the Cyber Present.* New York: St. Martin's Press, 2003.

Haight, Roger. *Jesus, Symbol of God.* Maryknoll, NY: Orbis Books, 2000.

Hanna, Nick. *The Millennium: The Rough Guide.* London: Rough Guides, 1998.

Harvey, David. *The Condition of Postmodernity.* London: Blackwell, 1990.

Hay, David, and Kate Hunt. "Is Britain's Soul Waking Up?" *Tablet*. London, 2000.

Hesmondhalgh, David, and Keith Negus, eds. *Popular Music Studies*. London: Arnold, 2002.

Heyward, Carter. *Saving Jesus from Those Who Are Right: Rethinking What It Means to Be Christian*. Minneapolis: Fortress, 1999.

Hick, John. *A Christian Theology of Religions: The Rainbow of Faiths*. Louisville: Westminster John Knox, 1995.

———. *The Metaphor of God Incarnate: Christology in a Pluralistic Age*. Louisville: Westminster John Knox, 1993.

Himanen, Pekka. *The Hacker Ethic and the Spirit of the Information Age*. New York: Random, 2001.

Hobsbawm, Eric. *On the Edge of the New Century*. Edited by Antonio Polito. Translated by Allan Cameron. New York: New Press, 1999.

Holden, Anthony. *William Shakespeare: His Life and Work*. London: Abacus, 1999.

Horgan, John. *Rational Mysticism: Spirituality Meets Science in the Search for Enlightenment*. New York: Houghton Mifflin, 2003.

Horrocks, Chris, and Zoran Jevtic. *Introducing Beaudrillard*. Edited by Richard Appignanesi. New York: Totem Books, 1996.

Hyman, Gavin. *The Predicament of Postmodern Theology: Radical Orthodoxy or Nihilist Textualism?* Louisville: Westminster John Knox, 2001.

Jarvis, Brian. *Postmodern Cartographies: The Geographical Imagination in Contemporary American Culture*. New York: St. Martin's Press, 1998.

Jencks, Charles. *What Is Postmodernism?* London: Academy Editions, 1996.

Jones, Tony. *Postmodern Youth Ministry: Exploring Cultural Shift, Cultivating Authentic Community, Creating Holistic Connections*. Grand Rapids: Youth Specialties, 2001.

Kellner, Douglas. *Media Culture: Cultural Studies, Identity, and Politics between the Modern and the Postmodern*. London: Routledge, 1995.

Kelly, Gerard. *Get a Grip on the Future without Losing Your Hold on the Past*. London: Monarch Books, 1999.

Kelly, Karen, and Evelyn McDonnell, eds. *Stars Don't Stand Still in the Sky: Music and Myth*. London: Routledge, 1999.

Kermode, Frank. *The Age of Shakespeare*. New York: Modern Library, 2003.

King, Ursula, ed. *Faith and Praxis in a Postmodern Age*. London: Cassell, 1998.

Kliever, Lonnie D. *The Shattered Spectrum: A Survey of Contemporary Theology*. Atlanta: John Knox, 1981.

Kotkin, Joel. *The New Geography: How the Digital Revolution Is Reshaping the American Landscape*. New York: Random House, 2000.

Lakeland, Paul. *Postmodernity: Christian Identity in a Fragmented Age*. Minneapolis: Fortress, 1997.

Langer, Susanne K. *Philosophy in a New Key: A Study in the Symbolism of Reason, Rite, and Art*. Cambridge, MA: Harvard University Press, 1942.

Lash, Scott. *Sociology of Postmodernism*. London: Routledge, 1990.

Lawrence, Bruce B. "From Fundamentalism to Fundamentalists: A Religious Ideology in Multiple Forms." In *Religion, Modernity, and Postmodernity*, edited by Paul Heelas, 88–101. Oxford: Blackwell, 1998.

Leach, Neil. *Millennium Culture*. London: Ellipsis, 1999.

Lechner, Frank J., and John Boli, eds. *The Globalization Reader*. Malden, MA: Blackwell, 2000.

Lecourt, Dominique. *The Mediocracy: French Philosophy Since the Mid-1970s*. Translated by Gregory Elliott. London: Verso, 2001.

Levine, Noah. *Dharma Punx: A Memoir*. New York: HarperSanFrancisco, 2003.

Lewis, R. W. B. *Dante*. New York: A Lipper/Viking, 2001.

Loughlin, Gerard. *Alien Sex: The Body and Desire in Cinema and Theology*. Oxford: Blackwell, 2004.

———. *Telling God's Story: Bible, Church, and Narrative Theology*. Cambridge: Cambridge University Press, 1996.

Lovejoy, Margot. *Postmodern Currents: Art and Artists in the Age of Electronic Media*. Englewood Cliffs, NJ: Prentice Hall, 1989.

Lynch, Gordon. *After Religion: "Generation X" and the Search for Meaning*. London: Darton, Longman and Todd, 2000.

———. *Losing My Religion: Moving on from Evangelical Faith*. London: Darton, Longman and Todd, 2003.

Lyon, David. *Jesus in Disneyland: Religion in Postmodern Times*. Cambridge: Polity, 2000.

Lyotard, Jean-Francois. *The Postmodern Condition: A Report on Knowledge*. Translated by Geoff Bennington and Brian Massumi. Minneapolis: University of Minnesota Press, 1979.

MacGregor, Neil, and Erika Langmuir. *Seeing Salvation*. New Haven, CT: Yale University Press, 2001.

Magnier, Mark. "Good Things in Small Packages." *Los Angeles Times*, May 23, 2003.

Maitland, Sara. *A Big-Enough God: A Feminist's Search for a Joyful Theology*. New York: Riverhead Books, 1995.

Manseau, Peter, and Jeff Sharlet. *Killing the Buddha: A Heretic's Bible*. New York: Free Press, 2004.

Marcus, Greil. *In the Fascist Bathroom: Punk in Pop Music 1977–1992*. Cambridge, MA: Harvard University Press, 1993.

———. *Lipstick Traces*. Cambridge, MA: Harvard University Press, 1989.

Mau, Bruce, ed. *Massive Change*. New York: Phaidon, 2004.

McClaren, Brian D. *A Generous Orthodoxy: Why I Am a Missional, Evangelical, Post/Protestant, Liberal/Conservative, Mystical/Poetic, Biblical, Charismatic/*

Bibliography

Contemplative, Fundamentalist/Calvinist, Anabaptist/Anglican, Methodist, Catholic, Green, Incarnational, Depressed-yet-Hopeful, Emergent, Unfinished Christian. Grand Rapids: Youth Specialties, 2004.

McDannell, Colleen. *Material Christianity: Religion and Popular Culture in America*. New Haven, CT: Yale University Press, 1995.

McGrath, Alister E. *The Future of Christianity*. Oxford: Blackwell, 2002.

McLuhan, Marshall, and Quentin Fiore. *The Medium Is the Massage*. New York: Random, 1967.

McRobbie, Angela. *Postmodernism and Popular Culture*. London: Routledge, 1994.

Milbank, John, Catherine Pickstock, and Graham Ward, eds. *Radical Orthodoxy: A New Theology*. London: Routledge, 1999.

Min, Anselm Kyongsuk. *The Solidarity of Others in a Divided World: A Postmodern Theology after Postmodernism*. New York: T&T Clark, 2004.

Moltmann, Jurgen. *How I Have Changed: Reflections on Thirty Years of Theology*. Harrisburg, PA: Trinity Press, 1997.

Mulhern, Francis. *Culture/Metaculture*. London: Routledge, 2000.

Myers, Tony. *Slavoj Žižek*. New York: Routledge, 2003.

Nash, Christopher. *The Unravelling of the Postmodern Mind*. Edinburgh: Edinburgh University Press, 2001.

Nelson, James B. *Body Theology*. Louisville: Westminster John Knox, 1992.

O'Connor, Maura R. "Twenty-first Century Kabbalah." *What Is Enlightenment?* November 2004–February 2005, 80–86.

O'Murchu, Diarmuid. *Quantum Theology*. New York: Crossroad, 1997.

Palahniuk, Chuck. *Fight Club*. New York: Henry Holt, 1996.

Pattison, George. *Art, Modernity, and Faith: Towards a Theology of Art*. New York: St. Martin's Press, 1991.

Peat, F. David. *From Certainty to Uncertainty: The Story of Science and Ideas in the Twentieth Century*. Washington, DC: Joseph Henry, 2002.

Phipps, Carter, and Craig Hamilton. "If Heaven Were a Place on Earth: A Pilgrimage to the 2004 World Parliament of Religions." *What Is Enlightenment?* November 2004–February 2005, 102.

Pine, B. Joseph, II, and James H. Gilmore. *The Experience Economy: Work Is Theatre and Every Business a Stage*. Boston: Harvard Business School Press, 1999.

Plant, Sadie. *The Most Radical Gesture: The Situationist International in a Postmodern Age*. London: Routledge, 1992.

Postman, Neil. *Amusing Ourselves to Death: Public Discourse in the Age of Show Business*. New York: Penguin Books, 1985.

Pountain, Dick, and David Robins. *Cool Rules: Anatomy of an Attitude*. London: Reaktion Books, 2000.

Poynor, Rick. *No More Rules: Graphic Design and Postmodernism*. New Haven, CT: Yale University Press, 2003.

Prothero, Stephen. *American Jesus: How the Son of God Became a National Icon*. New York: Farrar, Straus and Giroux, 2003.

Rahner, Karl. *Theological Investigations*. Vol. 20, *Concern for the Church*. London: Darton, Longman and Todd, 1981.

Rawlyk, George. *Is Jesus Your Personal Savior? In Search of Canadian Evangelicalism in the 1990s*. Montreal: McGill-Queen's University Press, 1996.

Ray, Paul H., and Sherry Ruth Anderson. *The Cultural Creatives: How 50 Million People Are Changing the World*. New York: Harmony Books, 2000.

Redfield, James. *The Celestine Prophecy: An Adventure*. New York: Warner Books, 1993.

Ridderstråle, Jonas, and Kjell Nordström. *Funky Business: Talent Makes Capital Dance*. London: Financial Times Publications, 2000.

———. *Karaoke Capitalism: Management for Mankind*. Harlow: Pearson Education, 2003.

Riess, Jana. *What Would Buffy Do?* San Francisco: Jossey-Bass, 2004.

Rifkin, Jeremy. *The European Dream: How Europe's Vision of the Future Is Quietly Eclipsing the American Dream*. New York: Jeremy P. Tarcher/ Penguin, 2004.

Riggs, John W. *Postmodern Christianity: Doing Theology in the Contemporary World*. Harrisburg, PA: Trinity Press, 2003.

Ritzer, George. *The McDonaldization of Society: An Investigation into the Changing Character of Contemporary Social Life*. Thousand Oaks, CA: Pine Forge, 1996.

Robertson, Ross. "Searching for a Postmodern Religion on the Set of the *Celestine Prophecy*." *What Is Enlightenment?* November 2004–February 2005.

Romanowski, William D. *Pop Culture Wars: Religion and the Role of Entertainment in American Life*. Downers Grove, IL: InterVarsity, 1996.

Rushdie, Salman. *The Satanic Verses*. New York: Picador Books, 1988.

———. *Step Across This Line: Collected Nonfiction 1992–2002*. New York: Modern Library, 2002.

Rushkoff, Douglas. *Exit Strategy*. New York: Soft Skull, 2002.

———. *Nothing Sacred*. New York: Three Rivers, 2003.

———. *Playing the Future*. New York: Riverhead Books, 1996.

Sardar, Ziauddin. *The A to Z of Postmodern Life: Essays on Global Culture in the Noughties*. London: Vision, 2002.

Schell, Orville. *Virtual Tibet: Searching for Shangri-La from the Himalayas to Hollywood*. New York: Metropolitan Books, 2000.

Schneiders, Sandra. "Religion and Spirituality: Strangers, Rivals, or Partners?" The Santa Clara Lectures, 2000.

Shakespeare, William. *Romeo and Juliet*. Reprinted edition. Edited by Roma Gill. Oxford: Oxford University Press, 1982.

Shulman, Alon. *The Style Bible: An A–Z of Global Youth Culture. The Influences, the Influencers, and the Influenced*. London: Methuen, 1999.

Shutt, Harry. *A New Democracy: Alternatives to a Bankrupt World Order*. London: Zed Books, 2001.

Silverman, David. *Qualitative Research: Theory, Method, and Practice*. London: Sage, 1997.

Sin, Stuart, ed. *The Routledge Critical Dictionary of Postmodern Thought*. New York: Routledge, 1999.

Smith, Huston. *Why Religion Matters: The Fate of the Human Spirit in an Age of Disbelief*. New York: HarperSanFrancisco, 2001.

Smith, Joan. *Moralities: Sex, Money, and Power in the 21st Century*. London: Allen Lane, 2001.

Sorokin, Pitirim A. *Social and Cultural Dynamics: A Study of Change in Major Systems of Art, Truth, Ethics, Law, and Social Relationships*. London: Transaction, 1985.

Spoto, Donald. *The Hidden Jesus: A New Life*. New York: St. Martin's Press, 1989.

Steiner, George. *Real Presences*. Chicago: University of Chicago Press, 1989.

Steinfels, Peter. "Swapping 'Religion' for 'Postsecularism.'" *New York Times*, August 3, 2002.

Stephens, Mitchell. *The Rise of the Image, the Fall of the Word*. New York: Oxford University Press, 1998.

Sterling, Bruce. "Every Other Movie Is the Blue Pill." In *Exploring the Matrix*, edited by Bruce Sterling, 16–29. New York: St. Martin's Press, 2003.

Storey, John. *Cultural Studies and the Study of Popular Culture: Theories and Methods*. Athens: University of Georgia Press, 2003.

———, ed. *Cultural Theory and Popular Culture: A Reader*. Athens: University of Georgia Press, 1998.

———. *An Introduction to Cultural Theory and Popular Culture*. Athens: University of Georgia Press, 1998.

Strinati, Dominic. *An Introduction to Theories of Popular Culture*. London: Routledge, 1995.

Sudo, Philip Toshio. *Zen Guitar*. New York: Simon and Schuster, 1997.

Sweet, Leonard. *Quantum Spirituality*. Dayton, OH: Whaleprint, 1991.

Tacey, David. *The Spirituality Revolution: The Emergence of Contemporary Spirituality*. London: Brunner-Routledge, 2004.

Tawney, R. H. *Religion and the Rise of Capitalism*. London: Penguin Books, 1926.

Taylor, Dennis, and David N. Beauregard, eds. *Shakespeare and the Culture of Christianity in Early Modern England*. New York: Fordham University Press, 2003.

Taylor, Mark C. *About Religion: Economies of Faith in Virtual Culture*. Chicago: University of Chicago Press, 1999.

Taylor, Steven J., and Robert Bogdan. *Introduction to Qualitative Research Methods: A Guidebook and Resource*. New York: John Wiley & Sons, 1998.

Tenner, Edward. *Why Things Bite Back: Technology and the Revenge of Unintended Consequences*. New York: Vintage Books, 1996.

Thiselton, Anthony C. *Interpreting God and the Postmodern Self: On Meaning, Manipulation and Promise*. Edinburgh: T&T Clark; Grand Rapids: Eerdmans, 1995.

Tickle, Phyllis A. *God-Talk in America*. New York: Crossroad, 1997.

Tomlinson, John. "Globalized Culture: The Triumph of the West?" In *Culture and Global Change*, edited by Tracey Skelton and Tim Allen, 22–29. London: Routledge, 1999.

Tsultim Gyeltsen, Geshe. *Mirror of Wisdom: Teachings on Emptiness*. Edited by Rebecca McClen Novick, Linda Gatter and Nicholas Ribush. Translated by Lotsawa Tenzin Dorjee. Long Beach, CA: Thubten Dhargye Ling, 2000.

Turner, Bryan S. *Religion and Social Theory*. London: Sage, 1983.

Twitchell, James. *Lead Us into Temptation*. New York: Columbia University Press, 1999.

Vanhoozer, Kevin J., ed. *The Cambridge Companion to Postmodern Theology*. Cambridge: Cambridge University Press, 2003.

Vattimo, Gianni. *After Christianity*. Translated by Luca D'Isanto. New York: Columbia University Press, 2002.

Vienne, Veronique. *Something to be Desired: Essays on Design*. New York: Graphis Inc., 2001.

Wallace, Mark I. "Earth God: Cultivating the Spirit in an Ecocidal Culture." In *The Blackwell Companion to Postmodern Theology*, New Edition, edited by Graham Ward, 209–28. Oxford: Blackwell, 2001.

———. *Fragments of the Spirit: Nature, Violence, and the Renewal of Creation*. Harrisburg, PA: Trinity Press, 2002.

Ward, Graham, ed. *The Blackwell Companion to Postmodern Theology*. Oxford: Blackwell, 2001.

———. *Cities of God*. London: Routledge, 2000.

———, ed. *The Postmodern God: A Theological Reader*. Malden, MA: Blackwell, 1997.

———. *True Religion*. Oxford: Blackwell, 2003.

Warner, Brad. *Hardcore Zen: Punk Rock, Monster Movies, and the Truth about Reality*. Boston: Wisdom, 2003.

Waters, Malcolm. *Globalization*. New York: Routledge, 1995.

Watters, Ethan. *Urban Tribes: A Generation Redefines Friendship, Family, and Commitment*. New York: Bloomsbury, 2003.

Webber, Robert E. *Ancient-Future Faith: Rethinking Evangelicalism for a Postmodern World*. Grand Rapids: Baker Books, 1999.

Bibliography

Wertheim, Margaret. *The Pearly Gates of Cyberspace: A History of Space from Dante to the Internet.* New York: Norton & Company, 1999.

Wilber, Ken. *A Theory of Everything: An Integral Vision for Business, Politics, Science, and Spirituality.* Boston: Shambhala, 2001.

Williams, Rowan. *On Christian Theology.* Oxford: Blackwell, 2000.

Wilson, Bryan R. *Religion in Secular Society: A Sociological Comment.* London: Watts, 1966.

Zetter, Kim. *Simple Kabbalah.* York Beach, NY: Conari, 2000.

Žižek, Slavoj. *The Fragile Absolute, or, Why Is the Christian Legacy Worth Fighting For?* London: Verso, 2000.

———. *On Belief.* New York: Routledge, 2001.

———. *The Plague of Fantasies.* London: Verso, 1997.

———. *The Puppet and the Dwarf: The Perverse Core of Christianity.* Cambridge, MA: Massachusetts Institute of Technology Press, 2003.

———. *Welcome to the Desert of the Real! Five Essays on September 11 and Related Dates.* London: Verso, 2002.

Zuckerman, Phil. *Invitation to the Sociology of Religion.* New York: Routledge, 2003.

Subject Index

Barry Taylor (PhD, Fuller Theological Seminary) is artist in residence for the Brehm Center and an adjunct professor at Fuller Theological Seminary, where he teaches a series of spiritually innovative classes on music, film, and contemporary theology. He also teaches in the school of advertising at Art Center College of Design in Pasadena and writes and performs music, including soundtrack scores for film. In addition, he is an associate rector at All Saints Episcopal Church in Beverly Hills. He has coauthored two books, *A Matrix of Meanings: Finding God in Popular Culture* and *A Heretic's Guide to Eternity*.